Practical Teaching Skills for Driving Instructors

Thirteenth Edition

Practical Teaching Skills for Driving Instructors

John Miller and Su McCormack

KoganPage

First published in Great Britain and the United States in 1993 by Kogan Page Limited
Thirteenth edition 2027

Kogan Page
Kogan Page Ltd, 2nd Floor, 45 Gee Street, London EC1V 3RS, United Kingdom
Kogan Page Inc, 8 W 38th Street, Suite 902, New York, NY 10018, USA
www.koganpage.com

EU Representative (GPSR)
eucomply OÜ, Pärnu mnt 139b–14 11317, Tallinn, Estonia
www.eucompliancepartner.com

Kogan Page books are printed on paper from sustainable forests.

ISBNs
Hardback 978 1 3986 3091 8
Paperback 978 1 3986 3090 1
Ebook 978 1 3986 3092 5

British Library Cataloguing-in-Publication Data
A CIP record for this book is available from the British Library.

Library of Congress Cataloging-in-Publication Data
A CIP record for this book is available from the Library of Congress.

Typeset by Integra Software Services Pondicherry
Print production managed by Jellyfish
Printed and bound by CPI Group (UK) Ltd, Croydon CR0 4YY

CONTENTS

About the authors viii

Introduction 1

01 How people learn 4

Structured training 5

The learning process 7

Transfer of learning 13

Skills training 20

Overcoming barriers 24

02 Communication 34

Instruction 36

Coaching 36

Verbal communication 39

Listening skills 45

Briefings and explanations 49

Body language 51

Feedback 59

03 Client-centred learning and coaching 62

Coaching or instructing 63

Principles of coaching 65

Benefits of coaching 65

Coaching skills 66

Effective questioning 70

Active listening – a few reminders 77

Learner feedback 78

Modifying behaviours in driving 82

Goals for Driver Education 86

Coaching – a summary 88

04 Structured learning 93
Goals and goal-setting **95**
Levels of instruction **101**
Route planning **104**
Fault assessment **107**
Hazard perception **111**
Learner involvement **115**
Visual aids **115**
The use of questions **117**
Risk management **117**

05 Driver training 122
Lesson structure **123**
Main car controls **124**
Moving off and stopping **132**
Use of mirrors **134**
Use of signals **136**
Turning and emerging at junctions **138**
Crossroads **140**
Meeting and dealing with other traffic **142**
Manoeuvres **145**
Emergency stop **149**
Pedestrian crossings **151**
Roundabouts and dual carriageways **154**
Making progress and road positioning **161**
Anticipating the actions of other road users **163**
Independent driving and use of sat nav **165**
Summary **173**

06 The ADI Standards Check 174
Lesson planning **176**
Competence standards examples **179**
Typical lessons **183**
Interpreting the assessment criteria **187**

07 Goal-setting and risk management 210
A Model for Goal-Setting and Risk Management **210**
Goal-setting **212**
Risk management **215**

08 Professional development 229
Benefits of CPD 230
Driver trainer competence framework 232
Business skills and customer care 234
Handling complaints 236
ADI national organizations 237
Driving standards 238
Driving instructor training 241
Driving instructor qualifications 242
Business opportunities 243
Summary 250

Appendix 1: Useful contacts 251
Appendix 2: Reference books 253
Index 254

ABOUT THE AUTHORS

John Miller was involved in the driver training industry for over 40 years and was an ADI for more than 35 years. For most of that time he ran his own driving school for both car and lorry drivers as well as an instructor training facility in Chichester.

Su McCormack has been involved in the driver training industry for nearly 40 years. As an ADI, she taught learner drivers, trainee and qualified driving instructors, and developed training materials and courses. Su has completed an MSc in Driver Behaviour and Education at Cranfield University, and scored 51 out of 51 in her ADI Standards Check.

As well as *Practical Teaching Skills for Driving Instructors*, John and Su are the authors of *The Driving Instructor's Handbook* (also published by Kogan Page).

Both books are listed by the Driver and Vehicle Standards Agency as recommended material for the ADI examinations.

Introduction

Practical Teaching Skills for Driving Instructors was originally published in 1993 as a follow-up and supplement to *The Driving Instructor's Handbook* and sets out, in a practical and straightforward way, the most effective practices for teaching driver training. The emphasis is on presenting up-to-date methods of teaching, learning, coaching and refresher training for Approved Driving Instructors (ADIs) and trainee instructors. Over the years the contents have been regularly revised and updated to reflect the changes that have taken place in the industry.

The original authors of *Practical Teaching Skills* were John Miller and Margaret Stacey who also co-authored *The Driving Instructors Handbook*. John Miller became sole author in later editions, ensuring it remained relevant to practical, in-car teaching.

Su McCormack joined John as co-author for the 11th and 12th editions, contributing to the continued development of its practical teaching approach. The new 13th edition closely complements the knowledge in *The Driving Instructor's Handbook* (23rd Edition), linking professional understanding with its application in the training vehicle.

Following John's death in late 2023, Su McCormack took on the responsibility of continuing his work on both *The Driving Instructor's Handbook* and *Practical Teaching Skills*.

This thirteenth edition has been updated to include information on:

- how to teach Advanced Driver Assistance Systems (ADAS);
- how to manage technology and distraction;
- eco-driving in an electric vehicle (EV) context;
- teaching neurodivergent learners.

Modern driver training increasingly takes place in a complex environment shaped by advancing technology, greater awareness of individual learning differences, and the need to prepare drivers for a lifetime of safe, independent decision making.

Much of the teaching in this book – particularly in relation to the latest updates on neurodivergence, advanced driver assistance systems (ADAS) and in-car technology – is most effective when delivered using a coaching or client-centred approach. In practice, this means actively involving the learner in the learning process, encouraging them to think, reflect and take increasing responsibility for their decisions.

Instructors who rely heavily on instruction alone may achieve short-term results, but often at the expense of deeper understanding and long-term independence. Coaching and client-centred learning, therefore, are not simply alternative styles of teaching; they are fundamental skills for the modern driving instructor.

As driver trainers, you are probably the only teachers whose 'classrooms' are travelling at relatively high speeds along busy roads. In this environment your control of the situation and your effectiveness as an instructor are vital factors with regard to the safety of your learners, yourself and other road users. Effective lessons are built around structured planning with clear goals that give each session direction and focus. At the same time, managing risk is essential – maintaining safety, anticipating hazards and supporting learners in developing their own awareness. Equally important is the use of appropriate teaching and learning strategies, helping learners to understand, reflect and become increasingly independent.

These three elements – lesson planning, risk management and teaching and learning strategies – form the foundation of professional driver training and underpin success in both the Part 3 test and the Standards Check. For these reasons *Practical Teaching Skills* is designed to help existing qualified instructors in preparing for the ADI Standards Check, as well as new instructors preparing for their ADI exams.

The practical teaching skills dealt with in this book are dependent on effective communication and coaching skills. Instructors who can communicate and coach effectively are more likely to succeed in transferring their own knowledge, understanding, skills and attitudes to their learners.

Knowledge of *The Highway Code* and the ability to drive with a high degree of expertise are not in themselves enough for teaching somebody else how to drive. As a professional driver trainer, you should be aiming to teach your learners 'safe driving for life' and not just training them to pass the test. This book focuses on showing you how to improve your teaching, coaching and communication skills so that you are better equipped to teach 'safe driving for life', whether you are a potential or a qualified ADI. The use of these skills in preparation for the ADI exams is dealt with in detail in *The Driving Instructor's Handbook*.

So, being a successful driving instructor relies on three key areas:

- Lesson planning (lesson structure)

  Planning and structuring lessons around clear, client-centred goals ensures sessions are purposeful, progressive and suited to the learner's needs. This includes identifying starting points, agreeing outcomes and reviewing progress, adapting the plan as necessary.

- Risk management

  Maintaining safety is fundamental to the learner achieving their goal. This involves agreeing the division of responsibility, making timely interventions and supporting learners in managing risk for themselves as their independence increases.

- Teaching and learning strategies

  Using effective client-centred methods helps learners understand, reflect and take responsibility for their learning goals. This includes appropriate questioning, feedback around the goal and adapting teaching to suit the individual.

  By using this book in conjunction with your practical training for either the ADI exams and Standards Check, or your Continuing Professional Development (CPD), you can learn how to improve your practical teaching, coaching and client-centred skills. This will benefit your learners, your own personal development and assist you in achieving the best possible grading on your Part 3 and Standards Check.

The development of this edition of *Practical Teaching Skills* has been supported by the Driver and Vehicle Standards Agency (DVSA), who have provided guidance and contributed to the accuracy of the content. Their commitment to maintaining high standards in driver training continues to shape the profession.

01
How people learn

Whether you are a trainee instructor or an ADI, you can develop and improve your practical teaching skills by understanding:

- why people learn to drive;
- what motivates learners;
- how learning takes place; and
- the factors involved in barriers to learning.

Your learners may be learning for a variety of reasons, including:

- social, domestic or leisure pursuits;
- business and employment requirements;
- personal satisfaction; or
- the need for independent mobility.

Once they have passed the test your learners will understand or appreciate how the other benefits gained will improve or enhance their quality of life by giving them:

- greater freedom and mobility;
- improved confidence and status;
- better employment or promotion potential; and
- increased earning power.

When these benefits are considered, together with the fact that a driving licence is effectively valid for life, driving lessons can be regarded as extremely good value for money. These benefits can be discussed with the learner right from the start of their lessons and in the context of the amount of training required for acquiring a life skill.

The main objective and motivation for most learners is to pass their test and obtain a full driving licence at the earliest opportunity, with the minimum of effort and at the least possible cost. In recent years, most young people have started their driver training as soon as they are old enough, but there are now some indications that a significant number of 17-year-olds are delaying their training and putting off lessons until they are slightly older. Some 10 years ago, about 50 per cent of all 17- to 21-year-olds held a full driving licence, but that figure has now dropped to about 26 per cent. The cost of learning, combined with the escalating costs of insurance for young drivers, may be influencing their decision.

The cost of insurance is one of the inhibiting factors for a young and inexperienced driver. New drivers in the 17–21 age group are six times more likely to be involved in a road traffic accident than any other group of drivers. For this reason, insurance premiums are increased significantly for newly qualified young drivers. However, several insurance companies offer substantial discounts for drivers who have a black box fitted.

Structured training

The main benefits of a properly structured programme of training with a professional trainer include:

- a good relationship that allows learning to be fun and engaging;
- a potential saving in time and possible wasted effort;
- a higher level of knowledge, understanding, attitude and skill;
- a better chance of passing the 'L' test and accomplishing safe driving for life.

To ensure your customers achieve these benefits you should have an understanding of how adults learn. You will then be able to structure a programme of learning to suit the individual needs of each of your learners.

During your normal working day you will find that your lessons involve using several different methods and strategies. This is part of what 'coaching' is all about – 'using all facilities and methods at our disposal'. Coaching and the principles relating to 'Goals for Driver Education' (GDE) are both dealt with in detail in Chapter 3.

Private practice

Although some people still learn to drive with friends or relatives it has been shown that most learners taking the driving test have had some professional instruction.

Sometimes they have their initial instruction with a professional to acquire the basic skills but, more commonly, they acquire the basic skills and then come to the professional just before the 'L' test saying, 'I just want to make sure I'm doing everything right!'

Unless the friend or relative carrying out the teaching has some form of instructional background, and is a reasonably good driver, it is a distinct disadvantage if the learner has received no lessons at all from a professional instructor. On the other hand, private practice of the right kind can be very helpful, particularly if it is carried out with your support.

Motivation

Finding out why your learner wants to learn to drive is as relevant to you as it is to them. People learn more effectively if they have clearly defined goals to aim for. If you understand some of the personal factors governing the learner's motivation, it helps you to structure an appropriate programme of lessons for their individual needs. Some people may indicate that they want to pass their driving test as quickly as possible.

Some of the reasons for wanting to learn include:

- Independence – they may feel trapped and that they must rely on friends or relatives to run them around; they may be fed up with using public transport to get to work every day.
- Employment – they may be out of work and recognize that a driving licence will increase their employment opportunities because it will increase their ability to travel further to get to work. Or they may be looking for work doing deliveries, for example.
- Self-esteem – they believe it will boost their self-confidence or help them establish or keep friends.
- Mobility – they may want or need to drive their family or friends around. Or they may live out in the country and getting around is very difficult when you must rely on public transport.
- Illness – a partner or family member becoming ill sometimes makes it necessary for people to learn to drive.

- Expectation – it is expected that they will learn to drive – either by their peers or their parents, for example. Everyone else can drive and they should also.

Holding a conversation with someone at the beginning of their driving lessons can be beneficial to draw out from them why they want to learn to drive. You will be able to remind them of their reasons if they are feeling despondent about their progress during their lessons or questioning why they are bothering. Keeping your learners motivated is crucial to their learning.

The learning process

Learning is individual

All learners start from their own position of knowledge and have their own personal set of experiences to draw upon. Each learner will have a whole lifetime of individual previous experiences behind them that will give them a completely different starting point from other new learners. They may have driving experience and they may already have had some driving lessons; they may have ridden a push bike or a motorcycle; they probably have been a passenger in both the front seat of the car as well as the back seat; they probably have been on buses and in taxis; they most certainly will have been a pedestrian; they may have been involved in a crash or know someone who has. In terms of their experiences unrelated to driving, they may have loved or hated school; they may find it easy or difficult to socialize and make friends; they might find learning difficult or easy. All these things set them apart from the next person and mean that, as a driver trainer, you should take your lead from them as to what their starting point is.

Learning is contextual

The context in which learners learn and operate affects how and what they understand. This is to do with giving meaning to the learning. For example, sitting inside the car isn't the only meaningful place to learn to drive. Because learning to drive involves far more than operating the controls of the vehicle, some of the learning could be done outside of the car. It is sometimes helpful to stand on a bridge and watch the traffic and discuss how it is behaving; or to watch a video of different traffic situations at home; or to be in a classroom situation with other people also learning to drive. If we make assumptions about the context needed for our learners to learn most effectively we could be restricting their ability to learn. Changing the environment can sometimes greatly enhance the learning.

Another aspect of the context is to do with the personal comfort of the learner. You may have noticed that you sometimes feel the cold more than your learners because they are struggling to learn something and it causes their body temperature to rise. Encouraging them to open the window or turn down the temperature is part of them taking responsibility and helps prepare them for driving on their own once they have passed their test. Also, recognizing that your learner needs to get out of the car and have a quick leg stretch is part of taking into consideration the learning context. Having a packet of mints available or a bottle of water is likely to help maximize their learning.

Learning is relational

To make sense and achieve an understanding of material and experiences, learners need to relate new information to existing knowledge and experiences. It is helpful to recap on what has already been covered in a previous lesson if it is going to be relevant to today's lesson because your learner can then link the new piece of information to the old. Asking your learner, rather than telling them, reinforces the learning that has already taken place. If your learner actually puts the previous learning into practice this really helps. For example, you are going to move onto emerging from junctions. Encouraging the learner to drive around a block of left and right turns concentrating on approaching to turn left or right into minor roads for 10 minutes first will make the world of difference to how well they learn.

Learning is developmental

Having made sense of new information and integrated it into an existing framework of understanding, learners can then make informed choices about what to do next and how to develop their understanding. Learning is most effective when people take responsibility for their own development. Even though you know what needs to be covered for your learners to be able to drive safely and pass the driving test, it is helpful to them if they can choose what they want to do next. This develops their ability to evaluate their progress to date and judge what would be most appropriate for them to learn next given their current skills. You would find it helpful to structure this kind of conversation using GROW (goals, reality, options, way forward) and this is covered in more detail in Chapter 3. When they are driving independently having passed the driving test, you will have helped develop decision-making and judgement skills, critical to safe driving.

Learning is experiential

This means we learn from experience, experimentation and self-discovery.

You may well be used to explaining with a briefing how to do something, possibly offering a demonstration and then going out and practising a new topic by talking your learner through what they need to do in order to be successful. This is just one way of teaching a topic and may not be the most effective way for all your learners to learn all of the time, especially when you consider the process of learning as detailed in the previous four points (individual, contextual, relational and developmental). In 1984 David Kolb developed a theory of learning, which cycles through four stages. Kolb's

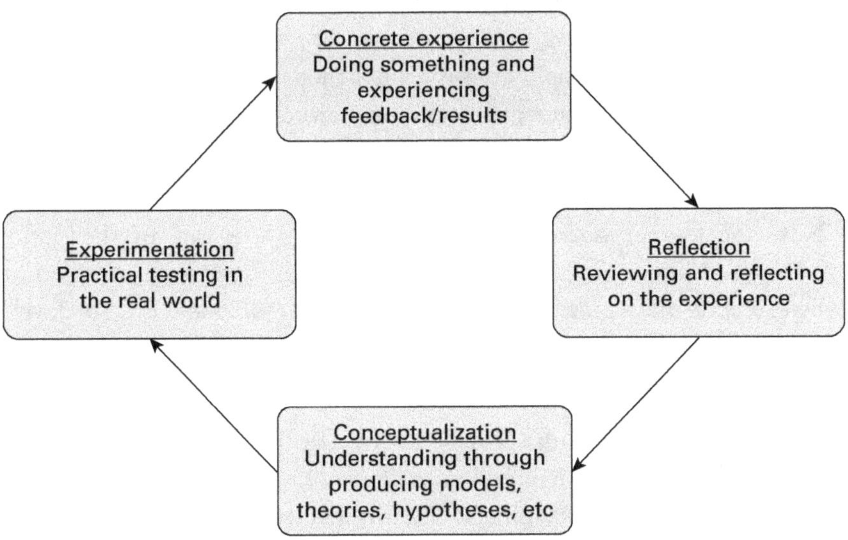

theory of learning gives us an insight into several different starting points when teaching a new topic to your learners or wishing to develop their existing set of skills.

1. Concrete experience
   Some learners are activists in their learning, which means that they need to have a go at something first before discussing it. To start with a briefing can be a waste of time because the information you are giving to them doesn't make any sense.
2. Reflection
   Having had a go at something and experienced the results, learners can then review and reflect on their experience by considering what went well, what didn't go so well and what needs improving. As a starting point this might mean the learner visualizes having a go at something and reflects on how they think it might go; or, the learner could watch you demonstrating first and then discuss it; or, they could observe a traffic situation and consider how they would behave in a similar situation.
3. Conceptualization
   Once the learner has had a go at something and reflected on the experience, they need to consider what to do next to either improve or develop. Here, they will need to consider several different options and, possibly, have a go at some of these in order to determine which is the most successful for themselves. As a starting point, you might, for example, introduce a manoeuvre and then ask how they think they would do this. They might draw a diagram or simply describe what they would need to do in order to carry out the manoeuvre safely. You should encourage them to come up with several different alternatives for themselves.
4. Experimentation
   Now the learner is ready to have another go at one of the options considered in the conceptualization stage. There may be a 'double loop' here where the learner experiments and returns to stage 3 to develop another theory or model before looping back up to stage 4 and experimenting again.

Kolb's learning theory links closely to the GROW model (for details see Chapter 3). One thing worth remembering is that most people benefit from a range of methods and teaching styles and will learn most effectively if you vary the techniques you use.

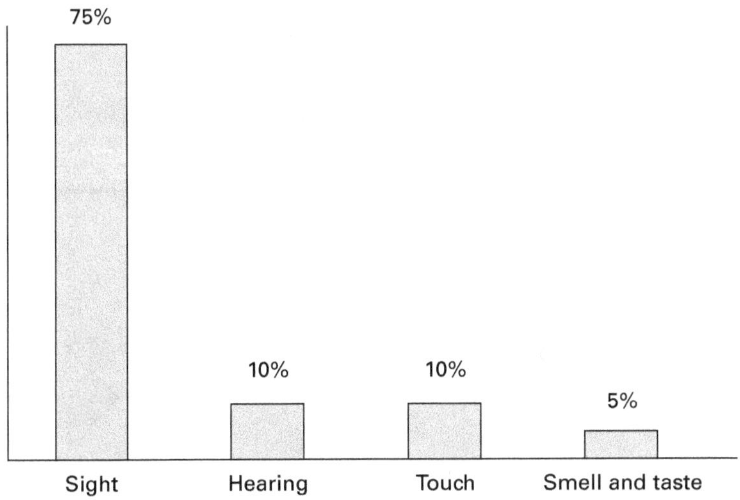

The proportions in which our senses gather information

The importance of sight

In the learning process, sight is the most important of the senses. This sense can be used in various ways to improve the quality of the learning taking place.

> Whether giving a demonstration, pointing out actual driving situations or using visual aids, any teaching that involves a learner's sense of sight will be most effective in fixing new information in their mind.

The above diagram shows the proportions in which our senses gather information. The diagram shows the effectiveness of sight in the learning process compared to simply explaining the numbers.

In driving, both hearing and touch can have an important role. For example, as well as seeing things, when listening and feeling as the noise of the engine changes and the clutch is raised to the 'biting point', learners will be developing the awareness and perception that go with these senses.

Awareness

Awareness is usually defined as knowing and understanding what is going on around you. In driving, awareness involves not only the perception and

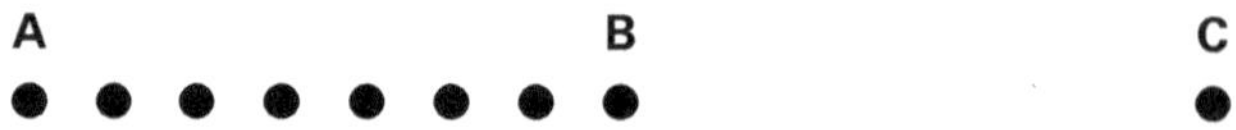

THE DISTANCE between A and B appears to be longer than that between B and C. The illusion occurs because the space between A and B is measured out in evenly spaced dots, filling the area for the eye. The distance between B and C can only be guessed at because there are no intermediate points.

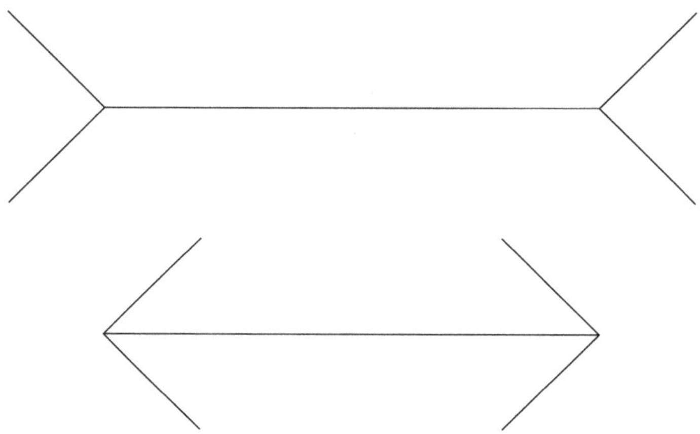

THE LENGTHS of the two horizontal lines appear unequal because of the directional arrows at the ends. Where the arrows branch outward, the line seems to be stretched out beyond its actual length. Where they branch in, the line seems to be strictly enclosed and shortened. Both of the lines are exactly the same length.

interpretation of one's own vehicle speed, position and direction of travel, but also the recognition of other hazards in time to take the necessary safe action.

Perception and awareness are the first steps towards performing a skill such as driving. Awareness is dependent on the interpretation and meaning the brain attaches to the information it receives from the senses. This involves not only looking with the eyes but also using the mind and calling upon existing knowledge from previous experience to 'see' with the mind.

What the eyes see is not always the same as what is perceived by the brain. Optical illusions offer evidence of this. They may be caused by distortion through perspective or by a lack of intermediate visual keys that help the viewer to gauge distance accurately.

This visual distortion, plus a weakness in a driver's ability to judge correctly the width of the vehicle they are driving, or that of approaching vehicles, can have very serious consequences.

What students perceive while learning depends not only on the individuality of their senses but also on how each person has learnt to see and interpret things.

Transfer of learning

This happens when a learner uses skills that have been acquired in previous experiences and in different environments. Examples include problem solving, decision making and prioritizing.

All of these are part of everyday life. You will often be able to relate or transfer your learner's existing skills to help in driving.

Incoming sensations are instantly compared with existing knowledge stored in the memory from previous experiences. The compatibility of these memories can either help or hinder learning of any new material. Where the new information is compatible with existing knowledge and thoughts, the established memories will be reinforced. For example, somebody learning to play tennis who is already a good squash player may find the learning less difficult because both sports are very similar. This is usually referred to as *positive transfer of learning.*

Sometimes previous knowledge can be a hindrance to learning. An example of this could be someone who decides to learn to drive a car and has been used to riding a motorcycle in scrambling trials, an activity where success depends on the frequent taking of risks. Put this rider behind the wheel of a car on the road and the difference in the steering, the width and length of the vehicle and the differing speed norms required may all hinder the learning process. This can be regarded as *negative transfer*. In this case, the learner is likely to be going for gaps that may be narrow, approaching hazards much too fast and struggling to master the steering at the same time.

It will take time for learners to establish the many thousands of memory connections needed to be able to drive safely, along with patience and understanding on your part.

Other basic requirements that are necessary for learning to take place are perception, attention, activity and involvement.

Perception

The senses vary from learner to learner and so does their perception. When you are driving along a wet road you will think that you 'see' a three-dimensional scene of slippery tarmac. What you actually see (the image in the eye) is neither slippery nor three-dimensional. This can only mean that you create in your mind a 'model' of what is there. You see the road as being 'wet' or 'slippery' because of the previous experience of such things you have 'fixed' in your mind.

A good example of this would be the lights of an oncoming vehicle on a dark country road at night. The amount of sensory information is very limited, but with your experience you should not have a problem interpreting it. You cannot see the vehicle, but you know that it is there! You will build an image of the type and size of vehicle to which the lights belong and decide whether any defensive action is required.

Drawing on your own experience, you will need to help your learners to 'fix' such things in their minds. This can be done by using question and answer routines regarding road surface, weather conditions, etc.

The first diagram on the next page gives an illustration of how the mind sometimes 'sees' things that may not really be there. The central triangle in each of the figures is an illusion. Although we see the edges as sharp and clear, they are not there. There is no actual brightness difference across the edges; the triangle must therefore be constructed in the mind of the observer.

In the early stages of learning to drive some learners will have difficulty in judging the width and length of the car they are driving, and the speed, distance and size of oncoming traffic. At night the problem for the inexperienced driver may be made worse by an optical illusion called 'irradiation'. This is a physiological phenomenon that occurs when the eye focuses on neighbouring bright and dark areas.

Although both squares in the second diagram are identical in size the image of the white square will, to most people, appear larger. Light-coloured cars can therefore, in some situations, appear to be larger and closer than dark-coloured cars of identical size.

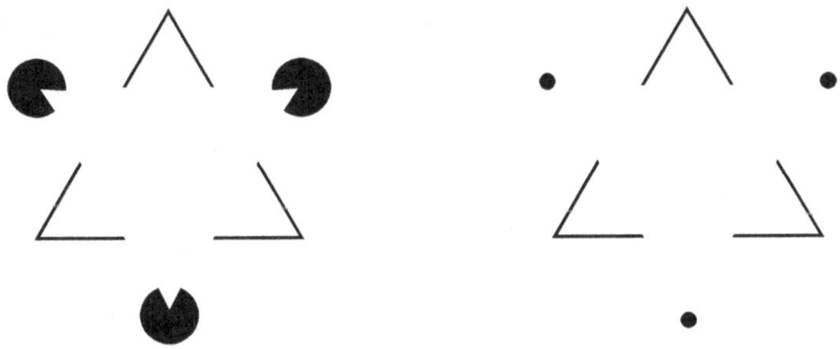

Optical illusions caused by irradiation

Attention

It is often quite difficult to maintain a learner's attention for a length of time without either a break or a change of activity. If you are involved in intensive courses, you need to take this into account and arrange the programme accordingly. Equally, you will need to consider your learners' attention span, whether your lessons are 50 minutes, 1 hour, 1½ hours, or 2 hours in length. Breaking the learning into small manageable chunks is going to be far more effective than giving a briefing at the start of the lesson and allowing the learner to drive for the rest of the lesson without a break. Repeating routes and circuits that take just a few minutes to complete, with time for reflection and development, will ensure that goals are achieved and that learning takes place. If you bear Kolb's learning theory in mind then you will appreciate that the time to reflect and come up with new ways of doing things is as important as the practice.

You should watch for non-verbal signals from the learner that may indicate boredom, impatience or fatigue (see the section on body language in Chapter 2).

Activity and involvement

The learner must be actively involved in the learning process. Avoid very long briefings or detailed explanations that do not require any active involvement on the part of the learner.

The more active and involved your learners are in the learning experience, the more they will normally learn and remember. Activity, however, should not be thought of as only physical. Learning to drive obviously involves a lot of physical activity but it is often the mental involvement that initiates the physical response to a situation. Effective instructors will help their learners to think and reason things out for themselves, leading them to the desired conclusion.

Use questions to test your learners' understanding of what they are doing and why it is important, and then through physically carrying out the task learning will take place. This practical involvement validates the teaching and can be done in various ways.

Using a more up-to-date method that includes coaching techniques means that the teaching/learning is much more 'learner-centred' than 'instructor-led'. This approach leads to a higher level of individual participation, with learners taking more responsibility for their own learning.

Memorizing

This is sometimes called *rote learning* or *parrot-fashion learning*, and is the method by which many of us learnt our times tables at school. Rote learning is rather limited in that it does not necessarily provide an understanding of the subject.

For example, a learner could memorize the overall stopping distances of a vehicle and be able to tell you, 'The stopping distance if you are travelling at 30 miles per hour on a dry road would be 23 metres'. The learner should then be asked to point out something that is 23 metres away! Even when learners can do this reasonably accurately, it is still necessary to test their ability to keep a safe distance from the car in front when driving at 30 miles per hour.

Memory is vital for those learning to drive as there is no point in learning something if it is forgotten in a short time. The ability of your learners to retain information and knowledge, and their capacity for forgetting what they have already learnt, will vary enormously from person to person. Engaging with the learner and varying the methods you use to communicate with them is very important because it will make the learning more fun and therefore more memorable.

Developing long-term memory

The first stage is to put the information in a form that can be more easily remembered by:

- breaking it down into its key components;
- using mnemonics – for example, M S M, P S L, L A D;
- painting pictures – 'What would happen if...?';
- using word associations like 'ease the clutch', 'squeeze the gas' and 'creep and peep';
- using visual keys – for example, 'round signs give orders, triangular signs give warnings', 'think of the thickness of a coin'.

When you have translated the information into a more memorable form, you could write it down and ask your learners to memorize it by rote. You could then check whether they have remembered it by asking questions at the beginning of the next lesson. If they have not learnt it, do not lose heart. Explain that it can be difficult to learn and encourage them to do some more studying. Repetition is a very good way of fixing information in the brain.

You should encourage your learners to study *The Highway Code*, *The Official Guide to Learning to Drive*, *The Official DVSA Guide to Driving: The essential skills* and *The Official DVSA Guide to Better Driving*. You will then need to confirm that this has been done by testing their knowledge. This can be achieved by setting simple multiple-choice questions that could be given as homework, thus helping them both to maintain interest in between their driving lessons and to prepare for the theory test.

Understanding

An effective way of finding out whether your learners understand something is to ask them to explain it to you: 'What are the reasons for looking round over your shoulder before moving off?' 'What must you do when you get to your turning point before you begin to reverse into a parking space?' And 'What is the reason for this?' 'What might happen?'

Understanding something means knowing its meaning, whether it is a statement of fact, a concept, or a principle. When a learner is learning to do something, it is important that, to begin with, the key steps are understood, and then practice takes place until mastery has been achieved. Rote learning will be of little help to the learner here and you need to use a technique that involves learning by understanding.

This method involves using mental processes as well as physical ones. It relies on the principle that the whole is greater than the sum of the parts. The easiest way to illustrate this is to use the analogy of a piece of music. Many of us often remember a catchy tune, to such an extent that we cannot get it out of our heads. It would be much more difficult, however, to remember just a few notes, and almost impossible to remember just one note, as this would depend on having perfect pitch.

When teaching learners how to approach junctions, you need to outline the complete manoeuvre and then break this down into its component parts. First of all, they need to understand the *mirrors–signal–manoeuvre* routine and then be able to break down the manoeuvre part into the *position–speed–look* and *look–assess–decide* routines.

Not only do learners need to understand the when, where, how and why elements involved in these sequences, but they also need to practise carrying them out until a reasonable degree of safety is achieved. No matter how well learners understand and can carry out any component parts of the junction routine, unless they can approach and emerge safely, very little will have been achieved.

So, the next teaching technique is to go back to whichever component part needs improving to get the learner to carry out the complete manoeuvre effectively. This may involve you in giving more explanation, possibly a demonstration and certainly more practice in order to improve performance. All these principles are dependent on the learners' understanding.

Asking questions to check knowledge and understanding

When deciding how to get information across to your learners you should ask yourself 'Where, when and how do we need to do that?' You will then need to ask the learners the same questions or discuss the reasons. Effective instructors will probably use a mixture of asking and telling to make lessons more varied. When using a question and answer routine, avoid making it sound like an interrogation as this will only annoy or demoralize, and you may lose the learner!

Relate any new information to what learners already know (teaching from the known to the unknown). This will allow them to build up a store of understanding. It is of little use for your learners to know how and when to do something if they do not understand why it is important.

For example, you may get learners who signal every time they move off when there are no other road users in sight. When you ask, 'Was that signal necessary or useful?' the reply might be: 'I've been told that you must always signal before you move off.' It is obvious from this response that there is no understanding of what signals should be used for, or how and when to use them. The learner's response can be followed up by supplementary questions such as 'Did anyone benefit from your signal?', which will lead to a useful discussion on the subject.

Open-ended questions that encourage active and creative participation, insight and contemplation will bring about better understanding by the learner rather than closed questions that only require a yes or no response.

Solving problems

Learning how to solve problems for themselves will help your learners to understand things and therefore take responsibility for their driving once they have passed the driving test.

Solving problems usually relies on learners being able to transfer to new situations any knowledge and understanding already stored in their long-term memory. This should assist them in working out different possible solutions to a particular problem. They can then evaluate these solutions and decide which is the most appropriate for the problem concerned. This is a valuable skill when they are driving on their own and will develop their ability to work out for themselves how to prevent risky and dangerous driving situations from occurring.

The technique of problem solving is particularly useful when analysing the driving errors made by learners, whether they are in the car (errors of control) or outside (errors of road procedure). An example of this would be a learner driver turning left and swinging wide after the corner. The cause of the error might be obvious to the instructor, but not so obvious to the learner, who may perceive several possible reasons. Perhaps the steering was started too late, there was a misjudgement of the amount of lock needed or the corner was approached at too high a speed, meaning that there was insufficient time to steer accurately enough to maintain the correct position.

Having recognized the fault, the effective instructor would help the learner to analyse it by using a discussion to arrive at the cause of it. The first question could be: 'Do you think you swung wide after that last corner?' After a series of supplementary questions such as, 'How can you avoid that situation on another occasion?' and, 'What, in particular, might you do differently?' followed by a discussion, the learner should eventually arrive at an answer that works for them.

Having arrived at a possible solution it would be helpful to take the learner round the block to have another attempt at turning the same corner. You might agree to give the learner a 'talk-through', particularly on when to start braking and how much to brake, in order to ensure that the corner is negotiated more accurately. When success is achieved, the learner should then be allowed to deal with similar corners unassisted, thus validating their understanding and skill.

Skills training

In learning to drive it is the practical application of the knowledge, understanding and attitudes gained that is most important. Whatever the situation, when learning to do something there are three basic steps:

1. *Determine the purpose* – what we need to do and why it needs to be done in a particular way.
2. *Identify the procedures involved* – the different alternatives of how it might be done.
3. *Practise the task* – do.

1. Determine the purpose

Learners must have a clear understanding of the reason for needing to be able to do whatever it is that you are teaching them. The reasons why things are done in a certain way are invariably to do with:

- safety;
- convenience;
- efficiency;
- simplicity;
- economy.

One example that covers all of the above would involve the use of brakes to slow the car rather than the gears:

- *Safety*: both hands are on the steering wheel when the weight of the car is thrown forward; the brake lights come on to warn following drivers.
- *Convenience*: there is less to do if you slow the car with the brakes rather than using only the gears.
- *Efficiency*: the car is being slowed by all four wheels rather than just two.
- *Simplicity*: it is easier to change gear at the lower speed.
- *Economy*: brake pads and discs are much less expensive to replace than clutches and gearboxes.

2. Identify the procedures

The most efficient way for a learner to understand how to do something is to break the skill down into manageable chunks or stages. This can be done by following a few basic guidelines:

- *Known to unknown*. Start with what the learner knows, understands and can do, before moving on to new skills and procedures.
- *Simple to complex*. Setting intermediate targets and moving gradually to more complex tasks will help the learner through the learning process.
- *Basic rules to the variations*. Once the basic rules for a particular procedure have been mastered, the learner will find it easier to deal with the variations.
- *Concrete observations to abstract reasoning*. Organizing a structured learning process is much less difficult if the learner can start with the more obvious facts before attempting to cope with more complicated or abstract matters.

For more detail on structuring the learning process, see *The Driving Instructor's Handbook*.

3. Practise the task

What I hear, I forget.

What I see, I remember.

What I do, I understand.

It is the **doing** that will give learners the greatest understanding; learners need to be given time to practise new skills.

Although some car driving routines could be taught initially by *rote* (for example, the M S M, P S L and L A D routines), putting them into practice requires an understanding that allows the learner to make connections with any previously established principles. For example, once your learner has carried out a basic manoeuvre using the criteria of control, observation and accuracy, it will be relatively easy for them to follow the same pattern in a similar, but slightly more complicated manoeuvre.

As an instructor you will be mixing learning methods to suit the needs of each individual learner, combined with the all-important practice. The skill of the teacher is to find a mix that works and to be prepared to change to a different mixture if necessary.

Defensive driving

You can contribute positively to reducing the risk of accidents by encouraging defensive driving techniques and attitudes. The development of a defensive attitude is as important as skill development. It is good to be able to get out of trouble when a potentially dangerous situation arises, but it is much more effective and sensible to avoid getting into trouble in the first place! The theory of defensive driving relies on the fact that human behaviour is generally motivated most powerfully by a desire to preserve one's own safety.

Defensive driving develops this concept by instilling in drivers an attitude designed to do just that, coupled with the advanced observation of potential accident situations. It may be defined as 'driving in such a way as to prevent accidents, in spite of adverse conditions and the incorrect action of others'. The need for teaching defensive driving skills is emphasized by the DVSA's use of 'hazard-perception' testing in the theory 'L' test.

An accident has been described as 'an unforeseen and unexpected event', but in many cases potential road accidents can be foreseen and avoided. In most cases, when accidents happen, they are caused by driver error. Everyone then asks who was to blame. Of far more value to driver education is to consider: 'Was it preventable?' A preventable accident is one where the driver – not necessarily at fault – could reasonably have taken some action to prevent it happening.

Some of the main factors involved in road accidents include:

- the driver;
- the vehicle;
- road conditions;

- visibility;
- weather conditions; and
- time of day.

Human actions that may contribute to accident situations include:

- committing a traffic offence;
- abuse of the vehicle;
- impatience;
- discourtesy;
- lack of attention.

The defensive driver will consider all the main factors in the first list. This involves making a continuous and conscious effort to:

- recognize each hazard in advance;
- understand the defensive attitude needed; and
- apply the skill required to take preventive action in enough time.

Encourage your learners to drive with full concentration to avoid potential accidents caused by other drivers and road users.

Teach your learners how to avoid confrontation with other drivers and how to keep a cushion of safe space around their vehicle. This includes advice about drivers who follow too closely.

Encourage your learners to continually ask themselves, 'What if... ?' In this way they will improve their anticipation skills and be able to take defensive action before a situation develops into an accident.

Teach them to consider using the horn to let others know they are there; just a gentle tap on the horn can sometimes prevent an accident. It is far better for your learners to sound the horn to alert another person than not to sound it and have to carry out an emergency stop, especially if there is a vehicle close behind.

As well as thinking defensively, develop positive attitudes towards:

- vehicle maintenance and safety;
- traffic law (for example safe use of speed, traffic signs and road markings, parking restrictions, drink/drive laws, dangerous driving implications);
- the more vulnerable groups of road users;

- reduced-risk driving strategies;
- further education and training for advanced/defensive driving;
- learning and studying.

Overcoming barriers

Learners all learn at different rates. Your training should be structured to take this into consideration and allow for the fact that some of them will experience barriers to learning. These barriers may affect the learners' studies for their theory tests, the rate at which they learn to drive or a combination of both.

There are various barriers to learning that your learners might need help with. Learning is the bringing about of more or less permanent changes in knowledge, understanding, skills and attitudes. Adults in general find that learning new skills and developing fresh attitudes are more difficult than gaining knowledge and understanding. Barriers to their learning may have to be overcome in any of these areas.

In adult learning the most frequently encountered barrier is previous learning.

Previous learning

Consider how you got on at school and which lesson or activity you enjoyed the most – was it Maths, English, Sport, Science, Cookery, Woodwork, History, Art, Music or French? In your class you will not all have got the same amount of information from all of your lessons. All of us will have taken something different from each of the lessons because each of us processes information through different channels. Most people are able to process information through several channels – visual (seeing), auditory (hearing) and kinaesthetic (feeling). However, a significant minority process information strongly through just one and possibly two channels, to the exclusion of the other channels of communication. In schools it is expected that most information will be learnt through reading and writing and yet this does not meet the learning needs of a large proportion of the population. The result is that lots of people go through school without feeling they learnt very much at all, and, possibly, blaming themselves for this because they didn't concentrate or pay enough attention. This creates a barrier to their future learning.

Similarly, in driver training, it is important to vary the means of communication to ensure that each customer is learning to the best of their ability. This means that the traditional form of 'explain, demonstrate, practise' is not always the most effective way to learn. Identifying how someone learns best (by asking them) and then choosing together what to do will ensure that learning takes place at a deep and long-lasting level because it has been specifically adapted to suit the individual learning needs of the client. Together, you could choose to let them have a go; get out of the car and look at the road layout; talk them through a situation; swap seats and encourage them to talk you through a situation; draw a mind map; draw a diagram; use a pre-printed diagram; or give a demonstration; or experiment with any other idea the customer might suggest.

Lack of motivation

This is also a barrier to learning. Each learner will have different reasons for wanting to learn to drive and helping them identify those at the start of their driving lessons will help keep them motivated. When they are despondent with their progress, asking them to remind you why they wanted to learn to drive can re-inspire them and re-focus them on their goals.

Colour blindness

This is likely to cause problems only when dealing with the different types of traffic light, controlled situations such as junctions and pedestrian and level crossings. Rather than focusing on the colours, you will need to base your explanation on the positioning and sequence of the lights and what each of them means.

Language difficulties

If the learner's understanding of English is very poor, this can be a barrier to learning and, in extreme cases, the learner might need the help of an interpreter. Provided the learner has some knowledge of English, the use of visual aids, demonstrations and getting to know what the limitations are, will help you to overcome these difficulties.

It is important, right from the start, for you to encourage learners to say if there is anything they have not understood. If there is someone in the family who speaks better English than the learner, it may be useful to have a debriefing with them present. This should enable you to clarify specific requests to the learner and also allow the learner to convey any queries to you.

Hearing difficulties

There are about 50,000 people in the UK who were either born without any hearing or who lost it during early childhood. There are several thousand others who have become profoundly deaf in adult life, well after they have learnt to speak, read and write. By the time they reach the age of 17 and are thinking about learning to drive, those with severe hearing problems may have had most of their education in specialist schools or units. Some will have speech, but this may be difficult to follow, especially for anyone who is not used to dealing with this type of disability. They will probably use sign language and may also be able to lip-read.

With understanding and patience from an effective instructor, people with hearing difficulties should be able to assimilate all that is necessary to learn to drive.

People who cannot hear do not regard themselves as being disabled. In fact, deafness is not classed as a driver disability, so no restrictions are placed on the full licence.

Most instructors are rarely asked to teach learners who have hearing problems and some are reluctant to take this type of learner. This is mainly because there is a widespread lack of understanding of the problems of people with hearing difficulties and the ways in which they are able to communicate. For many instructors the task may seem too daunting. As a result, people without hearing often find difficulty in obtaining expert tuition and tend to rely on parents and friends – people who may be good at communicating with deaf people but who are not necessarily able to teach safe driving for life. Driving instructors who are specialists in communication, have good practical teaching skills and who understand the effects of not being able to hear are better equipped to teach than friends and relatives.

After adapting your practical teaching skills for people with hearing difficulties, you will find the experience both rewarding and enriching. The problem for you will be to learn the best way to transfer your knowledge, skills, understanding and attitude to these learners.

It is not necessary for you to learn the British sign language used by people with hearing problems, but you must use simple, straightforward words that have only one meaning, avoiding those that might be ambiguous. As lip-reading depends as much on the clarity of the speaker's lip movements as on the ability of the learner, it is essential that you speak slowly and distinctly, and move your lips to form each word. Face-to-face conversation while stationary becomes more important than with a hearing learner. Don't shout – the learner cannot hear what you are saying!

With impaired hearing, sight and touch become a great deal sharper and this helps learners to overcome the disadvantage of not being able to hear. They are likely to be much more aware of what is happening on the road ahead and will quickly master how to assess risk.

People without hearing also develop great sensitivity of feeling over the normal course of living in silence. Consequently, they often acquire clutch control and coordination with the accelerator fairly easily. People with hearing problems often have better powers of concentration than learners with normal hearing.

When teaching people who have a hearing problem it is vital that a method of communication acceptable to both of you is established at the beginning of the first lesson.

As a large amount of learning will take place through the eyes, the task of teaching people with hearing difficulties becomes easier with the use of visual aids and demonstrations. Visual aids are not only invaluable, they are essential (see the section in Chapter 4 on visual aids). Face-to-face conversation, simple language and written notes should cover all the other needs of most learners.

Because you will not be able to use an effective question and answer technique while on the move, diagrams will be invaluable when teaching learners with hearing difficulties. More time will need to be spent parked somewhere safe so that non-verbal instruction can take place.

Other barriers to learning

Mere discomfort can be a barrier to learning. You need to be able to recognize whether or not your learners are comfortable. Discomfort can have many causes, ranging from toothache to sitting in an incorrect position, or being told, 'You must keep your heel on the floor when using the clutch' when the learner's feet are too small or legs too long to do this comfortably.

Allowances may have to be made for very tall people – they will need the seat as far back as possible with the back rake adjusted to give more leg room. If the tuition vehicle is very small, it may even be necessary for you to advise them to take lessons with another instructor who has a larger car with more headroom.

Learners of small stature may be assisted by securing cushions underneath and behind them, and pedal extensions may be needed for those with short legs or small feet. Your terminology may also need to be adjusted to allow for learners not being able to keep their heel down when controlling the clutch.

If a learner is not driving as well as usual, there may be some simple explanation. For example, was the driving seat adjusted properly on entering the vehicle, or was the learner in too much of a hurry to 'get going'? Make sure any necessary adjustments and procedures are carried out correctly otherwise you may both be at a loss as to the cause of the problems and the lesson may be wasted.

If the learner is having an uncharacteristically bad lesson, it may be due to something as simple as wearing different shoes, or as complicated as having problems at home. Ask tactfully if you think a learner may not be feeling well. The lesson may be completely wasted if a minor illness is causing a distraction. You could even be aiding and abetting an offence if the learner is taking medication that affects driving.

Other barriers to learning to drive can be related to the use of alcohol which, as well as being illegal when driving, can cause a false sense of confidence and impetuous risk-taking. If you think a learner has been drinking, ask tactfully and abort the lesson if necessary.

Anxiety, emotion and stress can all affect concentration. If a learner's driving is not up to the usual standard and they have recently had personal problems, it may be advisable to postpone the lesson.

For those who decide to learn to drive later on in life the going can be difficult. You should explain that it will be more difficult to learn and to remember new procedures. Things may be more easily forgotten and concentration more difficult to sustain. Problems may be even greater for older learners who have decided to learn to drive because they have lost a partner or close relative. You will need lots of patience and understanding if you are to help these learners attain their goal.

Physical disabilities

A physical disability need not necessarily be a barrier to learning to drive, but it is a subject that requires special skills from the instructor. These are dealt with in much more detail in *The Driving Instructor's Handbook*, with an overview in this section.

There are thousands of people with disabilities, some quite severe, who have passed the driving test. Many have proved their skill by also passing an advanced test. Teaching people with disabilities can be very rewarding as such learners usually have a considerable amount of motivation to learn and will often put in more effort than their able-bodied peers. If you are involved with people with any kind of disability, the practical teaching skills in this book will be particularly relevant in helping you to improve the quality of learning taking place. You will need to pay special attention to the following:

- *Flexibility* – being able to adapt your usual teaching methods to suit the perceived needs of the learner. Assess each learner's individual requirements and adapt your teaching methods accordingly.
- *Lesson planning* – being prepared to build in rest breaks and taking care not to spend too long on manoeuvres that may put physical strain on the learner.
- *Body language* – watching carefully for signs of strain or tiredness. Some people tire very easily as the day progresses, so arrange the lessons to suit the individual learner's needs.
- *Feedback* – offering feedback only on things that are controllable. Make allowances for limited mobility. Encourage feedback from the learner.

Neurodivergent Learners

Neurodivergence refers to natural variations in how people think, process information, and experience the world. This includes, but is not limited to, autism, ADHD, dyslexia and dyspraxia. For driving instructors, this is not a specialist add-on area – it is central to understanding how people learn.

Neurodivergent learners may process information differently, respond more strongly to sensory input, or require more time to integrate new skills. They may also demonstrate significant strengths, such as attention to detail, pattern recognition, or the ability to hyperfocus. Effective teaching recognizes and works with these differences, rather than attempting to normalize them.

A key principle is reducing cognitive overload. Driving places simultaneous demands on perception, decision-making and motor skills. Breaking tasks into smaller steps, allowing processing time, and avoiding excessive verbal input can significantly improve learning. Clear, unambiguous language is particularly important, as some learners may interpret instructions very literally.

Consistency and predictability support learning. Explaining what will happen during the lesson, using familiar routes where appropriate, and maintaining a structured approach can reduce anxiety and free up cognitive capacity for skills development. Equally, instructors should be alert to signs of overload – such as shutdown, increased errors, or emotional responses – and be prepared to pause or adapt the session.

Emotional experience plays a central role. Some neurodivergent learners may have a history of feeling misunderstood or judged, which can affect confidence and willingness to take risks in learning. A calm, non-judgemental approach, combined with specific and genuine feedback, helps to build trust and resilience.

Importantly, neurodivergent learners are not a homogenous group. There is no single 'method' that works for all. Your role is to observe, ask and adapt – developing an individualized approach that aligns with how each learner learns best.

Specific considerations – linked with the 17 competences of the Standards Check

This next section shows you how the 17 competences of the Part 3 and the Standards Check are demonstrated in practice, through your ability to adapt teaching to the individual needs of your learner. Throughout the following explanations, there are references that link directly to the relevant competence on the Standards Check (SC) marking sheet. See Chapter 6, The ADI Standards Check for a list of competences.

While neurodivergence is not a homogenous group, some broad patterns can help you anticipate potential needs. These should always be treated as starting points for observation and adaptation, not fixed assumptions. In all cases, your effectiveness as an instructor will be reflected in your ability to adapt to the learner (SC1 – SC3), communicate clearly (SC6 – SC8), and create a supportive learning environment (SC9 – SC11).

Autism

Autistic learners may experience differences in communication, sensory processing and predictability needs.

They often benefit from clear, literal instructions, which directly supports SC6 (clarity of instruction). For example, replacing vague guidance such as 'ease off' with 'slowly clutch up until the car starts to move. Feet still' reduces ambiguity and supports skill acquisition.

Planning and explaining the structure of the lesson in advance aligns with SC1 (Lesson planning) and SC2 (adapting the lesson plan). Using consistent routes and routines can reduce cognitive load and anxiety, enabling the learner to focus more effectively on the driving task.

You should also be alert to sensory overload and emotional responses, adapting the environment or pace accordingly (SC3). As some learners may mask confusion, techniques such as asking the learner to 'talk me through what you're thinking' support SC11 (analysing problems) and SC12 (clarifying learning outcomes), helping you accurately assess understanding.

A calm, non-judgemental approach is essential in building trust (SC16), particularly where the learner may have experienced misunderstanding in previous learning environments.

ADHD

Learners with ADHD may experience differences in attention regulation, impulsivity and working memory.

Maintaining engagement through concise, well-timed instruction supports SC6, while adapting the structure of the lesson to include variety and active participation reflects SC2. Long explanations are less effective; short, focused inputs given at the point of need are likely to be retained and applied.

Impulsivity may affect hazard perception and decision making. Encouraging learners to verbalize observations, eg 'What can you see developing ahead?' supports SC7 and promotes reflective thinking (SC11), helping them to regulate their responses more effectively.

Providing immediate, specific feedback reinforces learning (SC14) and helps maintain motivation. A positive learning climate (SC9) is particularly important, as learners with ADHD may be sensitive to criticism or frustration.

Dyslexia

Dyslexic learners may experience difficulties with sequencing, short-term memory and processing written information.

Adapting teaching methods to rely less on written material and more on verbal explanation and demonstration reflects SC2 and SC6. Breaking tasks into manageable steps supports SC4 (adapting the lesson plan) and reduces overload

For example, teaching a manoeuvre in clearly defined stages, with repetition and reinforcement, allows the learner to build confidence progressively. Where left/right confusion occurs under pressure and whilst reversing, adapting language to include physical or visual references demonstrates responsiveness to the learner's needs (SC3). For example, 'Steer towards me' or 'Steer towards your driver's door'.

Allowing additional processing time and checking understanding through appropriate questioning (SC12) ensures that learning is secure before moving on.

Dyspraxia

Dyspraxic learners may experience difficulties with coordination, motor planning and timing.

This may be evident in tasks such as clutch control, steering accuracy or gear changes. Adapting the pace of the lesson and allowing additional practice time reflects SC2 and SC3, ensuring the learner is not pushed beyond their current capability.

Breaking physical skills into smaller components and practising them in low-demand environments supports SC4 and SC5 (structured learning). For example, focusing solely on clutch control in a quiet area before integrating it into more complex driving situations.

Linking instructions to clear sensory or visual clues supports SC6, while encouraging the learner to reflect on what feels right or wrong in their control of the vehicle supports SC11 (encouraging self-evaluation).

Maintaining patience and a supportive atmosphere (SC9) is critical, as repeated difficulty with coordination can affect confidence.

A consistent approach

Across all neurodivergent profiles, effective instruction is characterized by adaptability, clarity and empathy. These are not additional skills, but core elements of the Standards Check: responding to individual needs (SC2 – SC3), using effective communication (SC6 – SC8), and building a positive learning environment (SC9–SC11).

In this sense, teaching neurodivergent learners does not require a different standard of instruction, but a more precise and responsive application of the same professional competences.

Neurodivergence and client-centred coaching

Effective teaching of neurodivergent learners requires more than minor adjustments to traditional methods. It demands a shift in approach. As an instructor, you must move beyond predominantly instruction-led techniques and adopt a coaching style that involves the learner in the learning process.

Coaching enables you to explore how the learner is processing information, to check understanding and to adapt the lesson in real time. This is particularly important where differences in attention, sensory processing, communication and motor coordination may affect how learning takes place.

Over-instruction can create dependency and mask a lack of understanding, particularly for learners who may already be managing a high cognitive load. A coaching approach, by contrast, supports the learner to think, reflect and make decisions – leading to more secure, transferable driving skills.

In this context, coaching is not optional; it is an essential part of meeting individual needs effectively. For more information see Chapter 3, Client-centred learning and coaching.

Labels and individual differences

While terms such as autism, ADHD, dyslexia and dyspraxia can be useful in helping instructors understand potential patterns, not all learners will have a diagnosis, and not all will identify with those labels. Two learners with the same label may learn in very different ways. In practice, the most important factor is not the label itself, but how the individual learner thinks, feels and responds to learning.

Relying too heavily on labels can lead to assumptions and inflexible teaching. Effective teaching is based on observation, questioning and adaptation – treating each learner as an individual and responding to their specific needs.

02
Communication

In this chapter we deal with the practical teaching skills of communication that help bring about learning. These skills include verbal, non-verbal and listening skills, all of which are covered in detail.

To become an efficient instructor and to pass the ADI exams you need to be:

- *Articulate*. This doesn't mean that you need to be a fluent public speaker, but it does mean that you should use language that is clear to your learners and that can be easily understood by them.
- *Enthusiastic*. Try to create a supportive learning environment by showing enthusiasm for the work and for your learners' efforts.
- *Encouraging*. Give encouragement to the learner when deserved, but balance this with criticism when required. Any criticism should be constructive and related to the requirements of the particular task or situation. Learners need to be encouraged to take on responsibility for their own learning and not be passively receiving instruction and information.
- *Friendly*. The way you approach the teaching of your learners should be in a friendly but professional manner, creating a relaxed atmosphere in which learning can take place and in which the learner can gain confidence.
- *Patient*. As with your own driving, show patience and tolerance, both with other road users and with your own learners when they make mistakes or are not as efficient as you would like them to be.
- *Confident*. Have confidence in your ability as a driver and as an instructor, but also develop the skill to help your learners build confidence in their own driving.

In addition to these qualities you also need to be a good listener, perceptive, aware and attentive, as outlined in Chapter 3.

Communication is a two-way process between you and your trainees. This means listening to the learners and observing their actions, as well as talking. Make sure that any communication from you to your learners is at a level that is easily understood by them.

Develop different ways of communicating effectively with your learners. You will often have to vary and adapt your methods and terminology to suit the needs of individual learners, so that each of them clearly understands your message or instructions.

As an effective driver trainer, you will use a wide variety of methods to communicate with the trainee, including:

- establishing an appropriate level of understanding for each learner;
- explaining any new principles in a clear and straightforward manner;
- using visual aids where appropriate to give the learner a clearer picture of what is required;
- considering whether a demonstration would be effective for a particularly complex procedure or manoeuvre;
- offering to 'talk through' any new procedures or routines to develop the learner's confidence;
- giving any directional instructions clearly and in good time, allowing the learner plenty of time to make decisions and respond accordingly;
- using positive feedback and praise where appropriate, to encourage and motivate the learner;
- using questions to ensure that the learner has a thorough understanding of the task;
- encouraging learners to ask questions and allowing enough time for them to respond.

Whatever means of communication you use, make sure that both you and the learner agree about what is required and be ready to modify your methods to suit the needs of the individual.

Use each lesson with a learner as an opportunity to practise your communication skills. At the end of each lesson, you should analyse your own performance with a view to improving your ability and skills. Reflect by asking yourself:

- 'Have I spent sufficient time looking at and listening to my learner?'
- 'Have I misinterpreted or not seen any silent signals?'
- 'Have I missed the learner's control faults or observational errors by not watching carefully enough?'

- 'Has my own body language been positive?'
- 'Have I encouraged or discouraged the learner by the way in which I reacted to their actions or responses to my questions?'
- 'Could I have communicated more effectively with the learner during the lesson?'

These points are dealt with in more detail later in this chapter.

Instruction

Instructing mainly involves telling the learner what to do and how to do it. This has the effect of personal and long-standing individual methods being passed on to the learner and perpetuated without considering any new methods or practices. The learner has no real involvement in the learning process and takes very little responsibility for any decision making. One of the problems with instructing is that we are generally not very good at learning by being told things because we do not remember them particularly well; we are usually much better when we actually do something.

Instructing is based on a hierarchy: 'I'm the expert, this is what you have to do.' With this method the emphasis is on the skill and expertise of the instructor being 'pushed' onto the learner. The result is that the learner is not sufficiently involved, other than practising what has been taught, and will generally be content to be told what to do in order to achieve a licence. This, of course, does very little to encourage any longer-term learning and often results in the learner simply learning enough to pass the test rather than generating a life skill.

Coaching

The skill of the effective coach is in extending and developing an individual's knowledge and skills by raising awareness and responsibility in the learner.

Coaching involves selling ideas and concepts to the learner and transferring responsibility; it should be an equal partnership between learner and instructor. In this respect, the objective is not to demonstrate how much the instructor or coach can do or how skilful they are, but to bring out the best in the learner. It is generally better to let the learner do what comes naturally, with steering for example, and then gradually guide the learner along the right lines.

Coaching has many benefits, particularly relating to retained and long-term learning. The instructor is no longer seen as the 'expert' in the traditional way – the coaching relationship is much more an equal partnership. Coaching puts learners in an active role and encourages them to identify their own goals and objectives, both in the long and short term. This is done by creating a situation where the coach finds out and establishes the prior knowledge and experience of the learner and builds on it.

Coaching (as opposed to instructing) can help to achieve a better performance because of the greater participation, willingness and satisfaction on the part of the trainee.

Coach or instructor?

With 'old-style' instructing, learners feel that the instructor is in control and that they are indirectly encouraged to take a passive role, simply following instructions. This is why, when instructors ask probing questions as part of the teaching/learning process, they often find that the learner is reluctant to answer or to be involved in detailed discussion. The learner's expectation is that the information will be provided. To overcome this situation, it is important to establish the relationship between coach and learner from the first lesson. This relationship should ideally be an equal partnership, with the instructor (coach) encouraging learners to set their own goals and to take more active responsibility in the learning process.

Coaching involves coaxing, questioning, motivating and listening. The most important of these is listening – not just listening but attending to exactly what is being said. The instructor (coach) should listen to, and pay attention to, the learner always and make sure that he or she is being given the coach's full attention.

There are two major benefits of coaching. The first is improved performance. Coaching brings out the best in individual learners – instructing does not necessarily do this effectively. The second concerns life skills. Coaching, with more emphasis on the active involvement of the learner, is more likely to provide the learner with longer-lasting skills ('safe driving for life'). Instructing is more to do with passing a series of tests.

Neutral and non-judgemental communication

We can sometimes find ourselves concentrating too much on fault-finding and correction, with an emphasis on learners' errors and in giving direct criticism. This can create tension and make the learner defensive. To overcome this, the effective coach/instructor/trainer should be neutral and non-judgemental with learners.

Try to balance the positives and negatives by offering information on the good points before dealing with any weaknesses. Rather than criticizing the learner, try to direct attention to the specific situation. Where possible avoid direct criticism (unless it is necessary) by using non-judgemental questions such as 'What happened...?' or 'What do you think caused...?'

Neutral communication means ensuring that what we are saying is not being misinterpreted by our learners. This comes back to self-awareness, which is the key to being aware of others and being able to empathize with them. Too often, what we say is misinterpreted by our learners because of our tone of voice or the words we have chosen to use. Being in rapport with our learners is about understanding how they learn, the kind of risks they are likely to take, and adapting the way we choose to communicate with them to ensure our message is received as it was intended. If we are going to adopt a uniform approach in the car with our learners, then we are not using neutral communication. A 'one size fits all' approach is not going to raise awareness and build responsibility in the learner driver.

Non-judgemental communication means avoiding criticism or blame, which can result in defensiveness and make the learner close up. It can be a challenge to understand how to avoid criticism within the context of driving instruction because of the focus we put on faults. However, if we aim to raise the learners' self-awareness, then we broaden the context to identify their strengths, limitations and development needs. It is important for learners to understand how their personality impacts on the way they control the car; and to recognize how they will cope with distractions, passengers and unfamiliar driving situations such as night, bends and motorways once they are qualified. Adopting a uniquely fault-based approach does not encourage learners to take responsibility for the whole of their driving because they sit back and allow themselves to rely on us for guidance and feedback.

With non-judgemental communication we ask learners what they think happened, and how they think it could be improved; we focus on the specific situation and we look for the positives first.

Coaching and instruction

It is sometimes said that coaching and instruction do not mix effectively and efficiently because instructing involves telling the learner what to do, whereas coaching deals much more with asking and discussing. However, in the context of driver training a mixture of the two methods is often necessary. For example, on the move in heavy traffic it may well be necessary for the instructor to take an active role to prevent potentially dangerous situations from developing. Here it is usually better to use only key words rather than a detailed instruction. This instructional intervention would, however, be followed by a period of coaching while stationary and a structured discussion about the particular situation. Even while on the move there is scope for effective coaching to take place. This can be done by using appropriate questions without distracting the learner from the main task, or by getting the learner to indicate developing hazards and then use this for subsequent discussion.

We may also find it useful to start the series of lessons with coaching methods to establish a partnership before moving on to instruction on specific routine matters. More instruction 'on the move' might follow but with an emphasis on coaching techniques once the skills have become more established.

All of the above can be regarded as 'coaching' because coaching is generally seen as being 'appropriate for the circumstances' and 'ensuring that the learner is put in an active role wherever possible'.

Coaching means discovering the individual's possibilities and developing them in a supportive and challenging way. Coaching therefore means communication not by telling, but by asking and involving the learner actively in the learning process.

Verbal communication

Speech should be used effectively and in such a way that your learners will hear and understand what it is that you need them to hear. For example, even though you may be frustrated or exasperated, you may not want your tone of voice to convey this to your learner. There are, however, certain times when for safety reasons you must get your point across reasonably forcefully. The elements of speech that help you to communicate effectively include:

- tone of voice;
- use of emphasis;
- content;
- use of figurative language;

- use of humour;
- speed of speaking;
- use of pronunciation;
- pitch of your voice; and
- use of implied speech.

The tone of your voice

It's important to put the learner at ease and to maintain their interest and attention. If they are not paying attention, it is doubtful whether they will learn anything at all.

Your tone of voice conveys your emotions and feelings, such as annoyance and pleasure, and supports the content of what you are saying. As the tone of voice often conveys the true meaning of your message, it is important that you sound friendly and relaxed even though you may be feeling the opposite!

Consider the following question: 'What made you decide to slow down?' If you pose this question in a harsh tone of voice, you will sound as though you are telling the learner off. If you ask the same question with a soft tone of voice, you are showing interest in the learner's actions. Practise asking the question in different ways and attempt to convey different meanings.

Vary the tone of your voice to ensure that your meaning is clear and to add variety to your delivery. This is essential if you are going to retain the learner's interest and attention. If you restrict yourself to only one tone, your delivery will become monotonous and it is likely that the learner will lose interest.

The use of emphasis

By putting greater stress on certain words, you can alter the meaning of a sentence. For example:

- '*What* are you looking for?'
- 'What *are* you looking for?'
- 'What are *you* looking for?'
- 'What are you *looking* for?'
- 'What are you looking *for*?'

Practise asking this question out loud and put the emphasis on the word in italics. In the first question, you are asking about the action of looking itself. In the second you imply disbelief that the learner is bothering to look at all. The third sentence queries whether it is the learner who should be looking – perhaps somebody else should be looking! In the fourth example you are questioning the action – perhaps there is no point in looking at this moment. In the last question you are probing the learner's understanding of what needs to be seen as a result of looking.

Now say each of the questions again, continuing to emphasize the word in italics, but try to vary your voice to express concern, anger and amazement. As well as saying the words in a particular way you can sometimes stress a particular consonant or vowel to accentuate your meaning, for example, '*Slooowly* let the clutch come up.'

People who are practised and skilled speakers, such as politicians or lawyers, often use emphasis to considerable effect not only to help the listener to understand the message but also to indicate hidden meanings. Sometimes it is only when a speech is heard rather than read that you understand what message is being conveyed.

The content of speech

As well as the tone and emphasis you use when speaking, the words themselves are vital if you wish to be effective in communicating.

The use of an unambiguous vocabulary is vital when teaching people how to drive. Try to match the words you are using to the level of understanding and ability of the learner. The skilled trainer will be able to put trainees at their ease by talking to them at an appropriate level. There is no point in using long and complicated words when teaching somebody who cannot understand them. The best advice is to keep it simple as this is more likely to bring about learning.

Getting to know your learners will help you to use suitable words and phrases that they will readily understand. One common criticism of less able instructors is that they tend to use inappropriate phraseology that is not easily understood. The use of jargon should be avoided where possible. If it is necessary, make sure that the expressions have been explained to the learner.

When dealing with the controls of the car it is best to explain to the learner not only what the control does and how it is used, but also the words that you are going to use when dealing with it. This will avoid your trainee becoming confused, with possibly dangerous results. For example, if you are going to call the accelerator the 'gas pedal', don't confuse the learner by then referring to the 'throttle'.

While communicating with learners, avoid talking about things that may be offensive to the person in question because this could interfere with their learning.

The use of figurative language

Try to make the content of your message interesting: there is nothing worse than boring your learner. You can avoid doing this in several ways by using figurative language. For example:

- *Metaphors*: used to imply a similarity between things or situations that are not necessarily associated – for example, 'crawling along at a snail's pace'.
- *Similes*: figurative comparisons using terms such as 'like' or 'as'. An example would be to say that a bad driver was 'driving like a lunatic'.
- *Hyperbole*: the use of deliberate over-exaggeration – for example, 'That gap is big enough to get a bus through'. (Be careful to avoid sarcasm.)
- *Analogies*: comparisons made to show a similarity in situations or ideas – for example, 'If you have time to walk across, then you will have time to drive across!'
- *Personal experiences (or anecdotes)*: these allow you to compare situations happening now with those that might have happened before. For example, if you had a learner who tried to emerge from a junction unsafely, you might use examples from your own driving experiences to illustrate the point.

By using these figures of speech you will make your lessons more interesting and the messages less likely to be forgotten. Take care not to overuse them to the extent that the intended content of your message is diluted or lost.

The use of humour

Instructors who are humorous often maintain their learners' attention and interest very effectively, but humour does not work for every learner or every instructor. If you try unsuccessfully to be funny you could lose your credibility. We all know someone who, when telling a joke, invariably forgets the punch line. You should not tell jokes during the lesson time as this will annoy most learners, and in no circumstances should you tell racist, sexist, religious or dubious jokes.

Some instructors can be extremely amusing without telling jokes. They can put a message across using wit but, again, not every learner will respond well to witty remarks and some may take offence, especially if they do not realize that you are trying to be witty. You can often bring a smile to your learner's face without trying too hard, simply by being alert and responding to a possibly difficult situation with a humorous remark. For example, you might be waiting at traffic lights that turn to green and your learner does not move – you could gently ask, 'What colour are we waiting for?' You should avoid using sarcasm, however, as it adds nothing to the learning process and could cost you a learner.

The speed of speaking

The speed at which you speak can help to maintain the interest of your learners. You can create anticipation by increasing the speed of speech as you build up to an important point. You can also use silence or pauses to allow things to sink in before you continue. If you pause while you are talking you can indicate a sense of deliberateness to give emphasis to certain key points. For example: 'Mirrors (pause), signal (pause), manoeuvre'.

You can also use pauses to give you time to think before delivering your next piece of information, but such pauses should not be excessive or you will lose your learner's attention completely. Try not to fill in the pauses with 'ums' and 'ahs' as this will irritate your learner and detract from what you are saying.

Slowing down the speed at which you say a single word can be useful in indicating the speed of action required. For example, '*Squeeeeze* the gas' or, '*Geeently* brake'.

Pronunciation

It is important that as an 'expert' you pronounce the words you use correctly. Your learners will expect you to be fully conversant with the subject you are talking about and if you mispronounce your words too often you could damage your credibility, distract your listeners from what you are saying and reduce their attention. If you come across new words when reading books on driving and intend using them but are unsure of their pronunciation, it is best to refer to a dictionary for guidance.

Pitch

Pitch is a combination of the tone you use and the loudness of the sound you make. Considerable emphasis can be given to the instruction or direction you are giving by varying the pitch of your voice. Pitch is particularly useful when you wish to convey urgency, caution or importance either to what you are saying or the way you wish your learner to react to the words you are using.

Take care not to over-exaggerate the pitch of your voice because it can be a distraction to your learner. Your speech should be a comfortable variation of harsh and soft tones and of loudness and quietness.

Speaking loudly will not always get the attention or response you want. You only have to think of British tourists abroad trying to communicate with somebody who does not speak English. In vain they end up almost shouting, 'Do you speak English?'!

Pitch is useful when using keyword prompts, particularly those that require urgent action such as 'wait', 'hold back', or 'stop'.

Implied speech

Speech can be used to convey your feelings and especially your attitude to a given situation. The dictionary meaning of the words you are using is not as important as what they imply. It is not only the words being used but also the way in which they are delivered that gets the message across.

Implied speech will sometimes be used to break the ice. For example, if you ask, 'How are you today?' it not only puts the learner at ease but also gives you some feedback, which might be useful when structuring the lesson content. If the learner is feeling good, then perhaps you will agree to set the goal for the lesson high. If the learner is not feeling good, then perhaps their sights will be lowered to maybe consolidating an existing skill.

When meeting people for the first time, we often talk about the weather or the journey we have had to get to the meeting. The person opening the conversation might genuinely not be interested in these things but is really saying, 'I wish to communicate with you, please respond.'

All these elements of speech can be developed. Whether teaching in the car, in the classroom or speaking to larger groups at meetings and conferences, it may be useful either to record or, better still (because you can also see what visual impact you are having), video the proceedings with a view to assessing and improving your performance.

There are certain speech distractions that should be eliminated where possible. The most common is the frequent use of speech mannerisms such as, 'OK', 'right', 'you know', 'I mean', 'well then'. This trait gives the impression of nervousness or a lack of confidence, neither of which will help to put the learner at ease or inspire trust. Also, the use of the word 'right' to mean 'correct' could be misleading and dangerous.

Talking plays a great part in teaching people how to drive and you should take every opportunity to further develop your speaking skills. Remember that, when speaking, you are not only giving a verbal message but also conveying your feelings and attitudes. By varying your speech, you can drastically change your listener's interpretation of what you are saying, whether you are talking on a one-to-one basis, or to small or large groups.

Other common mistakes that speakers make which, particularly when they are talking to groups, can cause their listeners to become bored and lose concentration, are repeating things and getting too technical for the audience.

Telephone conversations form a valuable part of your life, given that the initial contact with a potential customer is often made on the phone. Much of what has been said about speech also applies here. The problem is that you are unable to read the body language of the person you are speaking to. If you cannot see the gestures and facial expressions of the other party, you lose some insight into what they are thinking while they are speaking.

Communicating is not just talking but should be a two-way exchange of ideas and information. You will therefore need to develop your listening skills.

Developing the communication skills of speaking and listening will help you in presenting a driving lesson. Similar rules will apply to presentations to larger groups, but in the next section we will concentrate on listening skills and the one-to-one lesson.

Listening skills

We will learn more about our learners' needs by asking questions and listening to what they say than we will by talking to them.

As indicated in the section on coaching, the effective trainer listens very carefully to the learners' responses and attends all the time to exactly what is being said. Just as important, learners should be made aware that they have your full attention.

Pay particular attention to anything that your learners say voluntarily and try to look at them when they are talking so that you can pick up the silent signals as well. These non-verbal messages will often reinforce the verbal message and help you to understand what people are really feeling. This may often be at variance with what they are saying. You can then use questions like, 'You don't seem too happy with that. Is there anything that you don't understand?'

When people are listening, they tend to show their interest and attention both verbally and non-verbally. They will nod their heads, lean forward and say things like, 'Yes, I see', 'That's true', 'I absolutely agree' and 'Hear, hear'. On the other hand, if they are not listening, they do not look at you, they yawn, or they do not respond. Any of these responses will indicate to you that they are bored with the proceedings and that you need to alter your approach to this part of the lesson.

You can develop your listening skills in several ways:

- 'Listen' with your eyes as well as your ears. By looking at the speaker you will not only hear the words but detect the silent signals that help you to understand the true meaning of what the person is saying.
- Ask questions. If anything is unclear, do not be afraid to ask for it to be clarified, and if you disagree with the point being made, then say so, but give your reasons why.
- Use open-ended questions to test learners' understanding of anything you have explained to them and seek their views and opinions on what you are saying. When they respond, hear them out. Do not interrupt – wait until they have finished speaking before replying.

Let's look at five different levels of listening:

1. The lowest level of listening is where you are planning what to say instead of listening to what your learner is saying. This is the most irritating level of listening because the learner can tell that you are not listening. For example:

   Instructor: *'Hi, how are you today?'*

   Learner: *'Oh, feeling stressed. You know how it is...'*

   Instructor: *'Good, good. Today we are going to work on roundabouts.'*

   In this example you clearly focus only on your own agenda. Often it can be difficult to make the switch into client-centred learning because we get caught up in our long-held beliefs that this is how we were trained and therefore this is what we must do on each lesson. We have a set format to follow, which we know will get our customers ready for their test, and it is difficult for us to hear anything else. But, in a client-centred relationship, how the client is feeling is critical to their ability to learn and their ability to drive.

2 The next level of listening is where you give a reply that is about yourself and not about the learner. This is probably how the majority of conventional conversations are conducted. For example:

Instructor: *'Hi, how are you today?'*

Learner: *'Oh, feeling stressed. You know how it is...'*

Instructor: *'You think you're stressed! There's so much going on in my life at the moment you wouldn't believe. My son... blah, blah, blah.'*

If you were sitting with a group of friends chatting, then this would be an okay way of holding a conversation because communication in groups tends to meander and then make its way back to the beginning so someone would eventually ask the original person why they are feeling stressed. In a client-centred relationship the client is the important person in the conversation. How they are thinking and feeling will affect their ability to control the vehicle and also will potentially create barriers to their ability to learn. As driving instructors, it is important that we actively listen and stay on the client's agenda because learning to drive is about so much more than dealing with faults. We are not giving value for money and allowing learning to take place if we jump in and tell our own stories.

3 This level of listening is about giving advice that is still more about you, the instructor, than your learner, and can be close to the lowest level of listening in the irritation stakes if the learner is looking for a sympathetic ear rather than direction. For example:

Instructor: *'Hi, how are you today?'*

Learner: *'Oh, feeling stressed. You know how it is...'*

Instructor: *'Well, let's get these roundabouts sorted and then things will look a lot brighter', or, 'Cheer up, it might never happen.'*

In a client-centred relationship the word 'stressed' is like a golden nugget because it gives us an opportunity to explore with the client how their emotional state impacts on the way they handle the vehicle and how this could be an issue once they are driving unsupervised. It is important to listen to the words that clients are using and the way they use them, rather than to assume we have the answers and know how they are thinking and feeling; or, worse still, to dismiss what they are saying and move straight back onto our agenda.

4 The fourth level of listening is getting into active listening (see more on active listening in Chapter 3) and is moving onto the learner's agenda. It is about listening and inviting more. People often work things out while they are talking and a prompt from the coach/instructor may help the flow. For example:

Instructor: *'Hi, how are you today?*

Learner: *'Oh, feeling stressed. You know how it is…'*

Instructor: *'What are you feeling stressed about?'*

How easy is that? All that needs to be done is repeat the words the client used and you will find yourself right on their agenda. Often people get confused about coaching because they think they have to come up with complicated questions and spend their time planning their questions rather than listening. Repeating back allows both ADI and client to check meaning. The client hears the words they used and might respond: 'I didn't actually mean stressed ... I meant ...'. The ADI has focused on the words that were used and, in doing so, has not had the opportunity to wander off on a different track and has demonstrated to the client that what they are saying is valued.

5 The highest level of listening is all about listening behind and between the words; listening to the silences; using one's intuition. For example:

Instructor: *'Hi, how are you today?'*

Learner: *'Oh, feeling stressed. You know how it is…'*

Instructor: *'What are you feeling stressed about?'*

Learner: *'I have to book my theory test and I never seem to find the time to do it.'*

Instructor: *'What's getting in the way?'*

Learner: *'Oh, I don't know. I'm busy or someone else is on my laptop when I want to be. I don't seem to be able to stop long enough to work out how and when to do it.'*

Instructor: *'Is there anything else that's stopping you?'*

Learner: *'Actually, I keep putting it off because I don't want to book it.'*

Instructor: *'And why don't you want to book it?'*

Learner: *'Because I'm afraid I'll fail it.'*

What started off looking like a time-management issue ends up being about self-esteem. If the learner's self-esteem affects their ability to make decisions and gets in the way of their progress, then that is going to have a serious impact on both their learning and their driving.

One powerful listening technique is silence. Sometimes we take a lack of response from the learner as meaning they don't want to talk, when in reality they are still preparing what they want to say. If we sit and wait we will often be surprised by how much they will share with us.

Briefings and explanations

Although 'briefings' and 'explanations' are not strictly communication skills, they are included because they are examples of situations where good and effective communication skills are vitally important.

You will often give briefings in which you discuss what is likely to be covered during the lesson to come. These briefings will usually include a discussion with the trainee about the goals for the lesson, and a short summary of the key points of what is to be covered. The briefing will usually be followed by a more detailed explanation of how to do whatever is being taught, when to do it and, particularly, why it is important for the content to be dealt with in a certain way. Be careful not to 'overload' the learner. Information should be divided into the following categories:

- must know;
- should know;
- could know.

You should be able to identify the 'key points' of the message and then concentrate on making sure that the learner understands the 'must know' elements. Further information from the 'should know' and 'could know' categories may be given in response to discussion with the trainee or questions from them and can be added at a later stage. This can often be done 'on the move' as and when situations develop that require this further information to be given or discussed.

Making sure that learners know and understand everything that they need to know can be achieved by:

- breaking the information down into its component parts;
- using mnemonics or acronyms to make routines more memorable, for example, M S M or P S L (see Chapter 4);

- using word associations like 'creep and peep';
- using visual keys like 'Think of the thickness of a coin';
- slowing or quickening the speed of your speech to match that at which you want the action to be carried out;
- using pauses after important points have been made;
- using effective questioning techniques after each key point has been made to confirm the learner's understanding of what has been said; and
- using visual aids where appropriate and, if the subject is technical, giving handouts for learners to refer to after the lesson.

At the end of each lesson that has contained a briefing or full explanation, assess your own performance. Ask yourself, 'Has the learner understood all the key points that I have explained?'

Problems can arise during lessons if your instructions and directions are not given in a clear and unmistakable manner. You need to take account of all the previous points made about verbal communication, but you should also take special note of the following:

- Use language that will be readily understood by the learner to avoid any confusion.
- Avoid ambiguous words that might be misinterpreted by the learner. For example, 'right' meaning 'OK' or 'correct' could cause the learner to think you want them to turn right. 'Top', meaning top gear, could be misheard as 'stop', especially on a hot day with all the windows down and noise from traffic.
- When on the move give the instruction and directions early enough for the learner to do whatever is necessary without rushing.
- Match the level of the instruction to the ability of the learner. A novice will need almost total instruction in what to do, whereas a trained learner may only need the occasional 'keyword' prompt.
- Use the alert–direct–identify routine. For example: 'I would like you to... (alert) ... take the next road on the left please (direct). It's just around the bend' (identify).

Remember to take into account that less-experienced learners will take longer to react to the instruction or direction. An instruction given too late is likely to result in the learner:

- missing out important observations;
- losing control with feet or hands;

- assessing situations incorrectly;
- making poor decisions;
- losing confidence.

When teaching a learner who is at an advanced stage, you can transfer the responsibility of working out where the various junctions and hazards are by not giving too much help.

A very good way of transferring responsibility and finding out whether the learner is ready to drive unaccompanied would be to ask, 10 minutes before the end of the lesson, 'Do you think you could find your way back home/to college/to work from here on your own?' If the answer is yes, then let the learner drive back without any instructions or directions being given.

Once the learner is nearly at driving test standard you should make sure that you use phraseology similar to that of the examiner as a way of preparing for the test situation. It is extremely important that you 'sit in' on driving tests regularly so that you can reaffirm your understanding of how an examiner gives directional instructions and their timing.

One of the most common criticisms of ADIs is that of over-instruction. This happens because the instructor does not know when to 'drop out'. Are you guilty of 'over-instructing'? If so, what are you going to do about it?

At the end of each lesson ask yourself:

- Were the instructions and directions given to my learner in a clear and unmistakable manner?
- Did the timing of the directions given allow the learner to do all the things necessary to deal with situations?
- Was there any ambiguity in the instructions and directions given?

Body language

Whenever we communicate with others, we use body language – it is unavoidable and instinctive. Speech and the development of language began about 500,000 years ago but it is probable that body language has been used for at least 1 million years.

Because body language is so deeply ingrained in us, it is difficult to disguise. Even when you are not speaking you are sending messages to others, sometimes without even being aware of it. Your physical appearance, posture, gestures, gaze and facial expressions indicate to others your moods and feelings.

It is important to use positive body language and to interpret the body language of your learners. Because the body language of your learners may give you more information about their mood and receptiveness than what they are saying, being able to interpret accurately these silent signals will assist you in deciding whether to modify your delivery, back off, or even change the activity entirely. For example, should the face of your learner show frustration when failing to master a reversing exercise, you may decide to switch to something that is less demanding to boost the learner's confidence rather than destroy it.

The ability to interpret body language will also enable you to tell whether there is any difference between what the learner is saying and what they really think. The driving instructor needs to develop a high degree of perceptual sensitivity to read accurately the silent signals being sent by learners.

Body language is particularly important in interviewing, negotiating, selling and buying situations. Although the general rules regarding body language will apply at meetings, in the classroom or during social encounters, when you are giving driving lessons your skills will need to be adapted to take account of the fact that, on the move, you can only see the side of your learner's face. (We do not encourage our learners to look at us while they are driving!) Of course, while stationary you will often be able to see their eyes as well.

If you want to be able to use your own body language in a positive way and be able to read that of others, you need to recognize its constituents. There are seven main constituents, some of which are more relevant to driving instruction than others:

1. facial expressions;
2. gaze;
3. posture;
4. gestures;
5. proximity;
6. touch; and
7. personal appearance.

When teaching in the car, you will spend much time not only reading the road ahead but looking at the face, eyes, hands and feet of the learner. Although the hands and feet will tell you how well the controls are being used, the face and eyes will not only show where learners are looking but also what they may be thinking or feeling.

1. Facial expressions

In driving instruction, facial expressions are most useful. The face is highly expressive (even in profile) and can convey one's innermost feelings. Think of the expression on the face of someone who has just failed the driving test and then compare it with that of someone who has just passed!

The face is a very spontaneous communicator of messages and will generally convey the feelings of its owner in a uniform way. The face is, therefore, a reliable indicator of happiness or despair, pain or pleasure. Consequently, when teaching, you should ensure that your facial expressions do not contradict what you are saying – if they do, it will have a disturbing effect on your learners.

2. Gaze

When explaining things to your learner, or debriefing at the side of the road, or in a classroom situation, you will normally have eye-to-eye contact. The eyes can tell you a great deal about what people may be feeling but, with skill and practice, your eyes can tell others what you want them to think you are feeling. Poker players and salespeople use this technique to good effect, sometimes with high stakes to play for.

A strong gaze usually shows that you are being attentive and concentrating on what the other person is saying. However, in some cultures it can be impolite to stare. When people become embarrassed they will often break eye contact and look away.

Breaking eye contact may show that you have made an error or cannot answer a question, while a reluctance to look at someone at all may show your dislike or distrust of that person. However, establishing strong eye contact will show that you have a genuine desire to communicate and it will be seen by your learners as an invitation to speak. It is a cultural expectation that people look at each other when communicating. If you are reluctant to look someone in the face when talking to them, or continually shift your eyes around, you will not inspire trust.

Your emotions, attitudes and honesty, as portrayed by your eye contact, make gaze an important constituent of your body language. Aggressive stares and shifty looks should be avoided. You should try to develop a strong gaze, with an occasional blink or look away, which will make people feel more comfortable and receptive.

3. Posture

In the confined space of a motor car, when your feet and hands are occupied, posture is not quite as revealing as in a classroom situation where how you stand or sit and the position of your arms and legs will reflect your feelings and attitudes to others. A normal seating position, which allows learners to reach the foot and hand controls comfortably, will of course determine the 'angles' of their legs and arms.

You can display a warmth and liking for someone by leaning towards them slightly, with your arms relaxed. In contrast you can show your disgust at their actions by turning away and looking out of the window. Be careful not to hover over the dual controls with your feet as this will unnerve learners and destroy their self-confidence. Try to avoid continually looking round to check the blind spots on the move for the same reason. Careful and subtle use of your dual mirrors will achieve the same objective without worrying the learner.

In meetings or in the classroom, your posture becomes much more important. An erect posture will indicate a sense of pride, confidence and self-discipline, while stooping shoulders and head down may be interpreted as being slovenly or lacking in confidence. Your impressions of others and their impressions of you will be influenced by posture and gait. When walking across the room you should therefore adopt a confident, purposeful walk, which will indicate self-assurance and personal dynamism.

When giving presentations, you can use posture and body movements to help to bring your story to life, supporting any verbal message and thus maintaining the interest of those who are watching and listening.

4. Gestures

Gestures may be used instead of words in certain circumstances. If you are trying to communicate with someone who has hearing difficulties, or who does not speak English, gestures will help you to communicate. Your hands can be used to demonstrate how the clutch plates come together, for example.

A nod of the head or a wave of the hand are friendly, passive signals that may be given to other instructors or road users to acknowledge a courtesy, whereas a shaking of the fist conveys aggression. Sometimes your gestures will be involuntary. For example, scratching your head or chin may signal that you are uneasy or concerned about what your learner is doing. Driving instructors who constantly fidget or wave their arms about will give their learners the impression that they are nervous or worried. This will do little to build up learners' confidence! Gesticulations of this nature, or pen waving while going along the road, will also distract the learner from concentrating on the road and could be dangerous.

To control your gestures, you need to be aware of them, especially those that may be distracting to others. If you give presentations at meetings or in the classroom, a video recording of your performance will be invaluable in helping you to recognize those gestures that are weak and those that are effective in emphasizing and reinforcing your verbal messages. If you are uncomfortable using deliberately planned gestures, rehearsal and practice will allow you to deliver them in such a way that they appear to be spontaneous and natural rather than forced and awkward.

5. Proximity (personal space)

You should be aware that each learner needs a certain amount of personal space (a 'space bubble'). Encroaching on this personal space may make the learner feel uncomfortable and could even cause them to change to a different driving instructor.

Make sure that this space is not so great that your teaching loses its effectiveness. The diagram on the next page shows the different environments and situations and the amount of space required. You will see that the driving instructor is in the privileged position of being allowed to get closer than almost everybody else, with the exception perhaps of the family doctor!

The amount of personal space required sometimes depends on the cultural background of the person. In many Mediterranean countries and in Norway, for example, people feel comfortable almost rubbing shoulders. For most British people this would be quite unacceptable.

You will need to be very sensitive to the needs of each individual learner in this respect and generally should avoid getting too close wherever possible.

In the classroom, distance can be a barrier to communication, as can speaking from behind a desk or up on a rostrum. Avoid being seen as authoritarian and try to establish an informal atmosphere. For instance, it can sometimes be more effective to sit on the edge of the desk than behind it.

6. Touch

Formal touches are important when meeting someone for the first time, like a new learner. A firm (but not crushing) handshake will indicate self-confidence, which is especially important with new customers. A limp handshake implies weakness and it would be better not to give one at all.

At the end of a lesson a handshake is not always necessary and a wave or pat on the back might be more effective. These can also be nice gestures when the learner passes the driving test.

You must be extremely careful not to touch learners in the car unless it is for reasons of safety. Touching learners may make them feel uncomfortable or threatened and cause them to distrust your motives. Learners often change instructors because unnecessary physical contact upsets them. On

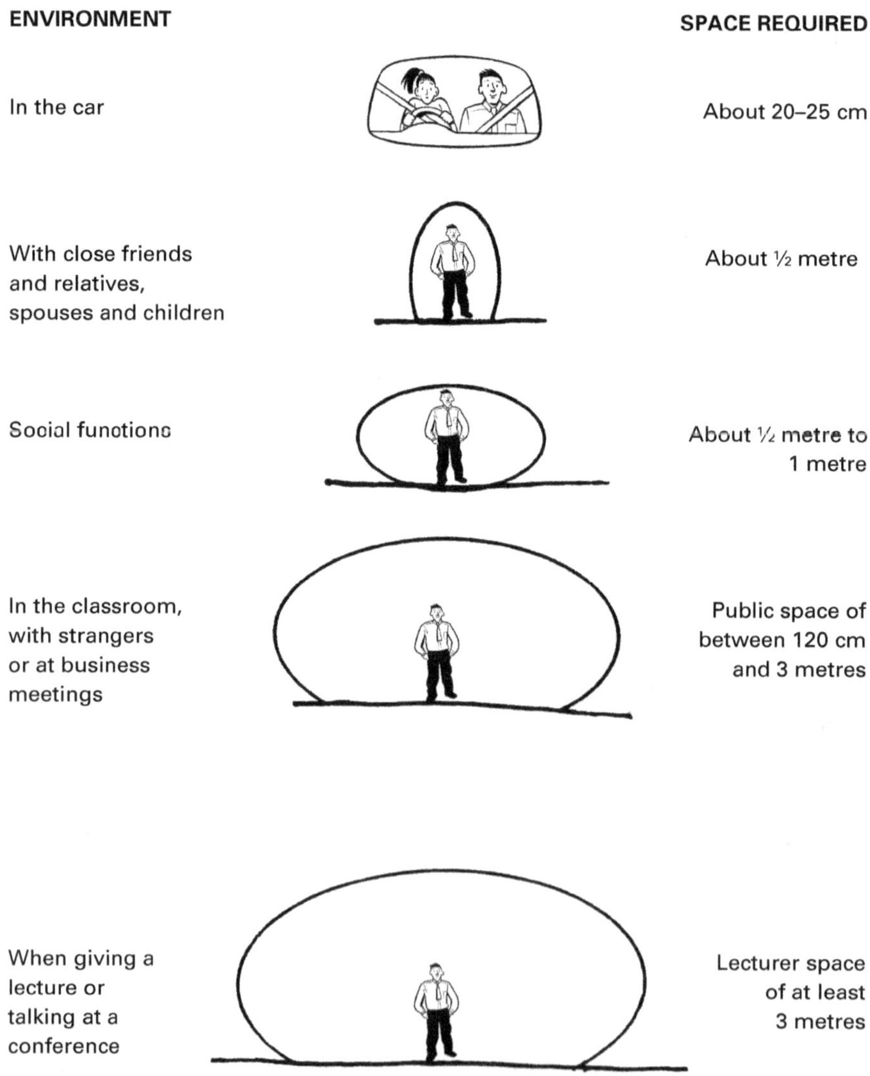

The space bubble

the other hand, in some cultures people continually touch each other during conversation.

7. Personal appearance

As a professional driver trainer you are under scrutiny from the public, particularly if you have your name on the car! Your appearance, dress and grooming may create an initial impression that is very difficult to change.

When considering body language, your personal appearance, your hair and the clothes that you wear are of great importance because you may well have more control over them than your facial features and posture. There is little we can do to change our shape, features and size, but much can be done to manage our appearance, the suitability of our clothes and the general impression that we convey.

When teaching people to drive, you do of course have to take account of the weather conditions and, while it might not be necessary to wear a three-piece suit, you can still dress casually but smartly. In the summer and winter you will need to dress for comfort, but never forget that your appearance can influence your impact on people and can help to create a favourable or an unfavourable impression.

Learners' body language

All the constituents of body language that we have discussed in the previous section may combine to present a positive image to those you meet. It is equally important that you recognize the silent or implied signals your learners give out. We have chosen common signs that your learners may give you to indicate the way they feel. Getting to know yo assist you in accurately interpreting their body lan rules generally apply.

Learners who are willing to listen:

- sit with their head on one side;
- look directly at you;
- rest their chin on the palm of their hand;

- nod in agreement;
- say things like, 'I see.'

Learners who are pleased:

- smile;
- use strong eye contact;
- can't stop talking;
- use humour in their speech;
- are polite and courteous.

Learners who are anxious to ask a question:

- lift a hand or finger;
- shift their sitting position;
- fidget with their ear or chin;
- look intently at you with their head on one side.

Learners who are annoyed with themselves:

- shake their heads;
- tightly cross their arms;
- hit the steering wheel;
- exhale loudly;
- frown.

Learners who have had a fright:

- cover their eyes with their hands;
- open their mouth and put their head back;
- bite their bottom lip;
- become red in the face;
- inhale sharply.

Learners who are disappointed:

- frown or scowl;
- drop their shoulders and let their head drop forwards;
- let their arms fall into their lap;
- droop their mouth.

Learners who are nervous:

- talk incessantly about nothing;
- tighten their grip on the steering wheel;
- lick their lips;
- bite their nails or chew their fingers.

Looking at your learners will not only allow you to see and interpret their body language, but also assist you in identifying faults being made that involve their feet, hands and eyes. If you do not see the fault, how can you suggest a remedy for it?

Feedback

Listening to what the client has to say about their driving experiences is the most vital part of feedback, as this is what tells you whether and to what extent they are learning. Driving is a task which involves a high level of reflection and self-evaluation if it is to be carried out safely. The process of feedback develops the student driver so that they can evaluate and reflect upon their driving when they are unsupervised. If a newly qualified driver is involved in a 'near-miss' incident and has been coached to develop self-evaluation skills, they will be able to reflect on this incident and determine how to prevent a similar one occurring in the future.

What sort of questions could you ask in order to elicit feedback from the learner on their own performance? Questions around scaling are effective because they encourage the learner to take responsibility for their own learning. You could ask, for example, 'On a scale of zero to 10 how confident did you feel when we were reversing around the corner, where zero is horrendously nervous and 10 is super confident?' or 'On a scale of zero to 10 how well do you think you controlled the speed of the car when we were reversing around the corner, where zero is very badly and 10 is brilliantly well?' It doesn't matter what number they give when scaling themselves because you are helping them to monitor their own progress so that they can take and remain in control and go on to establish new goals.

During a feedback session, scaling questions could be followed up with questions that look for evidence because evidence objectifies the feedback and ensures that it is constructive and can be built upon. The next question might be 'What evidence have you got for giving yourself that number?' You might need to use additional questions at this point to help your learner find the evidence that made them give themselves whatever mark they did. For example, when considering how well they controlled the speed, you might need to ask them what kind of gradient they were on to get them to consider whether they needed clutch or brake control. Alternatively, you could ask them what they need to do with the clutch to slow the car down; or, where was their right foot when controlling the speed of the car – on the gas or on the brake? These questions encourage the learner to recall precisely what their feet were doing in order to control the speed of the car and this raises their self-awareness and builds their self-evaluation skills.

Follow-up questions could be around development and goal-setting. This is all still part of the feedback process where you are coaching the learner to take responsibility for their learning. You could ask, 'What would you need to do to move up the scale one point?' (If they gave themselves a 10 from the outset, then the question might be, 'What would you need to do to maintain a 10?') The previous questions were around recalling what they did. Now you are asking them to visualize what they could do. If they say 'I don't know', you could refer back to the evidence they used to give themselves the score in the first place because within that evidence will probably lie the information about how to improve.

Other questions could be:

- 'What help do you need from me to move up the scale one point?'
- 'When would you like to have another go?'
- 'How long is it going to take you?' and
- 'How will you know when you have got there?'

This learner-centred approach to feedback ensures that newly qualified drivers remain safer than if they had simply been taught to pass the driving test.

The reason they remain safer is because they have practised giving themselves feedback on their own performance and this has developed their ability to self-evaluate and take responsibility for their driving.

Communication should always be two-way. Make sure that the learner is actively involved and that you respond to the learner rather than dictating. Most importantly, use your active listening skills.

03 Client-centred learning and coaching

Most people nowadays receive information in a completely passive way from a TV or computer, rather than taking an active part in the learning process. In the driver training context, they often expect to remain in the passive role and be taught 'how to pass the test'. Coaching and client-centred learning skills take the learner out of this passive role and encourage awareness and responsibility so that they can make safe decisions when driving on their own.

According to many experts, 'Coaching is a learner-centred method that develops awareness and responsibility with an equal relationship between coach and learner.' For example, with a complete novice you could establish how they learnt best and then use the most appropriate method to teach them. Rather than giving a lesson with an explanation covering the cockpit drill and all the controls of the vehicle you might agree to let the learner try the controls on their own. Alternatively, the learner might prefer to watch you demonstrate before having a go themselves. In this way we are using coaching right from the start of our learners' training process and actively involving them in taking on responsibility for their own learning.

Many experienced instructors ('driver trainers') do this anyway – but they have not necessarily called it 'coaching'.

The process of coaching involves:

- active listening;
- effective questioning;
- neutral and non-judgemental communication;
- giving and gaining feedback; and
- reflecting back.

Coaching skills include the use of the 'GROW' principle (goal, reality, options, way forward), which is explained in more detail later in this chapter. Most instructors will know about the principle, but will have probably used slightly different wording. For example, in *The Driving Instructor's Handbook* and in previous editions of *Practical Teaching Skills for Driving Instructors* we have used expressions such as:

- agree and set the objectives;
- set the baseline;
- establish prior knowledge and understanding;
- move from the known to the unknown and from the simple to the more complex;
- the different methods available to achieve the objective;
- what we might need to do to achieve the objective.

Coaching or instructing

Traditional methods of instruction are short term – they tend to help the learner to pass a test, but do not do a great deal for longer-term learning. Coaching focuses more on active learning which then fosters ongoing learning and prepares the learner for solo driving and more post-test learning.

Instructing is often seen as being quicker in the short term, but this kind of teaching only prepares the learner for passing the test and does little to encourage any ongoing awareness or responsibility for the learning. Coaching, however, has the advantage that the learner is involved in the learning process. This means that there is more chance of them being prepared for longer-term learning, and better able to make safer decisions when driving.

Some coaching experts feel that coaching and instructing do not mix. They stress that giving basic instruction has the effect of lowering the level of awareness and responsibility in the learner. An 'instructor' is, in effect, saying to the learner, 'I'm the expert, do as I say'. The overall effect is that any learning that takes place is minimal and short term. Others in the coaching industry, however, feel that there is sometimes a need to give basic instruction – especially in the early stages of novice driver training. What is clear is that there is a need for instruction in safety-critical situations. In other words, if the learner is unaware of a hazardous situation that is developing, the instructor must take appropriate action. This could be in the form of a question, '*Have you noticed that the lights have changed to red?*' or a direct instruction, '*Brake. The lights have changed to red*', or using the dual controls. Taking control like this affects the coaching relationship because the learner was no longer taking responsibility for the driving task at that point. However, it was necessary for safety reasons.

> 'Coaching means using all methods and facilities at our disposal.'

This means that in a coaching environment we can use explanations, demonstrations, instruction, direct intervention where appropriate or necessary but, at the same time, using all the recognized coaching techniques such as questioning, active listening, reflecting back and giving feedback.

However, starting with coaching methods as early as possible makes it much easier to encourage the learner to take responsibility for their learning and also makes it easier for you, the instructor, to address the higher levels of the GDE matrix right from the start. (The 'Goals for Driver Education' are dealt with in detail later in the chapter.)

To summarize:

- *Instructing* is mainly about telling. 'I'm the expert; this is what you have to do.' Giving too much training or instruction lowers awareness.
- *Coaching* is mainly asking. In particular, asking questions that the instructor (coach) does not know the answer to. The teacher/trainer/instructor becomes much more of a 'facilitator of the learning process'.
- *Mentoring* includes offering some advice based on the mentor's expertise or experience.
- *Coaching* encourages awareness and responsibility for the task.
- *Coaching* means using 'active listening' and 'effective questioning' as well as discussing, reflecting, offering feedback.
- An effective coach will always follow the learner's agenda.
- All training, instructing, coaching, mentoring must be learner-centred (following the learner's agenda and the agreed topics and goals or objectives). That is, responding to the learner's individual needs rather than 'following the set syllabus' and relying on what the instructor wants to impart.
- As a result of using coaching methods we will be drawing the information or skill out of the learner rather than 'pushing the information in'.

Principles of coaching

The main principles behind the concept of coaching include:

- The coach and the trainee have an equal relationship. The coach is no longer seen as the 'expert' as in instructing.
- Coaching raises awareness and responsibility in the learner.
- Coaching means that the learner or trainee is in a much more active role in the learning process.
- Coaching increases the learner's awareness of individual goals, aspirations, attitude and emotions as well as improving skills and knowledge.
- Coaching builds on the learner's prior knowledge and previous experiences.
- An effective coach communicates with the learner in a neutral and non-judgemental way.
- Coaching involves the use of effective questioning, active listening, giving and gaining feedback, and reflecting back.
- Coaching is not just about using question and answer techniques – it is also about using methods that are appropriate for the individual circumstances, making sure that the learner is actively involved in the learning.

Benefits of coaching

Coaching enhances the way we learn naturally. We learn many things without instruction – walking, running, throwing, catching, talking – and must take on awareness and responsibility to do each of these tasks. One example that is often used by coaching experts to illustrate the benefit of using coaching methods involves trying to instruct someone to stand up from a lying down position as if they have never done this before.

Main benefits of coaching:

- better self-awareness and self-reflection;
- increased long-term individual performance;
- higher motivation and commitment;
- clarity in purpose and meaning;
- greater responsibility for individual learning.

Coaching promotes:

- self-directed learning;
- personal growth; and
- improved longer-term performance.

Coaching can include the use of other forms of intervention such as a command in a real emergency situation or an explanation of how something works or a particular procedure, but we should revert to coaching as soon as possible.

Coaching builds awareness (particularly self-awareness) and responsibility in the learner from the earliest stages of learning.

Because it is difficult to accurately replicate the potentially risky circumstances that young or inexperienced drivers may be faced with it is sometimes necessary to use imagination exercises.

For example:

- 'What particular dangers or risks do you think there might be when you are driving on your own after passing your test?'
- 'If you were out for the evening with a group of mates and...'
- 'What would be significant about that situation?'
- 'Your car is full of passengers who might have had a few drinks and you are under pressure to get somewhere...'
- 'What could you do...?'
- 'What else could you do to alter the situation?'
- 'Would that effectively control the situation?'
- 'Are there any other...?'

Coaching skills

Rapport

We have previously looked at how people learn differently and how learning is most effective if we adapt the way we teach to suit the way the customer learns. In this next section we consider the effect the relationship has on the learning potential of the customer – that is, the rapport between the instructor and the learner. We also look at the difference between a traditional 'instructor-led' relationship and a coaching 'client-centred' relationship.

From a business point of view most instructors understand that it is entirely down to them to 'get on' with all their customers individually. If a learner expresses a view that you, personally, do not agree with it will not be good for business to show disagreement or disapproval. We need to be non-judgemental. This is fundamental to our business success – to 'get on' with our customers. This can be done in two ways: from an instructor-led point of view or from a client-centred perspective.

What does it mean to get on with our customers from an instructor-led point of view? Many instructors have great personalities and in the car they come across as larger-than-life characters. They would tell you that all their lessons are a great laugh and their learners love them. They tell jokes, tease and banter and expect their customers to behave in a certain way so that they will be able to take and pass their test. Their learners learn to drive and probably get to grips with the controls of the car and driving in different road, weather and traffic conditions in reasonable amounts of time. But they go away with little or no understanding of the higher-level goals in driver education. They will probably not understand how their personality, views, values and opinions affect the choices and decisions they make when driving independently with friends in the car. They may not realize how susceptible they are (or are not) to the effects of fatigue, or to peer pressure; how risky they are (or are not) and what their potential likelihood is (or is not) of driving under the influence of alcohol or drugs.

It can be appropriate to cover the effects of alcohol and drugs or the risks of distractions inside and outside of the car, but if the driving lessons have all been about the instructor putting on a show to get the learner to have a good time, then the teaching has all been one-sided. Some people will take on board the information and will process it effectively – these people probably share the same learning styles as the instructor.

Rapport is a key element in creating a learning environment where the customer feels safe enough to express how they really think and feel about things – things that are not always related to driving. This is important for them to develop an understanding of the inextricable link between behaviour, thoughts and feelings. How they think and feel affects the choices and decisions they make – always. They might not be clear what they think about things or how they feel about things. Often this is because their attitudes to driving, drink, drugs, sex, religion, road safety, seat belts, speeding, etc, are the result of a lifetime of influences from friends, family, the media, people they look up to. For example, being told 'you are stupid', or 'you will never make anything of yourself', or 'you are selfish' will affect the way we see ourselves and the world in a very different way from if we had been told 'you are going places', 'the world is your oyster', 'you are really bright'.

It is important to build a different relationship with each of our customers because each one has a different set of experiences, which will affect the quality of their learning. Some will really respond well to banter, joke telling and levity. Others will much prefer a studious silence without constant interjections. And most will be somewhere in the middle. However, the point is that until you are with your customer on their driving lesson you cannot decide how to communicate best with them so that they learn about how thoughts and feelings govern behaviour.

In a client-centred relationship the customer is treated as an equal and knows that their views and opinions are a crucial part of the learning process. The instructor's job is to be non-judgemental. As a result, the customer can work on developing their self-evaluation skills so that when they are out driving on their own they know how to recognize a near-miss, reflect on it, and put strategies in place to avoid it happening again.

How is client-centred rapport established? Mainly through non-verbal communication techniques, with the instructor taking their cue from the customer. It is necessary that effective learning takes place and for this to happen the instructor needs to use non-verbal communication techniques to relate on an equal basis and establish trust.

Eye contact: This doesn't mean staring into someone's eyes but it is about looking at the person when they are talking rather than looking down at some notes or straight ahead out of the windscreen. It helps establish equality and makes the person feel valued.

Body language: Ensure that your body language is open. When parked at the side of the road turn and face the customer.

Nodding, smiling: Nodding and smiling are part of active listening. These non-verbal communication techniques encourage the customer to open up further because they know they are being listened to.

Matching: Listening to the words that someone uses and adopting those types of words really helps build rapport. If you have an aural learner they may say things like: 'I hear what you're saying', 'That sounds like a plan', 'That rings a bell'. A visual learner might say: 'I see what you mean', 'That looks okay', 'I see what you are saying'. A kinaesthetic learner might say: 'That feels good to me', 'I get your drift', 'I'll give it a go'. By matching the words they use you are breaking down a potential processing barrier. If you don't adapt the language you use to suit the language of your learner, they have to work through and around your learning style before they can even get to theirs – many people give up on the way.

Matching tone of voice and speed of speech can also be very effective in establishing both rapport and an excellent learning situation.

Rapport is an essential coaching skill in a client-centred relationship because it puts the responsibility for learning on the learner (customer). This will accelerate their learning because rapport will ensure that barriers to learning are broken down. The instructor, by using their non-verbal communication techniques, will establish a relationship that is non-judgemental and equal. This means that the person learning will become more self-aware; that is, aware of how their individual and personal thoughts and feelings affect their behaviour.

Communication skills

To become an effective coach in driver or instructor training, you need to have excellent communication skills as outlined in Chapter 2, but specifically you need:

- to be observant and an active listener;
- to use non-judgemental verbal communication;
- to have self-confidence, so as to avoid slipping unnecessarily into an instructional or directive approach; and
- an open and honest working relationship with the learner.

Listening, questioning, clarifying, reflecting back, giving feedback are all essential skills for the coach (within a framework of goals, strategies and actions).

Awareness and responsibility

Building awareness and responsibility in the learner is at the heart of good coaching. The effective instructor/coach should be able to raise this sense of awareness and responsibility in the learner mainly by using effective questions. These will not only be based on 'What can you see?' but will be more probing in terms of feelings and attitudes.

The learner needs to have awareness of what is happening around them and also self-awareness, in terms of 'What do I feel?', 'How do I control this situation?' If the learner is not fully aware of both of these aspects, there will be a tendency for the situation to control the learner rather than the other way round.

A good coach can build awareness mainly through effective questioning, using appropriate questions such as 'What can you see?', 'What do you feel is happening?', 'How do you feel about...?' This line of questioning ensures that learners are gaining feedback from what is happening around them and what they might do to control the situation.

If the learner feels that the instructor is controlling the training by using too much basic instruction they will feel encouraged to adopt a passive role. If the learner/coach relationship is more of an equal partnership the learner is likely to be more relaxed and ready to take on responsibility for their individual learning.

Ideally learners should be encouraged to take responsibility from the start of their training. This does not necessarily mean that learners have to make the decisions about any major traffic or safety issues at an early stage, but that they should feel responsible for their own learning.

A sense of responsibility for their own learning can be developed in learners at an early stage in the learning process. This transfer of responsibility is much more effective if learners are involved in making decisions and identifying goals and objectives in partnership with the instructor/coach from the start of training.

Effective questioning

Just because you ask questions does not mean you are coaching. The use of effective questions is an important aspect of driving instruction because it involves the learner in the process and allows the instructor to check that learning is taking place. Coaching questions are very different from traditional instructing-type questions and this next section explores these differences.

We have previously considered the importance of rapport in a client-centred relationship and how active listening is all about listening behind and between the words, looking at body language, and helping the speaker explore their thoughts and feelings. By using a combination of skills such as building rapport and active listening, we can establish a balance between instruction and coaching – a balance that is critical in keeping the car safe. There are various questioning techniques that can be employed to help strike this balance but before we look at these techniques, we should look at the use of coaching questions.

Coaching questions are effective questions that target the thoughts and feelings that motivate behaviour. Questions such as '*What were you thinking as you approached that roundabout?*' or '*How did you feel as you drove along that road?*' are excellent conversation openers to use when parked up at the side of the road. It is important to ensure there is no negative tone attached to these questions so they should not be used when you know your customer has just made a mess of whatever they were doing. The questions need to be asked in a way that is neutral and non-judgemental. You don't know what answer the customer is going to give but you are curious and want to explore with them what they were thinking or how they were feeling. This is so that they can understand how these thoughts and feelings link to their behaviour. In fact, the questions can be even more open than the above example because, by mentioning the roundabout or the road they have just driven along, we are potentially restricting and guiding the learner's response. '*What have you been thinking about?*' or '*Describe your thoughts to me*' or '*How did that feel?*' or '*What were you feeling?*' are examples of wide open questions. If the rapport is good the client will have no problem in telling you that they were thinking about what they were going to be having for tea or how they are looking forward to going out at the weekend. These kinds of response open up a discussion about distractions and how distractions can interfere with the decisions we need to make when driving. This becomes a good example of how thoughts and feelings motivate behaviour.

Now let's look at the different types of questioning techniques we can use to maintain a client-centred approach:

1 **Goal questions**

This type of question is used to help the client in setting the goal and also to check what support is required from you to facilitate them achieving this. These questions would often be asked at the start of a lesson but could also be asked in the middle of a lesson where one goal has already been achieved and another one is being set. Normally, they would be used at the side of the road because they are useful in making sure the customer is in control of their own learning process.

Example questions might be:

- What would you like to achieve today?
- How do you learn best?
- How do you want to do this?
- What skills do you already have that will help you achieve this today?
- What support do you need from me?
- Where would you like to practise?
- How much time do you want to spend practising?
- Do you need me to do anything?
- Would you like a demonstration?
- How will you know when you have succeeded?
- How will you measure your success?

2 Closed questions

Closed questions are good for checking knowledge and facts. They have just one correct answer. For example, '*What is the speed limit on this road?*' These questions can be asked on the move because they are not generally too distracting. They also work well at the side of the road if the customer is a little reticent in opening up – by asking a couple of closed questions you help establish rapport.

One of the benefits of the goal-setting questions is that you will have established what level of support the customer requires during any practice. If the customer wishes to have a go on their own this doesn't mean you would step in and ask them questions to check where they are looking and what they intend to do. You would allow them to drive in silence. However, if the customer is, for example, practising raising their awareness of hazards then you might have agreed to ask them closed questions that draw their attention to particular hazards as they drive on their chosen route.

3 Safety-critical questions

Sometimes it will be necessary to step in and say something to keep the car safe even though you have agreed that the customer is going to practise something on their own in silence. You would ideally explain this before the car starts moving but if you haven't it is still crucial that you recognize the time to intervene with instruction. If you can do this in the form of a question, all well and good. However, it really doesn't matter when there is a risk of danger. Whether you ask a question or not you will still be instructing in this situation and will have taken the responsibility back from the customer for the driving task.

Examples of the type of safety-critical questions you might use are:

- Do you need to brake for this car emerging?
- Are you going to steer round this cyclist?
- Will you be stopping at this pedestrian crossing?

All these questions have an instruction in them and the response expected is in the form of an action rather than anything verbal. It would also be appropriate in these situations to have the dual brake covered or to be ready to go for the steering wheel.

The good thing about asking a question in these types of situations rather than giving an instruction is that you are endeavouring to keep the responsibility sitting with the customer. They still must decide how to respond to your question. Afterwards, it is important to discuss the situation at the side of the road. Remember, though, that timing is critical and if you have no time to ask a question then don't!

4 Open questions

Open questions have more than one correct answer. A question that can be answered with 'Yes' or 'No' is an open question. It could also be answered with 'Maybe', 'Sometimes', 'That depends', for example, so there are several alternative responses. Usually, the instructor does not know what answer the customer is going to give. These types of questions are asked to start a conversation where the customer is given the opportunity to explore their thoughts, values, opinions about something related to driving. The more open the question can be the better; however, sometimes a question that just gets a yes or no response is good because it then helps move the conversation forwards.

Example questions might be: '*What do you think about the speed limit on this road?*' or '*What are your views on alcohol and driving?*'

5 Task-specific questions

These questions are part of an exercise that has been agreed with the customer. They could be to do with reading the road ahead where you agree that you are going to ask questions about the signs and road markings. For example, '*What is the next warning sign?*' '*What is the speed limit on this road?*'

Another type of exercise is about distractions, where you might say to the customer that you are deliberately going to ask them questions that are unrelated to driving and that you will discuss with them afterwards how easily (or not) they were able to maintain their focus on the driving task. For example:

- Have you got a holiday booked this year?
- What are you going to do this weekend?
- How did you get on at college this week?

The most important thing about the use of questions is to recognize the outcome that each type of question is likely to produce. It is very easy to ask questions and struggle with this and therefore assume that coaching doesn't work. Some people do not like being asked questions and often this is because the questioner has bombarded them with questions rather than considering the rapport and using their listening skills. Client-centred questions need to be asked for a reason and the reason is to accelerate the learning of the customer by raising their self-awareness, building their responsibility and developing their self-evaluation skills.

To summarize

- Start with questions that link the current situation with any previous experiences: '*With your previous instructor did you...?*'
- Start broadly, with a general question: '*What are your main concerns today?*' and then move on to more detailed questions as a result of the learner's responses.
- Use 'open' questions: 'What...', 'When...', 'Where...', but be careful with the use of 'Why...', as this can often be seen as over-critical or too personal.
- Ask only one question at a time and listen very carefully to the answer before asking any follow-up questions.

Very often the most important questions are those that the instructor/coach does not know the answer to. For example, '*How do you/did you feel about...*', '*What do you understand by...*', '*What do you think would happen if...?*' and so on.

Questions – a few reminders

The effective instructor/coach should be able to raise awareness and responsibility in the learner mainly using effective questions. These will not only be based on 'What can you see?' but will be more probing in terms of feelings and attitudes.

Closed questions (those with only one correct response) should be used sparingly. Questions that the instructor/coach does not know the answer to are usually the most effective in raising the learner's awareness and responsibility.

Questioning technique involves: listening; probing; reflecting; discussing; feedback.

A typical Q&A routine:

Learner: 'I'm not sure what to do about...'.

a) Mentor: '*What I would do is...*'. (The reply is all about the speaker and is not particularly helpful to the questioner.) This kind of approach would usually be used by a parent or an amateur instructor.
b) Instructor: '*What you should do is ...*' (The answer is still mainly about the speaker and, as a result, the learner does not feel particularly involved.) This is the type of answer used in 'traditional' instructing methods.
c) Coach: 'What are you not sure about?'

Learner: '*How to...*'
Coach: '*What would you...?*'
Learner: '*Well, I would...*'
Coach: '*What do you think you might...?*'
Learner: '*I'd...*'
Coach: '*What effect do you think...?*'

(Note that the learner now sees that this discussion is all about their own situation and feels more involved.)

Some basic coaching-type questions

- 'What is your main concern today? Any other concerns? Do we need to go over any of those again?'
- 'What do you feel you need to do next?'
- 'What do you feel we need to do to change...? How do you think we can best achieve that?'
- 'Have you done this manoeuvre/exercise/routine before? How did it go?'

- 'What do you need to know to do...? Anything else?'
- 'What, in particular, do you need to watch out for/be aware of in this situation? What other road users do you need to be aware of?'
- 'What can you see/feel/hear? How do you feel about...?'
- 'Is there anything more we can/could do to...?'
- 'How will you deal with...? Are there any alternatives?'
- 'Where are you looking? Are there any other areas where you might need to look/be aware of?'
- 'How did you feel in that situation where...? What did you actually do? Anything else?'
- 'How did you think that went? Overall, what did you do well?'
- 'What could you do another time to change...?'
- 'What could you do that would make it easier/safer...?'

As previously indicated, all of these questions assist in raising awareness but they also allow learners to express themselves with their feelings. The coach's supplementary questions should then follow on from the learner's responses. This means that 'active listening' (see also the section in Chapter 2 on listening skills) is an important skill for the trainer/coach. Sometimes the more difficult part is knowing when to keep quiet and allow the learner time to consider a response.

Most of the time our listening consists of 'apparent listening'. It may appear that we are listening, but we are not actually concentrating fully on the content and meaning of what is being said. What we should be doing is using 'active' or 'effective' listening.

The ability to listen 'actively' is a key feature of any good communication and is essential in the process of coaching. As we can think much faster than we can talk, this speed of thought can be used to advantage in coaching. The available time can be used to consider what the learner has said, make sure in your own mind that you have fully understood, and consider what further questions or responses might be needed.

The effective coach is able to concentrate effectively and efficiently on what the learner says, possibly over a lengthy period of time. There is always the temptation to only half listen, or to assume when the learner is only part way through their response. In the same way, it is tempting to start formulating the next question or response too early and to risk missing the main point of the learner's response. Active listening is a skill that can be acquired, but only with planning and practice.

When listening to the learner and judging their response to your questions, make sure you look directly at the learner and use friendly facial gestures. This is particularly important when dealing with learners who are reluctant to answer or who have difficulty in expressing themselves.

During the questioning and listening process it is sometimes worth summarizing what the learner has said. Telling the learner what you think they have said can show that you have taken notice of any concerns and will usually assist in continuing the discussion in an appropriate way.

The effective coach listens to the learner's reply not only to check for accuracy, but also for any indication of uncertainty or a lack of confidence. The need is to listen carefully and to make an immediate interpretation of the meaning. In doing this, the coach/instructor will be able to decide on the next question or series of questions to put.

Active listening – a few reminders

One often-repeated quote – 'When you talk, you are only repeating what you already know. If you listen, you may learn something new.'

A few basic principles for listening:

- Listen more than you talk. Wait until the other person has finished – don't interrupt or finish the sentence for them.
- Even if the speaker pauses, still wait in case they have more to say. Even if you think you have understood what is being said, avoid cutting off the person who is speaking.
- Use gestures or nods to allow the speaker to continue.
- Maintain eye contact – show that you are actively involved in what is being said.
- Concentrate on getting the whole picture rather than just some of the information.
- 'Listen' with your eyes – be ready to pick up any non-verbal signals.
- Don't let the other person's mannerisms distract you from the actual content.
- Show the speaker that you are concentrating on what is being said by avoiding any unnecessary distractions on your part.

Learner feedback

So far we have looked at rapport, questioning and listening skills in terms of delivering client-centred learning as opposed to instructor-led teaching. In this section we look at feedback from the learner. Developing feedback skills in your customers is the key to safe driving. This is the most important skill; the whole point of building rapport, actively listening and asking effective questions is to develop the clients' ability to feed back to themselves how they are getting on.

With client-centred learning, feedback is used to raise the client's self-awareness of their strengths, limitations and development needs. It's also about how their thoughts and feelings impact on their behaviour. For this to be effective the instructor needs to be able to develop the client's ability to set their own benchmark, against which they can measure their performance. This process takes more or less time depending on the level of independent thinking the client is capable of. For example, when someone asks you, 'Would you like tea or coffee?' what is your response? Some people will say, 'Whatever is easiest for you'. This is often a conditioned and polite response but it betrays the fact that some people find it difficult to make choices. Being able to make choices, recognizing consequences and understanding the impact that choice will have on you, as an individual, is the result of effective self-evaluation skills – the ability to give oneself feedback.

When you ask your client how something went, the response may well be, 'I'm not sure'. This is not necessarily the time to dive in and give your opinion on how it went. It cannot be stressed enough how important it is to develop self-evaluation skills through the process of feedback. A newly qualified driver's inability to self-evaluate leads to errors of judgement. Developing in your clients the ability to consider how their driving is coming along, and giving them the skills to do so once they have passed their driving test, will enable them to recognize and reflect, in order to take steps to prevent further errors.

If someone blasts their horn at you how do you feel? Some people will feel a surge of rage, which will consume them for moments, and during those moments they could make decisions that are fuelled by their anger. In extreme cases, these decisions result in examples of road rage. Other people feel immediately embarrassed and assume they have done something wrong. This embarrassment is also consuming and may lead to decisions that are less than safe, such as sudden braking or swerving without checking the mirrors. Still others may feel fear, again resulting in unsafe actions. Do you know how you respond? Do your customers know how they will respond? Do they understand how their feelings affect their thought processes and therefore their actions? Understanding how our emotional state motivates our behaviour is the first step to anticipating the likely consequences of the choices and decisions we make. Knowing how to manage our emotions so that the choices we make are safe is the result of feedback and self-evaluation.

Making mistakes while learning to drive provides an ideal context to develop self-evaluation skills. With traditional, instructor-led driver training we focus on the core competencies of fault identification, fault analysis and fault remedy. By dealing with faults and through repetitive practice we bring people's driving up to a satisfactory level so that they can take and pass the practical test. On a behavioural level this works very well but it doesn't take into consideration the fact that our thoughts and feelings drive our behaviour. A learner driver behaves in a certain way because they will be rewarded by their instructor and allowed to go for their driving test. However, this behaviour will not necessarily remain in place and when put under different pressures – driving unsupervised – the now newly qualified driver will drive in a certain way according to their beliefs and motivation – and not because their driving instructor told them to.

So how can we develop self-evaluation skills in our clients? Let's take a brief look at reflection and scaling.

Reflection is arguably the most important process we can use because it reinforces learning and helps it to become long-lasting. It is through reflection that we can learn from our mistakes and move forwards. Some people reflect formally by writing everything down and keeping reflective diaries; others just spend a few moments thinking about what happened and breaking the whole thing down in their minds. An important part of reflection is to consider how you were feeling and what you were thinking because both feelings and thoughts play a part in the behaviour that is displayed. Developing these skills of reflection in your clients is about encouraging them to think about a piece of their driving and looking at what happened. They may need to draw a diagram or go back and look at the scene; they may need to drive the same route again or they might benefit if you drive. Ask them what they were thinking at that precise moment and then ask them what they were feeling. These questions help them analyse their actions and encourage them to take responsibility and put strategies in place to develop.

Great reflective questions for developing feedback skills are:

- What just happened?
- What were you thinking?

- How were you feeling?
- What do you need to do next time to develop?
- What help do you need from me?
- How will you know when you have succeeded?

Scaling is a means of reflection and a powerful feedback tool because it develops self-evaluation skills. It keeps the responsibility for the learning process sitting firmly with the person doing the learning, rather than the person doing the teaching. It doesn't matter what the scale is. It can be a ladder drawn on a page or a set of steps; it can be a numerical scale from 0 to 10 or 1 to 5; it can be a ruler held in your hand or theirs. The important thing is that the limits are defined. For example:

> 'On a scale of 0 to 10, where 10 is very good and 0 is rubbish, where would you put yourself regarding the bay parking you just did?'

The answer they give also does not matter – there is no need for you to comment. The next question is about their evidence for putting themselves at this point – encourage them to look for positive evidence. Even if they gave themselves a one they have at least got off the ground so you can ask:

> 'What was good enough to make you give yourself a one?'

The next questions are:

- *'So where would you like to be?'*
- *'How will you get there?'*
- *'Do you need any support from me?'*
- *'How will you feel when you have got there?'*

These questions keep the responsibility sitting with the client and you are just there to facilitate the process. Practised often enough, scaling becomes a feedback technique they can take away and apply in their driving once they have passed the driving test.

Scaling can be used very effectively on feelings:

- *'How tired/confident/stressed/focused are you on a scale of nought to 10?'*
- *'Describe a situation where you are at a much better point on the scale.'*
- *'What do you need to do to get there?'*
- *'How can I help you?'*

Scaling also works very well when giving feedback on the use of the controls, for example: 'On a scale of nought to 10 where 10 is amazingly smooth and nought is horrendous, where would you put yourself with the last gear change?'; *'Okay, so you say you are a three, next time aim for a four.'*

As far as client-centred learning and coaching are concerned it is not constructive or helpful to constantly be throwing away words like 'Excellent', 'Well done', 'That's great'. These do nothing to develop self-evaluation skills in your clients and often silence is far more powerful. They need to know how to congratulate themselves on their strengths and to also be able to identify their weaknesses and have the skills to develop and improve. Your job is to help them set a benchmark by which they can measure themselves. At times it is necessary to give praise, especially with someone who is not very good at evaluating their own performance, because this helps them set their own benchmark. You should, however, cut back on the praise you use as soon as you notice the time is right because you are restricting their self-evaluation processes by constantly chipping in with your opinion. Easing them into the process of self-evaluation so that they can take full responsibility once they have passed their driving test will help keep them safe for life.

Using a question and answer routine is only one way of giving and obtaining feedback. When teaching learner drivers you should give feedback on what they are doing well and what may need improving. Just as important is finding out from learners how well they think they are doing. They might think they are doing brilliantly when they are really struggling. Alternatively, learners might think they need extra tuition on a particular topic, whereas you might think this is unnecessary. Every learner will benefit from extra lessons, so never discourage them from booking more if they feel they need them.

Many driving instructors do not understand feedback and instead give constant criticism, which only destroys what confidence learners may have and leaves them feeling dejected and wanting to give up. Many potentially good drivers give up because they do not receive support and encouragement from their instructors. Invariably these learners will start learning again, if they really need to drive. However, they nearly always go to a different instructor. Never forget that if you are not fulfilling the needs of your learners, there are plenty more instructors for them to choose from.

Several guidelines can be followed when giving feedback to your learners:

- Feedback should always focus on what actually happened rather than on what should or might have happened.
- Suggest that learners comment on their own performance before giving feedback. They will often be more self-critical than you expect.

- Make sure that you balance learners' strengths and weaknesses.
- Concentrate on areas where you know that the learner is capable of improvement; don't dwell on points that you know they are not able to alter. This is most important when learners are aware that they have limitations.
- Be helpful rather than sounding judgemental. For example, rather than saying, 'You will fail your test if you do that', you could try, 'Your passengers will have a much more comfortable ride if you do this.'
- Try to 'round off' any feedback by stressing the good points.
- Above all, feedback should be seen by learners as being constructive and positive.

Hopefully these guidelines will help you to give feedback in a 'human' way, as this will build the confidence of your learners.

After each lesson, reflect on any feedback you have given. Decide whether you could have improved the way in which you presented the feedback to your learner. Think carefully about how your learner reacted to the feedback. Did you give the student an accurate indication of their performance or did you just criticize their driving?

Modifying behaviours in driving

GROW is a four-stage problem-solving model that focuses on behaviour. It stands for goal, reality, options and way forward.

Goal – What do you want to happen?

- Agreed in partnership with the learner.
- Learner takes more responsibility and 'ownership'.
- Must be challenging and measurable, but also achievable.
- Difference between the topic of a lesson and the outcome.
- May be a bite-sized part of a lesson.
- First agree the topic, then establish the goal.
- Must be realistic, and will come from the learner after discussion.
- Agreed, with small chunks of achievable progress. Sets the goal (or objective) so that the learner can finish the session/part of lesson with a measurable result.

Reality – What is actually happening now? Where are we now?

- A realistic assessment of the current situation.
- Using open-ended questions can clarify to learners exactly where they are.
- Reality needs to be clarified, agreed, fully understood and accepted.

Options – What could we do to make it happen? What are the alternatives?

- Coach helps the learner to generate the options and explore how to move forward.
- Coach's role is to assist learners in exploring for themselves the different options.

Way forward – What will we do to achieve the agreed goal? What is the most efficient strategy?

- Provides clarity on which of the options are most appropriate for the trainee and the goal and the level of certainty.
- Confidence in taking the agreed option forward.
- Job of the coach is to ensure that the learner has made a complete assessment of what needs to be done, and that the learner takes on responsibility for the outcome ('ownership').

Goals – What do we want to achieve?

Identifying and agreeing goals

Setting goals or objectives is an important principle in coaching. Rather than imposing a strict programme of goals on the learner, the coach helps the learner to identify their own goals at each stage of learning and then to realize them.

In driver training there are clearly some predetermined limits for the objectives – laws and regulations for example – but it is important for the instructor and learner to mutually agree the goals and that those goals meet the needs of the learner. For example, there is little point in the instructor having a fixed idea for the content of a lesson if the learner is concerned about an aspect of the previous lesson. In this situation the learner would feel uncomfortable about moving on to the next part of the syllabus without resolving the outstanding issues. The instructor should be able to recognize this and initiate a discussion and listen to the concerns and needs of the learner in order to move the learning process forward.

This way of working may need to be relatively formal in the early stages of training, particularly as the learner will not necessarily know or understand what goals or objectives are important to them. However, as the series of lessons continues the learner should be encouraged to identify their own goals or objectives and to work in partnership with the instructor. In practice, this often means that the learner's perceived goal is to do what needs to be known and done to pass the driving test. To get the learner to focus on the necessary attributes of awareness, responsibility, attitude and generally preparing for driving after passing the test can be more difficult, but can be achieved by using the appropriate coaching techniques.

If after a lesson the learner is not comfortable about a particular aspect, the instructor cannot agree or set the goals for the next part of the lesson. There will inevitably be interference caused by the learner's anxiety about the concern or doubt. This needs to be addressed before deciding on the next goal or objective.

As previously indicated, most young people are used to having instructions given to them. As a result, the learner's idea of setting goals may revolve around 'passing the test' and 'getting a licence'. The job of the effective coach is to guide the discussion towards agreeing on appropriate goals for each part of the training programme. To do this you need to be able to lead the discussion and encourage the learner to identify their own individual goals.

In order to clarify and define the goal and help the learner (or 'coachee') achieve an agreed objective, the instructor (or 'coach') might ask:

- What would you like to get from today's lesson?
- Which particular area would you like to develop today?
- What must happen today for you to get some benefit from the lesson?
- When you have done it, what will that enable you to do in the future?

Reality – Where are we now?

Prior knowledge and experience

We need to know and understand a lot about the learner's existing knowledge and prior experience before we can start on agreeing appropriate goals and effective objectives. Effective coaching does not start from scratch or by assuming that the learner is completely inexperienced.

All our learners will have had some previous non-driving experiences that will be useful in linking to the process of learning to drive. They will have been pedestrians; will almost certainly have been passengers with parents and other people; they will probably have ridden a bicycle and may have used a moped; and they could have had off-road driving experience. These experiences can, and should, be linked to the new learning experience.

In order to explore the reality of the current situation the coach might ask:

- What do you know so far?
- What is the potential gain/loss?
- What barriers could there be to achieving this?

Options – What are our alternative strategies?

Deciding on our options

- What are our options for making changes?
- What could we do to make them happen?
- What are our alternatives?
- Are we able to change or modify our strategy or method as appropriate or as required by the particular situation?

It is sometimes helpful to split this section into two parts, firstly to generate a list of options and secondly to take each option and evaluate it:

- What options have you considered so far?
- What other options are there?
- How/why might these options work/not work?
- What might be the consequences of each one?
- Let's rank the options.

Way forward – How are we going to achieve our goals?

- What will we do to achieve the agreed goal?
- What is the most efficient strategy for us to achieve the goal?

The final part of the GROW model is to establish and agree a way forward. One way to do this is to ask the learner for their thoughts on summarizing a plan:

- Could you summarize for me the actions you are going to take?

- How will you make this happen?
- What are you going to take away from this session?
- What do you need from me to achieve this?

Used effectively in driver training the GROW model can raise self-awareness and develop responsibility, making our newly qualified drivers safer in the long term.

Goals for Driver Education

A brief overview

The Goals for Driver Education (GDE) are summarized in a framework or matrix, consisting of four levels and three columns. Levels 1 and 2 are addressed in traditional driver training and are sufficient to prepare someone to pass their driving test.

Level 1 is all about the vehicle – its controls and how to use them, maintenance, vehicle regulations. **Level 2** is about driving the vehicle in traffic, dealing with different road and weather conditions as well as different amounts of traffic, forward planning, hazard management and the effects of

GDE matrix

(Goals for Driver Education)

(Hatakka, Keskinen, Glad, Gregersen, Hernetkoski, 2002)

Level	Knowledge and skill	Risk-increasing aspects	Self-assessment
4. Goals for life and skills for living	Lifestyle, age, group, culture, social position, etc, vs driving behaviour	Sensation seeking Risk acceptance Group norms Peer pressure	Introspective competence Own preconditions Impulse control
3. Goals and context of driving	Modal choice Choice of time Role of motives Route planning	Alcohol, fatigue Low friction Rush hours Young passengers	Own motives influencing choices Self-critical thinking
2. Driving in traffic	Traffic rules Cooperation Hazard perception Automatization	Disobeying rules Close-following Low friction Vulnerable road users	Calibration of driving skills Own driving style
1. Vehicle control	Car functioning Protection systems Vehicle control Physical laws	No seatbelts Breakdown of vehicle systems Worn-out tyres	Calibration of car-control skills

Level	Knowledge and skills	Risk-increasing factors	Self-evaluation
Level 4 The person	Who am I? What goals and ambitions do I have? What skills do I have? What views and opinions do I hold? What do I enjoy most about driving? Why do I want to learn to drive?	What type of personality do I have and what are the risk-increasing factors of being a thrill seeker, or aggressive, or anxious and nervous? What are the risks for me when I've passed my test?	How well do I manage myself? Am I able to reflect? Do I understand consequences to actions? How will I cope with driving once I've passed my test?
Level 3 The journey	What do I need to know about planning my journey? What mode of transport should I use? What is the best time of day to travel? What roads should I avoid? What do I need to know about distractions, passengers, alcohol and drugs?	What risks are involved with drinking and driving, speeding, being distracted, using my mobile phone and driving, driving when tired, driving my mates?	How good am I at navigating and route planning? How does tiredness affect my concentration? What strengths do I have in dealing with peer pressure? What are my weaknesses?
Level 2 The road	What do I need to know to drive in traffic, negotiate busy junctions, forward plan, read the road ahead, anticipate hazards, as well as driving in different weather conditions and at night?	What are the risks of driving at night, or in adverse weather conditions? What could go wrong if I don't look properly or forward plan?	How good am I at dealing with other traffic; what strengths do I have and what weaknesses?
Level 1 The vehicle	What do I need to know to operate the controls smoothly, move away and stop, complete manoeuvres, deal with basic junctions, as well as maintain my vehicle and carry out basic checks?	What if I didn't wear my seatbelt, or check my tyres, or carry out basic checks; what if I brake harshly, or accelerate fiercely, or steer sharply – what could go wrong?	How good am I at operating the controls? What weaknesses do I have? How well do I choose the correct gear or time my gear changes?

driving on the environment. Levels 3 and 4 are not addressed in traditional driver training. **Level 3** focuses on the how, why, where and when of driving in recognition of the fact that driving involves choice and decision. While learning to drive the learner is often robbed of any opportunity to make decisions for themselves. Even choosing what they want to do on their driving lesson is a step in the right direction towards taking ownership and control of the driving task. **Level 3** also includes other influences that affect the decisions the driver must make, such as passengers, distractions and the effects of alcohol and drugs.

Level 4 acknowledges how the personality, values, opinions and beliefs of the driver influence the way they handle the vehicle, drive in traffic and choose when, how and where to drive every time. Depending on the personality of the driver, they will respond in different ways to the effects of peer pressure, for example. If they are tired this can affect the way they handle the vehicle and the decisions they make. One person might be fine with three or four mates in the car having a good time, while another might find it impossible to concentrate and feel quite stressed in this situation. Understanding how they might respond in different situations gives them the ability to make choices about their safety.

The three columns of the Goals for Driver Education matrix on page 94 show the competencies the driver needs to be able to apply across the levels. These are, for each level:

- the knowledge and skills the driver needs;
- awareness of the risk-increasing factors; and
- the ability to self-evaluate.

Traditionally, the bottom left-hand corner of the matrix is covered – levels one and two and the first two competencies.

Another version of the GDE matrix is shown on page 95, populated with the kind of questions you could ask your learners to help address the goals for driver education.

Coaching – a summary

So far, we have looked at essential coaching skills and shown how these skills, when used in client-centred learning, raise awareness and build responsibility in the individual learner.

- **Rapport**
  This is all about the relationship between you and your customer. The relationship must be equal, and the customer must trust that you will be non-judgemental. Being non-judgemental is critical in empowering the customer to be themselves. Customers must believe that they can express how they think and feel about things knowing that you will not be dismissive or defensive in your response.

  This equal relationship enables the customer to learn how the way they think and feel about things influences the choices they make. The learning environment is such that they feel comfortable exploring and experimenting with different strategies to manage their emotional state and help them make decisions that are safe for them.

  Rapport is not necessarily created through banter or even establishing common ground. It is created through non-verbal communication techniques, such as the use of eye contact, nodding, smiling and matching body language, tone of voice or use of words.

- **Listening**
  There are several levels of listening, most of which are ineffective when aiming to create a client-centred relationship. Active listening is about focusing entirely on the customer's agenda and almost seeing yourself as a blank sheet. As the coach, you have no idea where the conversation is going to go and simply facilitate the process.

  There are several techniques you can use to do this, such as repeating back parts of what has been said, paraphrasing and summarizing. These techniques enable the customer to check that what they have said is what they meant. Listening is very important when developing the customer's ability to set their own goals and determine for themselves how they learn.

- **Questioning**
  Effective questions target thoughts and feelings. They are open questions and may start with words like what, where, why or how; or explain, or tell me. Coaching or client-centred questions are very different from the use of questions in an instructor-led relationship. Coaching questions do not check knowledge and understanding. They focus on the underpinning things that motivate behaviour. They help the customer recognize how individual they are and how the decisions they make are affected by their state of mind.

- **Feedback**

  There are many forms of feedback. In client-centred learning the most powerful form is one that develops effective self-evaluation skills in learners. Feedback is all about the customer identifying a set of skills, against which they can measure their performance. They need to be aware of their strengths, weaknesses and development needs and they need to understand how their emotions impact on their behaviour and their ability to rationalize. Their measure of 'good' and 'safe' will be very different from yours because they think and feel things differently from you. 'Drive like me and you will always be okay' is not helpful to an individual when all their life experiences, conditioning, peer groups and influences have developed them into human beings who do not resemble you in one tiny little way. They can 'drive like you' up to their test and pass but post-test they will always 'drive like them'. Effective feedback is about developing their ability to make choices by evaluating the potential consequences of those choices and deciding whether this is what they want or need to do.

  Consider two different emotional states: happiness and sadness. Reflect on how you feel when you are happy; where that feeling of happiness sits; how it affects the way you carry yourself; how you feel when you smile or laugh; how you relate to other people. Now consider the same points when you reflect on how you feel when you are sad. Now imagine you are sitting waiting to emerge at a busy junction in a sad state and then in a happy state. Does your emotional state affect your judgement of a safe gap? The answer is 'Yes' but the extent to which it affects your ability to make a decision depends on you and will vary from individual to individual.

  For example, in order to make a safe decision to go I have to consider my emotional state and understand how it influences my thought processes and my behaviour. I will drive differently depending on how I feel and I will develop strategies to help my decision-making process based on my recognition of my emotional state. Sadness slows down my ability to make decisions. I am more hesitant. Happiness may encourage me to take more risks and I may emerge into gaps that are too small.

  It is the use of essential coaching skills that empowers our trainee drivers to recognize how their thoughts, feelings and behaviour are inextricably linked. Finally, there is one more essential coaching skill we should think about and that is the use of intuition.

- **Intuition**

  As driving instructors, we use our intuition in many ways. We recognize when our customers are feeling nervous as their shoulders tense and the grip on the steering wheel tightens or they sit forwards in their seat when the demands of the task suddenly increase. The physical tension will make them tire more quickly and affect their ability to focus on the hazards and risks outside of the car. We know instinctively when they are thinking about changing gear before they have even done so or when they have mis interpreted our instructions and are about to signal left when they should be going right.

  It is important that we use our intuition to develop coping strategies in our customers. They need to understand how their behaviour is a reflection of their thoughts and feelings. If something becomes too difficult for them to manage and we notice this in their behaviour, then we need to identify this to them so that they can work out for themselves the link between the way they are thinking and feeling and the way they are behaving.

  For example, let's imagine that one of your customers struggles with busy junctions and roundabouts. Often, she will end up stalling. You notice that, on the approach to these junctions, she takes her left hand off the steering wheel and places it on the handbrake. When you pull up to discuss this you use your intuition – you know that her hand going down to the handbrake is because she feels nervous about the busy junction and wants to make sure she can stop the car. The problem with this is that she is 'thinking stop' whereas she really needs to be 'thinking go' and getting the car ready to go by slipping into first gear and holding it on the bite. You could tell her all this and she would practise it and get it. However, she wouldn't have had the chance to reflect on her nervous state and appreciate how this emotion was governing her behaviour. So, instead, you scale her on how nervous she felt approaching these junctions and she says she rose from a 4 to a 9. You then ask where she was on the scale when her hand went down to the handbrake. After practising this for a couple of junctions she can identify that when she gets to a 9 her hand goes to the handbrake. Only once she realizes that her behaviour is a direct result of her feelings is she able to rationalize her fear. She realizes that her fear is producing risky behaviour – the opposite of her intention. By encouraging her to keep her hand on the wheel until she needs to change gear and getting her to 'think go' she is now able to bring her nervousness back down to 4 and keep it there. In this case, her behaviour now governs her emotions.

Intuition, therefore, is about recognizing a mis-match between behaviour, thoughts and feelings. Someone might start yawning when you are giving them a briefing. Your intuition tells you that they are no longer paying attention and processing what you are saying to them – they have stopped learning and you need to change your methods.

To become good coaches and always remain client-centred, we need to develop our ability to use these five essential coaching skills. This can only be done by constant practice, reflection and evaluation and it is a long process that will not happen overnight. When you come across someone who you think cannot be coached, ask yourself whether you have been using these essential coaching skills effectively enough.

04
Structured learning

The specific requirements for presenting the lesson on the ADI exam are covered in *The Driving Instructor's Handbook*. The exam is a slightly artificial situation compared to a normal lesson in that there is a strict limit to the time available for the lesson and you have an ADI Examiner (ADIE) observing you.

Treat it like a normal lesson with a real learner where you and your learner agree the goals and make effective use of the time available.

The most effective way to start is to think of the learner's needs and their current level of ability, knowledge and skill. Then ask yourself a series of questions involving what, why, how, where and when. This is best done by holding a conversation with your learner and asking them a few questions, such as:

- What do you already know?
- What are you going to need to learn?
- What do you need to have included?
- How are we going to get the message across?
- Where will we need to go to carry out the lesson in an appropriate environment?
- When should we get to the main content of the lesson?
- How are we going to manage the available time?

Once you have answered the questions you will be able to organize the planning and presentation of the lesson.

In any teaching/learning situation the lesson should be properly structured and 'learner-centred'. For you and the trainee to achieve any mutually agreed objectives or goals you will need to involve the learner. Effective use of coaching and communication skills will help you achieve this.

Through discussion with the learner, agree for each lesson what you are going to deal with and why you are going to teach it, where the lesson is going to take place, how the available time is to be utilized, and how the lesson is going to be structured.

An effective instructor should:

- have a clearly defined plan of what is going to be taught;
- consider the level of ability of the learner when agreeing the goals for the lesson;
- have an idea in advance what activities and techniques could be used to help keep the learner interested and attentive;
- be prepared to modify the lesson plan if the need arises during the lesson;
- have specified learning goals for the student;
- vary the teaching methods to suit those goals and the characteristics of the student;
- demonstrate a range of skills when using these teaching methods and any visual or learning aids;
- carefully manage the time, structure and content of the lesson;
- adapt the lesson to suit the perceived needs of the student where necessary;
- identify, analyse and correct faults;
- identify any problem areas, taking remedial action or recommending further training where necessary;
- always take account of the safety of the student, the passenger and any other road users;
- offer feedback to the student during and at the end of the lesson, where appropriate;
- link forward to the next lesson; and
- encourage reflection to evaluate what learning has taken place.

To appreciate the variety of lesson plans that are needed, consider how you would plan a lesson for each of the potential learners listed below – what type of routes you would choose and how you would vary your level of instruction:

- an absolute beginner;
- a partly trained learner;
- a learner at about 'L' test standard;

- somebody who has recently passed the 'L' test but has never driven on motorways;
- somebody who passed the 'L' test a few years ago but has not driven since;
- a full licence holder who wishes to take an advanced test;
- someone who has a full licence for cars with automatic transmission but has not driven a vehicle with manual gears;
- a company driver taking a 'defensive driving' course;
- the holder of a full foreign licence who has never driven in this country or on the left-hand side of the road;
- somebody who is just about to appear in court on a traffic offence and who needs an assessment and report;
- somebody who will need to retake the driving test as part of a court order;
- somebody who must take an extended test as part of a court order.

At the end of each driving lesson, you should ask yourself:

- Did the lesson plan help the learner to achieve the goals that were agreed at the start of the lesson?
- Did I involve the learner in the lesson sufficiently?
- Should I have changed the lesson plan to take account of perceived problems?
- Did I give the learner enough feedback on how well they were doing?
- Did I plan the lesson thoroughly?
- Were the routes chosen correctly?
- Was the level of instruction pitched appropriately for the learner?
- With hindsight, was there anything I should have done differently?

Goals and goal-setting

One of the most effective ways to learn to drive is through goal-setting. There are several important reasons why your customers need to learn how to set goals for themselves:

Goal-setting breaks learning into bite-sized chunks

Creighton Abrams famously said, 'When eating an elephant, take one bite at a time.' When your customer feels overwhelmed, it helps to look at the whole learning to drive task with all its commitments and actions as bite-size, or fun-size, goals. Remind them that they have choices about what they say 'yes' and 'no' to, and when and how they move forward. This shifts the focus away from the driving test and means that they can achieve goals without them having to be 'test standard'. What is meant by this is that we often look at our learners' achievements and measure them against the standard expected in the driving test. This undermines what has been achieved on that occasion. If the only goal is the driving test, then think how long it can take before the customer experiences a sense of achievement.

Goal-setting identifies strengths and development needs

If you know what you are good at you can choose to channel your decisions through your strong points. Lots of people have a way of talking ('I'm rubbish at that', 'I could never do that', 'I can't do it') that is a clear reflection of how they think about themselves. Their choices and decisions are all about running away from what they are bad at, rather than positively focusing on what they are good at and basing their choices on this. In learning how to set their own goals your learners will also be learning to identify what they are good at and what they are weak at; what they need to do to improve; and what improvement/success will feel like to them.

Goal-setting raises self-awareness

Do your learners know how they learn best? Do they know how their emotions fuel their decisions, judgements and behaviour? Do they know what (if any) barriers to learning they are inclined to put up? Learning how to set goals for themselves will raise your customers' self-awareness in these areas. In many cases, barriers disappear as soon as someone is encouraged to determine their own goals for the lesson. They no longer feel defensive or insecure or fearful.

Goal-setting builds self-responsibility

Self-responsibility is all about taking ownership of the learning process as well as the driving task. This leads to more effective decision-making skills as well as an ability to be self-determining. By setting the goal the customer is taking control of their learning. Many instructors feel understandably nervous about this aspect of goal-setting in particular. Taking responsibility is an exciting, challenging and, sometimes, nerve-racking experience for the individual involved. It is not about the learner driver driving amok. You are ultimately responsible for their safety – they are learning to become responsible for their learning and together you will share the responsibility for the driving task.

Goal-setting develops skills for life

Learning how to set goals leads to the development of skills for life – in particular, self-evaluation skills. Naturally, this links closely with the Goals for Driver Education (GDE) framework where Level 4 is entitled 'Goals for life and skills for living' and is about self-evaluation or self-assessment. This is about learning how to give an accurate assessment of strengths and weaknesses in terms of judgement and decision making. For example, when you have to emerge from a busy junction, is your decision to go different depending on whether you are hungry, tired, happy, sad or angry? If you recognize that you are functioning in a particular emotional state do you have strategies to ensure your decisions are still safe and objective?

Goal-setting moves towards realizing full potential

In terms of Abraham Maslow's Hierarchy of Needs, widely published in 1954, human beings have five needs:

- Biological and physiological needs – air, food, drink, shelter, warmth, sex, sleep, etc.
- Safety needs – protection from elements, security, order, law, limits, stability, etc.
- Belongingness and love needs – work group, family, affection, relationships, etc.
- Esteem needs – self-esteem, achievement, mastery, independence, status, dominance, prestige, managerial responsibility, etc.

- Self-actualization needs – realizing personal potential, self-fulfilment, seeking personal growth and peak experiences.

According to Maslow, each of us is motivated by needs. Our most basic needs are inborn, having evolved over tens of thousands of years. Maslow's Hierarchy of Needs states that we must satisfy each need in turn, starting with the first, which deals with the most obvious needs for survival itself. Only when the lower-order needs of physical and emotional well-being are satisfied are we concerned with the higher-order needs of influence and personal development.

Learning how to set goals moves individuals towards being able to realize their full potential.

These points about goal-setting are important in ensuring that you are giving value for money in your lessons and that learning is taking place.

When discussing and agreeing goals and objectives it is important that both the instructor and the learner agree what they are to be, and that some record is kept of progress made. Using this system gives an immediate progress chart for each learner and will also act as a memory prompt for you so that you will be able to remember which particular item is the next one to be covered.

By using a log book or progress report, another instructor would be able to pick up where the previous instructor has left off.

As well as giving each learner feedback on their progress on a record or appointment card, you should also keep a master list in the car so that each learner's progress can be monitored. Progress sheets can be filed on a clipboard in alphabetical order by surname or the information can be recorded on an iPad or tablet.

Do not lose sight of the fact that as well as giving learners an individual 'test-related' programme of learning, we are also preparing them for a lifetime of safe driving. The requirements of the test go further than performing the set exercises. Knowledge, understanding and attitude all come into it as well as practical skill. Your course of instruction should cover all of these.

With the more traditional old-style conversations the instructor decides on the objectives for the lesson. With a client-centred approach the conversations will be very different, as shown in the following examples:

1: T-junctions

At the start of a lesson an old-style instructor might say:

'Today we are going to deal with emerging at T-junctions. Is that OK with you?'

'Fine.' (Learner thinks: 'Oh no! I'm dreading this because I can't even deal with turning corners yet. I don't know how I'll cope with all the other traffic.')

Using a coaching dialogue:

'OK, we've got a one-hour lesson today. What do you feel we need to achieve by the end of the session?'

'Well, I don't know – that's up to you isn't it?'

'Is there anything left over from last time that you feel could be improved?'

'Well, quite a lot, I suppose.'

'Anything in particular?'

'Not sure.'

'How did you think the last lesson went?'

'Reasonably well.'

'Were you happy with the way you were turning basic corners and dealing with the limited amount of traffic that we met?'

'Yes, I think so.'

'Do you feel that you're ready to take it a little further and deal with slightly more complex junctions and a bit more traffic?'

'Possibly.'

'So, if we spend a little time in consolidating what we did last time and then move on to, say, emerging at junctions you'd feel that's what we should do?'

'Yes, I think I'll be happier with that.'

'Right, so that means that the goal for today is to be able to emerge properly at T-junctions?'

'Yes, that's fine.'

'You're happy with that goal that you've set yourself?'

'Yes.'

'Fine, let's make a start, shall we?'

(Thinks: 'I'm pleased that we're going to do it that way and that I was able to make up my own mind about how the lesson was going to be structured.')

2: Reversing

Old-style instructor:

'Your regular instructor has told me that today we are to deal with reversing' or, 'If you remember, last time I saw you I told you that today we would be making a start on reversing.'

'Yes, OK.'

'Right, this is what we do.'

(Thinks: 'How can I tell him that I know half this stuff he's telling me?')

Coaching style:

'Just going back to our previous lesson, do you remember what we said we would be doing today?'

'Er, I think we said reversing.'

'Oh yes, that's right. What do you know about reversing?'

'I know that it's part of the test.'

'Yes, but we don't need to worry about that yet – have you got any thoughts about what we're going to do?'

'Well, yes. And in fact, at the weekend, I had a chance to do a bit of manoeuvring in my Dad's car in the big yard at the back of the house.'

'Oh good – how did you get on?'

'Well, quite reasonable, I think.'

'You probably know quite a bit about handling the car then, so what we'll do today is build on that.'

'Good.'

'What do you think will be the big difference between what you did at home and what we're doing today?'

'Well – er – other traffic, I suppose – pedestrians, cars and so on.'

'That's right, so those are the things that we'll have to deal with in today's lesson. At the same time though, we'll check your control of the car and the accuracy of the reversing.'

'That's fine.'

'OK, so let's imagine that we've now got to park on the right-hand side of the road. Are there any rules about what we do? For example will it be safe to reverse in this area or might we be affecting other traffic?'

(Thinks: 'What a good job I was able to explain what I'd done.')

These are all examples of client-centred learning that involve:

- coaching principles;
- learner involvement;
- use of Q&A;
- persuasion;
- most of the elements described previously in this book.

By using this style and method of teaching, your learners will be more likely to develop self-awareness and they will be encouraged to take more responsibility for their own learning. Both of these are important elements of an effective coaching environment.

When teaching by goals you will need to ask yourself at the end of each lesson:

- Were the goals set at a realistic level for the learner?
- Am I concentrating too much on 'getting them through the test' instead of teaching safe driving for life?
- Am I paying enough attention to knowledge, understanding and attitude, or spending too much time on skill training?
- Have I kept my learner's progress chart or driver's record up to date?
- Have I kept my own progress chart for this learner up to date?

Levels of instruction

There are three levels of instruction:

- Talk through or Guided: teaching new skills;
- Prompted: consolidating partly learnt skills;
- Independent: assessing skills already learnt or partly learnt.

Some lessons may contain a mixture of some or all of these activities. Many instructors make the mistake of trying to cram too much into one lesson to the detriment of the learning process.

As well as planning the content of the lesson to be given, you need to consider carefully the routes and areas chosen and the level of instruction required for each particular learner.

One of the problems for instructors is knowing when to 'drop out' and transfer to the learner the responsibility for solving problems and making decisions. The sooner your learners start to think things out and make decisions for themselves, the sooner they will be ready to drive unaccompanied.

For many learners, the first time they ever drive 'unaccompanied' will be on the 'L' test, when the examiner is there purely as an observer.

The skilful instructor knows when to stop talking. Of course, in most driving lessons, you will need to give directions, but it would be very beneficial to the learner if you say, 'Let's see if you can drive home on your own, without me saying anything at all. You make all the decisions and pretend that I am not here.' You would, of course, be prepared to step in and prevent any safety-critical situations from occurring, either by telling them what to do or by using the dual controls.

This exercise will boost the confidence of the learner in achieving their goals, and give you a measure of the learner's readiness to drive unaccompanied. At the end of the 'unaccompanied drive' it will be useful to ask the learner: 'How did you feel about driving on your own then?'

Some feedback would then need to be given to the learner. Two very common instructional errors arise from instructors not matching the level of instruction to suit the level of ability of their learner: over-instruction or under-instruction.

Over-instruction

This often occurs when the instructor is teaching a new skill or has identified a problem area and is giving the learner a complete 'talk-through' on a subject. The new skill will probably be mixed in with the skills that are already learnt or partly learnt.

For example, the instructor may be talking the learner through a difficult junction, with the added problem of roadworks. When the junction has been negotiated, the learner is asked to pull in and park somewhere convenient, so that they can discuss what happened. The instructor forgets that the learner knows how to park unaccompanied and says: 'Gently brake to slow; clutch down; gently brake to stop; apply the handbrake; select neutral.'

The learner may have parked a hundred times unaided, without any problem. What has happened is that the instructor, who has got so involved in the 'talk-through' mode, has forgotten when to keep quiet.

You should therefore try to restrict your prompted practice or talk-through to those aspects of driving that are new to the learner or are as yet unaccomplished. Over-instruction is particularly common when the learner is approaching test standard. It is as if the instructor is reluctant to 'let go of the reins'. Always remember that at this level your learners will learn a lot more by doing it themselves, even if they get it wrong, than by listening to you telling them what to do.

Under-instruction

This is particularly common when the learner is in the novice stage or is only partially trained. When teaching new skills it can help the learner learn more effectively if you control the practice so that, where possible, the learner gets it right first time. There is nothing more motivating for learners than success, even though that success may be the result of you prompting or talking them through the task. Some learners will learn most effectively if you talk them through each stage of the operation, skill or exercise until they develop the ability and confidence to do it for themselves.

The possibility of the need for a full talk-through is greater in the early stages of learning a particular task so as to lessen the risk of vehicle abuse and inconvenience or danger to other road users; and where it matches the particular learning style of the learner, or they are especially nervous.

The talk-through must give the learner enough time to interpret and execute your instructions comfortably. The speed with which each learner will be able to do this is likely to vary. You therefore need to match the level of instruction and the timing of your delivery to the needs of the learner.

Knowing when to drop out is important. If you leave the learner on their own too soon, resulting in a poor execution of the task, it can be very demotivating. However, when you consider the learner is ready to take personal responsibility, you should encourage them to do so. Some learners will need plenty of encouragement to act and think for themselves. Others will make rapid progress when left to work on their own initiative.

Prompting is the natural progression from controlled practice and will largely depend on the ability and willingness of learners to make decisions for themselves.

If conditions become too busy for the learner's ability, or if potential danger is a factor, then the learner may be reluctant to make any decisions at all. Where these situations arise, you may need to be prepared to step in and prompt when required.

The use of detailed instructions should decrease as the ability of your learners increases, thereby transferring the responsibility from you to them for making decisions and acting on them.

In the last few lessons leading up to the driving test, it should not be necessary for you to prompt the learner at all. If this is not the case, then you have a selling job to do. You need to either sell more lessons and the necessity for further practice or postponement of the test.

At the end of each lesson ask yourself:

- Did I match the level of the instruction given to the ability and needs of the learner?
- Did I over-instruct on things that the learner should need no instruction on?
- Did I leave the learner to do things without prompting or should I have given more help?

Route planning

Route selection and planning is itself a practical teaching skill and is an essential part of lesson preparation and planning. Part of an instructor's role is to create a situation in which learning can take place, and the selection of routes is an integral element in this process.

The ideal route would be one that takes account of the character and level of ability of the learner. It should be designed to stretch them but not be daunting.

Using training routes which are not relevant to the needs of the learner or not appropriate to the requirements of the lesson plan can have an extremely negative effect on the training.

The confidence of some learners can be destroyed because they are taken into difficult situations that require good clutch control before they have mastered this skill. Imagine how you would feel if you were sitting at a red traffic light on your first driving lesson and you stalled the engine a couple of times!

If new drivers are unnecessarily exposed to road and traffic conditions with which they are unable to cope, it is quite likely that the amount of learning taking place will be reduced. In the most extreme case, the learner's confidence will be severely affected, with a detrimental effect on learning or even a reversal of the learning process.

At the other end of the scale, restricting experienced learners to inappropriate basic routes will not encourage them to develop their skills.

When planning routes, you should consider some of the main requirements:

- the specific goals for the lesson;
- the standard and ability of the learner combined with the need to introduce or improve any skill or procedure;
- any particular weaknesses or strengths of the learner;
- any hazards or features that you may want to include or avoid in the overall lesson plan;
- the length of time available for the lesson;
- whether any danger or inconvenience might be caused by using a particular area at a particular time.

Ideally, you should have a thorough knowledge of the training area and any local traffic conditions. However, as this is not always practicable or possible, you will need to take care to avoid any extreme conditions.

If, because of the road layout and the limited time available, complex situations cannot be avoided, consider whether you should drive the learner to a more appropriate training area. In this event, use the drive to give a demonstration of any relevant points and to include a 'commentary' of what you are doing.

Training routes and areas tend to fall into three main categories: nursery or basic, intermediate and advanced. There will not be a clear division between the three groups and there will often be a considerable overlap from one group to another. Nevertheless, it is important that you have a clear idea of the appropriate routes within your own working environment.

Nursery routes – these will normally include fairly long, straight, wide roads without too many parked vehicles and avoiding pedestrian crossings, traffic lights and roundabouts. This type of route will incorporate progressively most of the following features:

- roads that are long enough to allow for a reasonable progression through all the gears and for stopping from various speeds;
- several upward and downward gradients suitable for starting and stopping;
- left- and right-hand bends to develop speed adjustment and gear-changing skills;

- left turns from main roads to side roads;
- left turns from side roads to main roads;
- right turns into side roads and onto main roads.

Intermediate routes – these should include busier junctions and general traffic conditions. At this stage, try to avoid dual carriageways, multi-lane roads and any one-way systems. Some or all of the following features might be incorporated in the routes:

- crossroads and junctions with 'stop' and 'give way' signs;
- several uphill, give-way junctions;
- traffic lights and basic roundabouts;
- areas for manoeuvring.

Try to avoid too many complicated traffic situations – for example, right turns onto exceptionally busy main roads or complex junctions.

Advanced routes – these will incorporate most of the features of the intermediate routes and should be extended to give a wider variety of traffic and road conditions. They should include, where possible, dual carriageways, multi-lane roads and one-way systems as well as residential, urban and rural roads. A properly planned 'advanced' route will provide the opportunity to conduct mock tests without using actual test routes. You should be able to find routes that include:

- different types of pedestrian crossings;
- roads with varying speed limits;
- level crossings, dual carriageways and one-way streets;
- multi-lane roads for lane selection and lane discipline;
- rural, urban and residential roads.

Starting with nursery routes, try to introduce new elements and situations at a controlled rate, bearing in mind the needs of the individual learner and their level of ability. Get used to what seems to be 'their own pace' – one at which the learner feels comfortable.

There may be occasions when a mixture of all types of route may be incorporated into one lesson – for example, when making an initial assessment of a new learner who has previous driving experience.

Ideally, you should start off with a fairly wide selection of routes. This will give you the opportunity to vary and extend them with experience.

Retain a certain amount of flexibility in using the planned routes because you may, for instance, need to spend more time than anticipated on a topic that the learner is finding more difficult than expected.

If a specific problem is identified, you may need to bring the learner back to a particular junction in order to 're-create' a situation.

Excessive repetition of identical routes will often lead to a lack of interest or response from the learner. This in turn will lead to slow progress in learning and may also be counterproductive. Some variation of routes is essential to the learning process and will sustain the learner's interest and motivation. Chunking your lessons, however, by repeating short circuits that last perhaps five or six minutes can give your learner the opportunity to drive independently towards the end of the lesson as if you weren't in the car. This gives them a sense of achievement and means they are more likely to achieve the goals agreed at the start of the lesson.

Remember that training routes are often a compromise between the ideal and the reality of local conditions in the training area. The nature of traffic conditions can vary enormously from time to time and from lesson to lesson. You may find that a carefully planned route may unexpectedly prove unsuitable and you are faced with a situation that the learner is not ready for. Careful route planning can, however, keep these incidents to a manageable level. Be ready to extend the length of a lesson for a particular learner if appropriate training routes are not readily available in the immediate vicinity.

At the end of each lesson, ask yourself:

- Did I choose a route that was suitable for the level of ability of the learner and for the goals agreed?
- Did I vary the route sufficiently to sustain the interest of the learner?
- Am I using routes that stretch the ability of the learner without destroying their confidence?

Fault assessment

This section deals with fault recognition, assessment and correction.

Driving faults normally fall into two separate categories: in the car (control skills) and outside the car (road procedure errors).

You will often find that 'in-car' errors will lead to errors of road procedure, lack of accuracy or failure to respond correctly to traffic situations.

You will need to use your eyes, dividing your attention between what is happening on the road ahead, what is happening behind and what your learner is doing with their hands, feet and eyes.

Try not to: watch the learner so intently that you miss important changes in the traffic situation ahead to which your learner should be responding; or watch the road and traffic so intently that you miss faults that are happening in the car.

An effective way of coping with all the visual checks required is to use the M S M, P S L and L A D routines – but from an instructor's point of view. For example, when approaching a hazard, you should check that your learner:

M – checks the rear view mirrors; look in your own mirror to confirm what is happening behind and check that your learner acts sensibly on what is seen;

S – is signalling properly, when necessary and at the correct time;

M – carries out the manoeuvre correctly;

becomes:

P – positions the vehicle correctly for the situation;

S – slows down to a suitable speed and selects an appropriate gear when necessary;

L – is looking early enough, at the correct time, and that the observations are effective and include use of the mirrors;

becomes:

A – assesses the situation correctly;

D – makes a good decision as to how to deal with the hazard.

Continuous assessment should be sensitive to the learner's needs and is concerned with improving performance. In the last few lessons leading up to the 'L' test, the continuous assessment should give way to 'objective' or 'mock' testing. The purpose of this is to assess the learner's readiness to take the test and it should be matched to the requirements of the test itself.

Grading of errors

Don't think of errors as being black or white. In driving, there are many shades of grey, and the circumstances surrounding the error need to be considered. When assessing driver error, you should take into consideration the following: an error can involve varying degrees of importance; some errors are of a more serious nature and can result in more severe consequences than others.

Driver errors will generally fall into one of four categories:

1 Not marked – this is where the fault is so slight that you decide not to mention it.
2 Minor – this is where the fault does not involve a serious or dangerous situation. No other road user is potentially or actually involved.
3 Serious – a serious fault is one that involves potential risk to persons or property.
4 Dangerous – this is where the actions of the learner cause actual danger to persons or property.

There is a need for some standardization between the consistency of assessments made during driving lessons and those used for the driving test.

Having said this, there is no need to grade errors exactly to test criteria. Remember that we are teaching safe driving for life. Consequently, some instructors may aim for a much higher overall standard of ability than that required on the 'L' test.

This can be beneficial to their learners. It would be true to say that most learners do not perform as well on the driving test as they do while out with their instructor on lessons. Learners who have been trained to a higher standard should therefore stand a better chance of passing. Even if they do not drive as well on the test as on previous lessons, they are still likely to pass, provided that there are no serious or dangerous errors. In any event, the extra training before taking the test will mean that these learners are better prepared to drive unaccompanied after passing.

To give maximum benefit you need to:

- recognize the fault;
- analyse the fault;
- correct the fault.

Fault recognition

Having recognized a fault, you should identify it as being minor, serious or dangerous. Minor faults can normally be corrected on the move. However, if a recurring pattern of minor faults is identified, you will need to spend some time on dealing with them before they become more serious.

Minor faults could include errors in coordination and inefficient or uneconomic driving style, slight inaccuracies in positioning (either travelling along the road or during the set manoeuvres) and harsh use of the controls.

Serious or dangerous faults will need to be discussed more fully. This discussion should be carried out while parked somewhere safe. Do not get into discussions at road junctions, or while learners are trying to negotiate hazards – this will only confuse them, which could lead to even more serious faults being made.

Fault analysis

When analysing faults, you need to compare what your learner is doing, or has done, with what you would be doing or would have done in similar circumstances.

A useful approach would be to ask the learner: 'How do you think that drive/manoeuvre went?'

It may be that the learner realizes that a mistake has been made, in which case you could help them to analyse the fault.

You should:

- discuss what was wrong (both the cause of the error and its effect and consequences);
- discuss what should have happened;
- discuss and explain why it is important (paying particular attention to how the error could affect other road users).

Consider using a visual aid if you need to recreate a difficult situation or explain incorrect positioning on the road or illustrate how other road users were involved. Diagrams, models and magnetic boards are useful aids.

Whilst analysing the fault, use questions to make sure that the learner understands what went wrong, what should have happened and why it is important. This will then lead to the last, and most important, part of the routine.

Fault correction

You should be able to offer remedial action while the fault and the improvements needed are still fresh in the learner's mind. It is of little use to say that you will come back to the fault on the next lesson as by that time the learner will have probably forgotten what happened and what to do.

If the fault involved the way in which the learner dealt with a particular hazard or junction, the most effective way to correct it would be to get the learner to approach the same situation again. Depending on the fault, you may agree to talk the learner through the situation, or just prompt on the points that need improving. The main thing is that success is achieved. If time allows, a third approach to the same situation will help to validate your instruction, this time leaving the learner to deal with it entirely unaided. Feedback must be given when improvement has been made.

At the end of each lesson, ask yourself:

- Did I identify all the main faults made by my learner?
- Did I correct all the minor faults on the move and stop to analyse the major faults as soon as convenient?
- Did I analyse the faults made with regard to what went wrong, what should have happened and why it was important?
- Did I offer appropriate remedial action, bringing about improvement?

Hazard perception

Hazard perception is part of the theory test for learners and the ADI Part 1 exam. It is a subject that instructors need to be expert at both in theory and practice.

The driving skills involved include:

- scanning the road well ahead;
- anticipating the actions and reactions of other road users;
- being aware of following traffic;
- planning an appropriate course of action;
- maintaining a safe and appropriate distance behind the vehicle in front;
- driving at a speed that is appropriate to the conditions.

However, the main element is concentration!

As an instructor, your own perception of hazards is even more important. You should also be able to develop these skills in your learner drivers by utilizing a variety of practical teaching skills, but mostly by effective question and answer techniques.

A 'hazard' is usually defined as anything that might result in a change of direction or the speed of the vehicle. Some of these will be static hazards such as road junctions or bends; others might be moving hazards, such as pedestrians, cyclists, horse-riders, motorcyclists and other vehicles.

Using your Q&A techniques you should be able to help your learners to improve their skill in recognizing and dealing with all types of hazard.

The ultimate aim of your instruction will be to enable your learners to:

- scan the road ahead and behind effectively;
- anticipate the main points of danger;
- recognize that what they can't see is often more important than what they can see;
- think about what might happen as well as what is happening;
- give themselves time and space to carry out a particular manoeuvre or to avoid a problem;
- maintain absolute control of their vehicle while carrying out correct driving procedures.

Encouraging your learners to look well ahead, keeping their eyes moving all the time and continually looking for clues as to what might happen, helps achieve this.

Demonstration

A demonstration can sometimes be useful in that learners will be able to see a model of correct behaviour which they can then imitate. Complex tasks can be broken down into component parts that can be demonstrated before the learner practises and repeats them until mastery is achieved.

There are several advantages in giving a demonstration, including:

- you can adapt the demonstration to suit the specific needs of the learner;
- you are there to answer any questions the learner may wish to ask.

The demonstration must not be used to impress the learner with your own expertise. The key points in the preceding briefing or explanation should form an integral part of the demonstration by way of an abbreviated commentary.

A learner may often be genuinely unaware of a mistake. A demonstration will help to show them where they are going wrong and what is needed to correct the problem. This is especially so when the learner's perception of safety margins, the need for 'holding back' procedures, and speed approaching hazards, is poor.

You might mention slowing down approaching a hazard and get no response from the learner if their understanding of 'slow' is different from your own. Under these circumstances a demonstration can be a valuable aid in persuading learners to modify what they are doing to fit in with how you want the driving task carried out.

It may be helpful to learners if you simulate what they are doing so that they can appreciate the difference.

This technique would be particularly useful when giving feedback on the learner's performance in the set manoeuvres.

Points to remember:

- Explain beforehand what you are going to demonstrate and give the reasons for the demonstration.
- Pitch the demonstration and the commentary given while carrying it out to the correct level for the ability of the learner.
- Make the demonstration as perfect an example as possible of what you want the learner to do.
- Restrict the commentary to key points only and those that are necessary for that particular learner.
- Consolidate afterwards with a debriefing and controlled practice.

The demonstration should be concluded with a summary of the key points, which might then lead to a Q&A session to identify any aspects of the task that the learner still does not understand.

Demonstrations can be carried out in different ways depending on the learning style of your learner. For example, if your learner has told you they learn visually and process information most effectively this way, you could carry out the demonstration in silence having previously discussed what your learner needs to look at and watch. If your learner has an auditory learning preference then you could give them a commentary while you demonstrate, or you could ask them to talk you through as if they were the driving instructor. A kinaesthetic learner might benefit most from no demonstration or explanation at all – just let them have a go.

Practice

Having demonstrated a particular skill or manoeuvre you should then allow your learner to practise it. You could find that there is a need for prompting if the learner is encountering difficulties or deviating from what they should be doing. For example, if the learner is bay parking you may need to offer some prompting on where to look.

Establishing good habits in these early stages while practising the manoeuvre will pay dividends for the learner later.

When the learner is practising new skills, check on the body language for signs of stress, frustration or despair. Be prepared to intervene if necessary. Encouragement and reassurance may be needed. Be prepared to change your lesson plan and go back to consolidating previously learnt skills to boost flagging confidence.

Controlled practice will allow the learner to remain safe, and not be too unsympathetic to the vehicle. It involves the learner in following simple verbal instructions to carry out the component parts of the skill which, when brought together, form complete mastery.

The speed with which the learner interprets and responds to the instruction needs to be considered. This may vary from learner to learner. With some learners it may be necessary to carry out tasks more slowly than normal.

The instructions given should eventually be reduced to prompting. As soon as the learner appears to be able to cope independently, the instruction should gradually be phased out.

The amount of prompting given will depend on the ability and willingness of learners to make decisions on their own. Some learners will require a lot of encouragement to act and think for themselves.

The ultimate objective is to get the learner to carry out each skill under all normal traffic conditions with no prompting from you at all.

Many learners complete their programme of training being able to carry out all the driving tasks required of them, but unable to do any of them particularly well. This is not helpful to the learners, who may themselves feel that 'all is not well'.

The sequence of development should be:

- controlled practice;
- prompted practice;
- transferred responsibility;
- reflection;
- revision.

Prompting should not be necessary where the learner is about to be presented for the 'L' test!

Learner involvement

To help maintain the interest and attention of your learner you need to bring the lesson to life, personalizing it and making it enjoyable. At the end of any lesson your learners should leave the car feeling not only that they have learnt something and achieved the objectives of the lesson, but also that they have enjoyed themselves.

A proportion of your learners will probably come to you having had lessons with another instructor. Why is this? It is often because they feel they were not making progress with the previous instructor or were not enjoying the lessons.

Don't forget that each learner is an individual. Use first names during the lesson and make eye contact when discussing things while stationary. Use the different speech elements discussed in the previous chapter – metaphors, hyperbole and similes – to add interest and perhaps a touch of humour to the lesson.

Use visual aids when explaining things, and make sure that learners can actually see what it is that you are showing them. If instructors accidentally cover up what they are showing with their hands, learners cannot see or understand the points being made!

Visual aids

A learning aid is any medium you might use to enable you to present your ideas, concepts, knowledge and skills in a manner that is more easily understood by your learner.

Learning aids can assist the learning process by helping to hold learners' attention and generate an interest that stimulates the desire to learn.

It has been said that 'The purpose of a learning aid is to liberate the teacher from the limitations of their own speech.' But, while learning aids may help to make a good instructor even better, they will not compensate for bad teaching.

Learning aids range from a simple notepad and pencil to sophisticated driving simulators. Between these two extremes, there is a vast range of aids available to the instructor, many of which are visual. ADIs may also use applications on mobile phones or tablets. In this section we will concentrate on those aids of a visual nature that can be used in the car.

'A picture paints a thousand words' – provided it is a good picture! It is amazing how many instructors say to their learners, 'I am not very good at drawing, but I am going to draw you a diagram to explain what I mean.'

The visual aids you use are limited only by your imagination. You can use your hands to explain how the clutch plates come together; you can use your fingers to show 'the thickness of a coin' when explaining the biting point; you can produce pre-prepared diagrams to assist you in explaining various aspects of road procedure, manoeuvres, etc.

Visual aids offer the following benefits:

- they add structure to your lesson;
- they provide a change of activity for the learner;
- they will assist you by reminding you what needs to be explained;
- they will allow the learner to recall and visualize previously encountered situations;
- they can help to clarify difficult concepts or show specific positions required when manoeuvring or dealing with hazards;
- they stimulate the interest of the learner and help to maintain attention.

By being skilful in designing, creating and integrating visual aids in your presentation, you will be able to bring the lesson to life.

When using visual aids in the car you should:

- avoid just reading from a script;
- talk to the learner and not to the visual aid;
- turn the aid around so that the learner can see it – it is for their benefit, not just for yours;
- avoid covering the visual aid with your hand – you may need to hold it with your right and use your left hand, or a pen, to point to the key parts;
- avoid 'pen-waving' because it can be threatening to the learner;
- put the visual aid away once you have used it, before it becomes a distraction.

The 'A to E' of visual aids:

Accuracy – try to ensure that the visual aid accurately recreates the situation you are trying to depict.

Brevity – keep drawings/diagrams simple and avoid having too many words or unnecessary detail.

Clarity – ensure that letters or words are big enough to be seen by the learner.

Deletion – use them then lose them, otherwise they become a distraction.

Emphasis – make sure that the visual aid stresses the key points.

At the end of each lesson ask yourself:

- Did I take every opportunity to use visual aids in order to assist the learning process?
- Were the visual aids stimulating and effective?
- Did I identify any situations where a visual aid could have been useful? If so, should I think about designing one for future use?

The use of questions

The question and answer technique (Q&A) is an important aspect of driving instruction because it involves the learner in the process and allows the instructor to check that learning is taking place.

It is the combination of key skills of questioning, building rapport and active listening that enables the driving instructor to establish a balance between instruction and coaching – a balance that is critical in keeping the car safe. There are various questioning techniques that can be employed to help strike this balance.

For details of different types of coaching questions, see the section on effective questioning in Chapter 3.

Risk management

Some learner drivers may fail to recognize potentially dangerous traffic situations in time to employ the necessary procedure or defensive strategy.

As instructors, you must read the road well ahead. You must also learn to anticipate a learner's incorrect response to risky situations and be prepared to manage this, either by verbal or physical action.

When giving driving lessons you must manage the risk to maintain a safe learning environment for your learners by:

- planning routes that are suitable to their ability;
- forward planning and concentrating on the overall traffic situation – front, rear and to the sides;

- being alert and anticipating learners' incorrect actions or lack of activity in difficult situations;
- giving clear instructions in good time for them to respond;
- overriding learners' decisions when necessary;
- being prepared to intervene verbally or physically.

Many learners show a reluctance to slow down, give way, stop or hold back when necessary. This is usually because they have an innate fear of stopping. If they stop, they know they then have to get the car moving again – one of the most difficult things for learners to do in the early stages!

This reluctance to deal with hazards defensively may cause the situation to develop into an emergency. Where the situation is allowed to reach this critical level, there are two possible unwanted reactions: the learner may do nothing and remain frozen at the controls; or the learner may over-react at the last moment, resulting in harsh, uncontrolled braking, the effect of which is difficult to predict.

It is in situations like this that expert instructors prove their worth. By intervening, either verbally or physically, a possible accident situation can be avoided.

There are four main reasons why you should intervene:

1. To prevent risk of injury or damage to persons or property (including the driving school car).
2. To prevent the learner from breaking the law, which could lead to you being prosecuted for 'aiding and abetting'.
3. To prevent excessive stress to the learner in certain unplanned circumstances (for example, an emergency situation).
4. To prevent mechanical damage to the vehicle (for example, in the event of an injudicious gear change).

Because intervention can undermine confidence and inhibit the progress of the learner, it should be kept to a minimum. Verbal intervention should, if time allows, be used before considering the use of physical intervention or the dual controls.

Verbal intervention

A verbal instruction or command will usually be successful in dealing with most traffic situations or driver errors, provided it is given early enough.

Verbal instructions and memory prompts will be used more frequently in the early stages of learning to drive and may take the form of more specific instructions such as: 'Use the mirrors well before...', 'More brake!', 'Ease off the brake' and 'Clutch down'.

These more positive commands will often be needed to make sure that your learner slows down early enough on the approach to a potential hazard.

'Hold back!', 'Give way!' and 'Wait!' are other examples of positive instructions that require a positive response or reaction from the learner, but which also leave some freedom of judgement.

When using this type of command, the pitch and tone of your voice should be used to convey the degree of urgency to the learner.

The use of the word 'Stop' should generally be restricted to those occasions when other instructions have not been followed by the learner or when the learner has not responded positively. Incorrect use of this command could mean that your learner over-reacts and stops too suddenly or in an unsuitable position. Unnecessary and too frequent use of the word 'Stop' – for example, when parking – could have the effect that learners will not respond quickly enough in urgent situations.

Physical intervention

Use of any form of physical intervention, or the dual controls, should be restricted to situations when the verbal instruction has not been followed or there is insufficient time for it to be given or acted on.

In these situations, you may need to consider the main alternatives: use of the dual brake and/or clutch; assistance with the steering.

Using the dual brake/clutch

The following points need to be considered:

- Avoid sitting with your legs crossed when teaching. When approaching hazards, keep your right foot discreetly near the dual brake but not riding on it.
- Avoid unnecessary or 'fidgety' movements of your feet as this may unnerve your learner.
- Make effective use of the dual mirror before using the dual brake.
- If your learner has 'frozen' on the gas pedal, avoid using the dual clutch as this could cause a blown head gasket.

- Give the learner time to use the brake before intervening. If you both use the brake at the same time, this could cause problems.
- Consider using the dual brake to help you to 'buy time' if you have to help with the steering. This applies particularly where the learner may be trying to turn a corner too fast.

Assistance with steering

This should only be used to make slight alterations to road position. It would be better for you to tell the learner to 'Steer to the right' or 'Steer to the left'.

Bear in mind the following points:

- Minor corrections with steering are usually more practical and safer alternatives to using the dual brake.
- Use only your right hand when assisting with steering.
- Avoid physical contact. If you get hold of the learner's hand or arm and he or she lets go of the wheel, you have lost control.
- If you wish to steer to the left, hold the wheel near the top so that you can 'pull down'.
- If you wish to steer to the right, hold the wheel near the bottom so that you can 'push up'.
- If the situation is such that more drastic turning of the wheel is required, it would be safer and much less worrying for the learner if you used the dual brake.
- Never get into a fight with the learner over the wheel – you might lose!

There may be occasions when assistance with both steering and braking are required. For example, it may be essential to hold the steering wheel while using the dual brake to prevent the learner from over-steering. In order to gain more time, you may need to reduce and control the speed of the vehicle with the dual brake, particularly when the learner has 'frozen' on the gas pedal.

In any potentially dangerous situation, you will need to use your experience to decide which method of intervention is required. You may need to use the dual clutch at the same time as manipulating the gear lever to prevent an inappropriate gear change. This will allow your learner to concentrate on maintaining the correct speed and position.

Examples of other types of physical intervention that crop up from time to time include:

- selecting a missed gear at a critical time or place;
- preventing an incorrect gear selection by 'covering the gear lever' until the correct speed is reached;
- covering the dual clutch to be ready to prevent the car moving off at an inappropriate time;
- rectifying an error with the handbrake when there is no time to tell the learner to do so;
- switching off the engine to prevent mechanical damage;
- cancelling an injudicious signal with safety in mind when there is no time to tell the learner to do so.

The need for any kind of intervention can be kept to an absolute minimum by careful route planning and matching the road and traffic conditions to the ability of the learner.

You may encounter some resentment towards any form of physical interference or the use of the dual controls. This could result in learners losing confidence in themselves and in you as a teacher. You should therefore make sure that:

1. You do not get into the habit of using physical intervention or the dual controls excessively or unnecessarily.
2. Having used any physical intervention, you fully explain to the learner what you did to control the car, and why it was necessary to do it!

05

Driver training

Teaching driving as a life skill in today's traffic conditions is a challenging occupation. So that your learners become safe and competent drivers, as well as being able to enjoy their future driving, you need to:

- understand and be able to apply all the coaching and client-centred skills covered in this book;
- be able to develop confidence and safe attitudes in your learners;
- structure your training to follow the 'known to the unknown' and 'simple to complex' rules of learning.

In this chapter some of the subjects are dealt with in a relatively formal way, including an introduction, objectives and so on. With others, we give examples of how to set up more of a coaching approach by way of a dialogue with the learner to encourage more self-learning, self-awareness and motivation. With other topics we simply offer a few guidance notes on the important key points.

With experience, you should be able to decide for yourself the method and approach that will best suit your own style and one that will be most appropriate for any individual learner or specific circumstances.

This chapter contains a training programme that follows a logical sequence incorporating the above principles. It focuses on the various topics involved in driver training and not necessarily on the requirements of the ADI exams. If you learn how to apply these effectively, you should be well prepared to teach drivers at all levels of experience and ability.

Beginning with the introduction of the car's controls and how to move off and stop, we progress through the different stages of learning to drive in a logical sequence.

Depending on your local road and traffic conditions, as well as the individual needs of your learners, you may need to teach some of the subjects in a different sequence. Always be ready to adapt your lesson to suit the level and ability of the learner, and the amount of time available.

You can do this by:

- using your client-centred learning skills to work to an agreed programme;
- adapting your teaching method to suit progress made by a learner during the lesson; and
- ensuring positive learning takes place through practice within the time scale.

Whatever the subject or level of ability of your learner, your aim should always be to ensure that learning takes place and to encourage your learner's development and long-term learning.

Lesson structure

Every lesson, no matter what the subject matter is, should follow a similar pattern. There should always be a beginning, a middle and an end.

The main ingredients should be:

Beginning

- greeting;
- recapping on the previous lesson;
- agreeing the content, process and goals of the session;
- establishing prior knowledge and understanding.

Middle

- working from the known to the unknown;
- applying the appropriate teaching, instructing and coaching skills;
- creating opportunities for learning to take place through practice and reflection;
- using feedback.

End

- encouraging reflection in a summary, and giving feedback;
- looking forward to the next lesson.

Main car controls

Objectives

The main objectives for this lesson:

1. To get to know your learner by finding out what has motivated them to want to learn and why they have chosen you as their instructor.
2. To let the learner get used to you and your style of teaching, and for you to gain their confidence.
3. To introduce the main controls of the car and, if possible, let the learner have some experience in moving off and stopping.

Getting to know your learner

One of your main aims, when meeting a learner for the first time, is to sell yourself by promoting a caring and understanding image and ensuring that you inspire confidence. To do this, try to imagine how your learner may be feeling about learning to drive, and being in the confined space of a car with a stranger.

For this lesson, you will need to drive to an area that is reasonably quiet, with as long a stretch of straight road as is available to practise moving off and stopping (see route planning in Chapter 4). The area you use will depend on the locality of the learner's pick-up point and the likely content of the lesson. You will sometimes have to adapt your instruction to suit less than ideal conditions – this is often the case on the instructional ability test.

During the drive to the training area find out if your learner:

- has a valid and signed driving licence;
- can read a number plate at the prescribed distance;
- is studying for, or has already passed, the theory test.

Get to know a little more about your learner by asking questions such as:

'Why do you want to learn to drive?'

'How did you hear of me? Was I recommended by someone?'

'Do you have any experience in driving a car?'

'Do you ride a motorbike?'

'When you've been a passenger, have you been watching what the driver was doing?'

If your learner is a little shy, you may have to 'back off' a little. However, try to avoid silence – this will only make a nervous learner even more tense.

Part of your job as an instructor is to gain the confidence of your learners and put them at ease.

Driving deliberately and a little more slowly than usual, give a simple commentary on what you're doing. Focus mainly on the application of the M S M routine and its application to the various situations you meet.

You are your best salesperson – make sure your driving is impeccable.

Select a training area that is safe, legal and will cause as little disruption to other drivers as is possible – in other words, convenient. Park where:

- you can safely carry out your explanation of the main controls;
- the learner can get some stationary practice in their use; and
- there is plenty of opportunity to learn how to move off and stop.

Vehicle familiarization

It is usually more practical to get the learner into the driving seat so that you can explain where the controls are, and they can practise using them. This makes the most effective use of your time and avoids unnecessary repetition. It means you have plenty of time for the learner to get practical experience at moving off and stopping before the end of the lesson, which in turn should help to meet some of their expectations.

With an absolute novice, for instance someone with no experience of cars as a passenger, you may decide to give the explanation from the driving seat. This will ensure that the learner is not tempted to fiddle with any of the controls.

The first thing you need to get your learner to think about is getting out of the passenger seat, around the car and into the driving seat safely. This should include:

Checking around before opening the passenger door. You could ask something like: 'Is anyone near the car on the pavement?'

Making sure it's safe to walk into the road, around the car and to open the door, ask: 'Is there any traffic coming up that might make it unsafe to step out or that you will affect by opening the door?'

Entering the car and getting into a correct seating position is commonly called 'The cockpit drill' and includes:

- Doors – ensuring they are properly closed.
- Seat – correct adjustment of seat, back rake, head restraint and other ancillaries as are available and necessary such as steering column and seat height.
- Steering – hands can be comfortably moved from top to bottom of the wheel.
- Seatbelts – correctly put on and removed (no twists); driver's responsibilities.
- Mirrors – all mirrors are correctly adjusted.

Main controls

These fall into three categories:

1. foot controls;
2. hand controls;
3. ancillary controls.

It is not essential to cover these in the sequence listed. However, it does help learners if you deal mainly with those controls that will be used to make the car go and stop – that means the foot controls. Apart from the indicators, the ancillary controls you will need to cover should depend on the weather and light conditions.

Foot controls

Unless you are teaching in a car with automatic gears, confirm that there are three foot controls:

- accelerator;
- footbrake; and
- clutch.

Ask your learners if they know which foot operates which pedal and what each does, for example:

'Do you know what the pedal on the right does?'

'What's the pedal in the centre for and which foot will you use to operate it?'

'Do you know what following drivers should see when the footbrake is used?'

'What's the pedal on the left for?'

If you are teaching in a car with automatic transmission, then you will need to explain that the right foot is used for the two pedals. You will also need to explain about the gear selector.

Accelerator Because you will sometimes need your learner to respond quickly to a request, for example to start slowing down, it's easier to say, 'Off the gas' than it is to say, 'Off the accelerator'.

If you ask, 'What does the gas pedal do?' most learners will say that it makes the car go faster. Very few will realize that it is also the first means of starting to slow down the car. However, this point should become clear if you use a simple comparison such as how a tap works, explaining that when the pedal is pressed down more fuel will flow into the engine to make it go faster; and when the pressure is eased the flow will slow down. The pedal is sensitive and should be used gently.

Footbrake Operates on all four wheels to slow the car down and eventually bring it to a stop.

Discuss a few important points such as:

- a mirror check should be made before braking;
- this is also a sensitive pedal and should be used gently and progressively;
- the stop lights will be activated as soon as pressure is applied to it.

Clutch Consider asking questions such as: 'Do you know what the clutch does?'; 'Do you know when you'd use it?'

Depending on the learner's responses, using a visual aid, either confirm or explain in simple terms the clutch's main purpose. This is to disconnect the engine from the gearbox to make smooth changes from one gear to another and to ensure that the engine keeps running when the car has been stopped.

Hand controls

Explain that, although there are lots of dials, switches and gadgets in the car, there are three main hand controls:

- steering wheel;
- handbrake; and
- gear lever.

Steering wheel You can use coaching skills to find out which hand position is most comfortable for your learners. First, get them to place their hands on the wheel at around 'ten to two' or 'quarter to three' and encourage them to hold it gently with the thumbs along the rim rather than around the wheel. Ask how it feels when they slide their hands to the top and bottom. If it's not comfortable, get them to drop the hands a little and try again. Try this procedure until the learner can move the hands comfortably around the wheel – provided they aren't at rest too near the top or bottom.

Turning the steering wheel using the conventional method of 'pull–push' does not come naturally to most new drivers and everyone's body and range of movements are different. Use common sense and be flexible about the way the steering wheel is used.

Although 'pull–push' is the officially recommended method, the main point is that the car should be under complete control and in the correct position on the road. You should also be aware that 'rotational' steering generally results in a much quicker response in most emergency situations and in correcting skids.

Describe how it's natural for the hands to follow the eyes. Ask your learners if they've ever experienced a situation when they've been walking along and something to the side has caught their attention and when they've looked forward again, they've gone off course. Confirm that this can happen while driving and that's why it's so important to look well ahead up the road at where they want to go.

Handbrake Confirm that it secures the car once stopped by locking up the rear wheels. As well as for parking, it should be used for stops of longer than a few seconds, on hills to prevent rolling forwards or backwards, and for safety when stopped for pedestrians on crossings. (When driving automatics, the handbrake should be used more often to compensate for the tendency to 'creep'.)

You will need to ensure the car is secure. You can either apply the dual footbrake or, because you also need to encourage an understanding of the relationship between the two braking systems, you could say something like: 'Press the middle pedal down with your right foot.'

The handbrake has three positions: on, off and, when the button is pressed, ready to release. Discuss how to properly release and apply the handbrake and then allow the learner to practise this a couple of times.

Gear lever Find out what learners know about the use of gears. Usually if they have ridden a bike they will have a little understanding. However, in order to develop your practical teaching skills, we will deal with the subject as it should be taught to someone with no knowledge.

First, explain about the power to speed ratio and, while serving as a memory jogger for you, a visual aid may assist your learner in understanding this principle (see visual aids in Chapter 4).

Confirm that, because of the weight of the car and its occupants, you will need more engine power to get moving. The lower gears, first and second, are the most powerful and normally first is used for moving off. Second is useful for moving off down hills where gravity will help in getting the car rolling more quickly. We will need to accelerate to build up speed and then change up into the higher gears. These allow us to drive at a wider range of speeds while using less power.

To assist in the learner's understanding, you might ask:

'When you're walking uphill what happens to you?'

'Do you start to slow down and then have to put in more effort?'

'If you were cycling up a hill, what would you have to do?'

You will then be able to confirm that this is exactly what happens to the car by saying something like: 'Because of the hill slowing the car down, we will need to give it more power by changing into a lower gear.'

You should also discuss the point that, because all cars differ in size and power, the speed at which the gears will need to be changed varies. However, after a few lessons they should become familiar with the sound the engine makes as it 'tells' them when a change is required. Confirm that you will help them to recognize these sounds and to build up their vehicle sympathy so that they will eventually feel the car is part of them.

As one of the main objectives of this lesson is vehicle familiarization, you should allow plenty of stationary practice so that the learner will be able to 'find' all the gear positions while looking ahead. This can be done without switching on the engine, but it might be useful to get the learner to push down the clutch to establish the relationship.

Allow your learner to take an initial look at the lever and identify the different gear positions. It might help, in the early stages, to relate the position of the first four gears in the form of the letter H to the position of the road wheels so when a change is necessary, and without looking down, they should be able to move the lever in the appropriate direction.

The gear lever in most modern cars is usually 'spring-loaded'. As well as demonstrating (with your right hand) how to select the gears using the 'palming' method, you will also need to emphasize this bias as you talk the learner through the various changes.

Allow the learner to practise gear change combinations. That is, as well as showing how to change in sequence up and down, explain about selective changing and talk through these changes with a couple of examples of where they might be used.

This practice is very important because, the more confident learners become with gear changing while stationary, the easier they will find it when they are on the move.

Other hand controls

Indicators

Remember – new drivers will have been pedestrians and passengers and will be aware of the use of indicators. To avoid being patronizing try to get them to discover for themselves where they are and in which direction they will need to be operated. Use questions such as:

'What are the orange flashing lights for on the front, rear and sometimes the sides, of cars?'

'When do you think they should be used?'

'Which of the controls on the steering column do you think is the indicator switch?' If the learner has a problem, follow this up with: 'OK, find the switch with the arrows on.'

'If you're intending to turn right, which way will you turn the wheel? Now tell me which way you think the indicator switch will need to be operated.'

Allow the learner to practise switching the indicators on and off (preferably using the fingertips while keeping the hand on the wheel), confirming that the indicator should normally self-cancel after going around corners. Explain the audible and visible warnings that will tell the driver when the indicators are operating.

Horn

Confirm that this is a warning device and should only be used when there is possible danger or potential damage. Discuss one of the main rules about not using it when stationary unless under threat from another moving vehicle. You could then ask them to check up on the other rules because you'll be asking some questions on their next lesson.

Ancillary controls

As your learners must take on board lots of information on this lesson, it's very important to consider how much of it is likely to be remembered. Overloading them at this stage with information they are unlikely to remember in any case, is going to inhibit their progress and confidence.

Only cover those ancillary controls that are necessary according, mainly, to the weather and light conditions. If it's not raining and light conditions are good, you won't need to cover the lights, washers, wipers or demisters. Confirm that you will show the learner where these are and how they work on another lesson.

Stationary practice Demonstrate how to check that the handbrake is firmly applied and that the gear lever is in neutral. Ask your learner to make these checks and then allow plenty of stationary practice in:

- setting the gas;
- covering the brake pedal;
- finding the 'biting' point.

Moving off and stopping

You would normally have time to include moving off and stopping on the first lesson.

Confirm that your learner understands about the main controls by asking a couple of questions such as:

'Do you feel happy with what we've covered so far?'

'Is there anything you're not sure about?'

'Is there anything in particular you feel you need to practise?'

Agreeing the goals

You are now ready to continue the lesson by agreeing the next goal. This is to learn how to move off and stop the car safely. If your learner is preparing for their theory test, ask if they know anything about the M S M routine and give praise if they have even only a little knowledge. In any case, you will need to give a breakdown of the routine to ensure that all the important points are covered.

Mirrors

Discuss the difference between the flat glass of the interior mirror and the convex glass of the exterior ones. Confirm why any decisions must be based on the true image seen in the interior mirror.

Confirm that not all areas to the rear and sides are covered by the mirrors and demonstrate what a 'blind area' is by selecting a point, such as a driveway, to the learner's right. Confirm why it's important to look over the shoulder before moving away to make sure no one is at the side of the car. For example, there may be a cyclist or someone emerging from a driveway or side road.

Signal

Introduce *The Highway Code* requirements and discuss the use of signals to warn or inform other road users of your intentions.

Discuss whether there is a need to give a signal if no one is going to benefit from it. Explain that you will help with these decisions to begin with.

Manoeuvre

This means any change in speed or direction. Moving off involves getting the car moving, building up speed and getting into the normal driving position; and stopping involves slowing down, moving back towards the kerb and stopping.

Practice

Moving off and stopping

Make sure the learner knows and understands how to:

- make safety checks before starting the engine;
- prepare the car to move;
- take full all-round observations;
- move the car when it's safe;
- stop where it's safe, legal and convenient;
- move off on the level and on uphill and downhill gradients (where suitable opportunities arise);
- move off, building up speed and changing through the gears; and
- slow down and stop.

At this stage it is useful to practise stopping from different speeds and in different gears (without changing down!). Controlled stops – for example 'By that next lamppost' – will reinforce the point about slowing and stopping by using the footbrake rather than gears.

Be patient and give help where necessary, particularly with the less able. As skill increases, start dropping off your instruction. However, always be ready to come back with more help when needed.

Fault identification, analysis and rectification

Be positive when you make corrections and give your reasons. Common errors during these early stages of learning are:

- Moving away before or without checking blind areas. Ask: 'Is there anyone in the blind area?', 'Can you see that pedestrian?'
- Lack of coordination between gas and clutch. By being totally in tune with your car, and giving positive instruction, you can do much to ensure your

learner's confidence is built up. By encouraging your learner to listen to the sound of the engine and feel for the biting point, you can do much to prevent a stalled engine and, at the same time, start to develop vehicle sympathy.

- Looking at the controls. Confirm that the hands will follow the eyes and that's why we need to look well ahead up the road when we're driving.

Feedback

Throughout the lesson, give praise for routines carried out correctly. End the lesson by confirming where progress has been made. Look forward to the next lesson when more practice will take place prior to learning how to apply the M S M routine to turning left and right.

Use of mirrors

Objectives

The main objectives of this lesson are to ensure your learner fully understands the importance of correct mirror adjustment and effective use of all mirrors.

Examples of agreed objectives:

- able to adjust all mirrors so that you have the maximum possible view around the car with the minimum of head movement;
- awareness of the areas not covered by the mirrors;
- understand the importance of responding properly to what you see;
- able to apply the M S M routine.

Confirm what your learner has remembered from previous lessons by asking questions such as:

- 'When you get in the car, how should you adjust the mirrors?'
- 'Tell me which is the offside and which is the nearside mirror.'
- 'Do the mirrors cover all areas around the car?'
- 'What is important about checking over your shoulders before moving off?'
- 'What do you need to consider before deciding on a signal?'
- 'What routine would you apply for moving off, passing parked cars and stopping?'

Give praise for correct answers and discuss where knowledge or understanding is weak.

Make sure the learner understands that, when a change in direction is involved, the mirrors should be used in pairs. For example, before moving out to pass a parked car a check of the interior mirror should be made, followed by a check in the offside door mirror. Before moving back in to the left, the interior mirror should be re-checked and this should be followed by a check in the nearside door mirror. Similarly, before turning left, as well as checking the interior mirror a check should be made to the nearside for any cyclists.

Discuss why it's important to check the mirrors well before deciding when to signal. For example, before signalling to turn right, it's important to know what's behind, how fast it's travelling and whether anyone is going to overtake you. In this case, applying a signal too early may cause confusion all around so it would be better to delay it until the vehicle's gone by. On the other hand, if you intend to turn left and there's someone following closely, giving an early signal will be of benefit as it will give the other driver plenty of warning of your intention and time to react to you slowing down.

This is another subject where practice rather than demonstration will help develop your learner's awareness and skill in mirror use.

Practice

Unless the learner has had several lessons, some prompting may initially be required to establish the need for regular checking of all the mirrors. Encourage general mirror checks every few seconds so that eventually, when there's a hazard that requires a change in speed or direction, checking will become automatic.

As your learner's mirror work develops, drop off your instruction but when any lapses occur, give a reminder. You can do this by either physically watching them or by using an extra mirror trained on their eyes. The latter can be beneficial in that you can avoid giving hints to your learner to check the mirrors by not having to look directly at them at the appropriate time.

One of the basic ingredients of safe driving is being aware of what's happening all around and responding safely. To establish safe routines, it's extremely important that you identify any weaknesses in learners' mirror use during their early stages of learning. You will need to watch for learners:

- not adjusting mirrors correctly;
- exaggerating head movements when checking the mirrors;

- making late mirror checks;
- checking mirrors at the same time as signalling;
- not checking mirrors before speeding up, slowing down, changing direction or stopping;
- playing about with the anti-dazzle setting;
- not checking blind areas;
- not using door mirrors;
- not responding correctly to what is happening.

Always try to give reasons for using the mirrors effectively by explaining the consequences for other road users of incorrect responses.

You then need to create opportunities where you can emphasize the need for using the mirrors correctly and responding safely. This may sometimes mean using prompted instruction until you can see that the learner's understanding is improving.

Feedback/recap

Give praise where improvement has taken place and confirm by looking back over a few of the situations that arose, where any weaknesses must be worked on.

Remember that feedback is a two-way process. At the end of the session confirm, by using effective questions, that the learner understands the importance of correct mirror use and ask if there are any points they are not sure about. Discuss with the learner where any misunderstandings may be occurring.

Use of signals

The use of signals, and response to those given by others, is not a subject that you can teach in isolation. It should be taught from lesson one and as part of the general routine for driving.

Make sure that your learners are aware of the many ways in which drivers communicate with each other, including:

- indicators;
- arm signals;

- brake lights;
- horn;
- headlights;
- road positioning;
- eye contact;
- signals given by police officers and school wardens.

The emphasis here should be on the need to give signals to warn or inform other road users. If no one will benefit, make a conscious decision not to give a signal. This will encourage more effective use of mirrors and all-round observations.

Sample questions to assess the learner's knowledge and understanding:

- 'How can we tell other road users of our intentions?'
- 'How does a following driver know when you're slowing down?'
- 'When could you use the horn?'
- 'What does *The Highway Code* say about using hazard-warning lights?'
- 'When would you signal to move away or stop?'
- 'Do you always need to signal to pass parked cars?'
- 'When might you use an arm signal for slowing down?'
- 'Apart from the indicators, how can you tell following drivers that you're going to pass parked vehicles?'
- 'If you wanted to allow another driver out of a side road when it's busy, how could you do this without waving them out?'
- 'Why do you think it might be dangerous to beckon pedestrians onto crossings?'
- 'If someone flashed their headlights at you to turn in front of them into a side, would you automatically assume that your way was clear?'

During learners' early lessons, you should ensure that they get plenty of practice in applying the M S M routine in all situations. As the basic car control skills improve and the learner becomes more confident, encourage them to judge when to use signals. They should learn to:

- look all around and check the mirrors before moving, working out whether anyone will benefit from a signal;
- make regular checks of all mirrors and decide on the best way to tell others of their intentions to pass parked vehicles, for example moving out earlier;

- use the brake lights as an early indication of slowing down for lower speed limits;
- respond correctly to other road users' signals for moving off, stopping and turning;
- check for themselves that it's safe to proceed when others beckon them on;
- use eye contact;
- work out when a short beep on the horn might be used to warn others, for example when they see someone reversing out from a driveway or where there is a blind summit.

As this subject will apply to every lesson, you should give the appropriate praise when the correct routines are applied and good discrimination is demonstrated, and positive advice on where more practice is required.

Turning and emerging at junctions

As with all topics, first agree the goals for the lesson so that you can pitch the instruction at the correct level. Remember, in this chapter we are dealing with how to teach the subject to one of your regular learners who has no experience of it. You can set the baseline, therefore, by asking a few questions relevant to what was covered on the previous lesson. Examples:

- 'Do you remember our discussion on the last lesson about the routine for moving off, stopping and passing parked cars?'
- 'Why do you think that it's important to use the mirrors before signalling?'
- 'What if there is some traffic behind, for example, a motorcyclist who is about to overtake? How would that influence your signalling?'
- 'What do you think you should you look for when you're turning into a side road?'
- 'What does *The Highway Code* say you should do if there are pedestrians who are about to cross the side road?'

Early in the learner's training you should ensure that your instruction will result in the correct routines being applied. To do this, you will need to start giving your instructions early enough to allow the learner plenty of time to carry out each individual element comfortably.

As they are less difficult, begin with left turns into and out of T-junctions. Do a few circuits of these and then, as the learner's skill improves, and their confidence increases, introduce turning right following a similar pattern of circuits.

Where there are any weaknesses or misunderstandings you must create opportunities for more practice on appropriate junctions so that positive learning and improvement can take place. To achieve this, you may find that you have to drive from one area to another to avoid the learner having to deal with situations that are too complex for their ability. It might be helpful to use these opportunities to give a demonstration with commentary, keeping this to a level that will suit the learner's capabilities.

For all types of junction make sure that:

- the mirror–signal–manoeuvre routine is applied correctly;
- signals are properly timed, considering any following traffic and the location of the junction;
- road position is appropriate for the direction being taken, the width of the road, and the presence of other road users;
- full control of the car is maintained by effective use of the brakes;
- any downward gear change is done only after slowing down with the brakes – this should be emphasized from the start, otherwise the learner mistakenly gets the impression that gears are needed for slowing down;
- the car is secured with the handbrake when waiting to emerge for more than a few seconds;
- full all-round observations are made. Keep checking that your learner is looking effectively, as well as making sure that it will be safe for them to complete the turn or to emerge.

As skill increases, transfer the responsibility for decision making and introduce more difficult and busier junctions.

Always bear in mind that, no matter what their level of ability, you are responsible for the safety of all your learners, other road users and, of course, yourself. Don't let an unsafe situation arise and put someone else at risk when it could easily be avoided by giving a simple instruction such as 'Wait' or, if necessary, 'Stop'.

At the end of each lesson offer a summary, including a few questions such as:

- 'Why do you think that we should look into a junction before turning in?'
- 'How would you deal with a slightly more complex situation such as...?'
- 'Why was it necessary for us to...?'

As well as your use of effective questions to recap on the lesson, allow time for the learner to ask questions. Make sure your learners go away with an understanding of the principles covered during each lesson.

Finally, 'look forward' by briefing the learner on the next training topic. This would probably cover 'crossroads' as an extension of junction work or, if progress is slow, maybe a lesson consolidating junctions.

Crossroads

The introduction to this subject should include a brief recap on turning left and right into and out of minor roads.

A few questions to recap will be appropriate, particularly if there has been a gap between lessons and if the learner is normally getting private practice. Here are a few examples:

- 'Have you been able to get some practice in?'
- 'How did you get on?'
- 'Why do you think that it's more appropriate for us to slow down by using the brakes, rather than using the gears as your brother/father/mother says?'
- 'If we can see that we're going to have to stop – for instance at a red light – do we need to change gear?'
- 'Did you check on that *Highway Code* rule regarding pedestrians – what did it say?'

To introduce the subject of crossroads you might use the following types of question:

- 'Have you dealt with crossroads at all while you were practising?'
- 'Compared with a T-junction, what extra observations do you think you'll have to make?'
- 'Who has priority at a crossroads if we are going ahead and the oncoming traffic is turning right?'
- 'Can you explain the sequence of traffic lights?'
- 'What do you think "amber" means?'
- 'Which is potentially more of a problem – a light that's green as we approach, or one that's been red for some time?'
- 'Why do we need to look to the right when we are about to turn left?'

Before introducing more complex situations such as traffic light-controlled junctions, allow for practice at various types of less busy crossroads and include turning:

- left from main roads into side roads;
- left onto main roads;
- right onto main roads;
- right from main roads into side roads.

When the learner is applying all the principles, particularly the extra observations required at crossroads, select routes where there are different types of traffic light-controlled junctions.

Remember that your job is to produce skilled and safe drivers. This means that you not only have to work on their practical ability, but you also need to develop in them sensible attitudes towards other road users in situations that aren't always straightforward. An example is at traffic light-controlled crossroads where there are no markings and decisions need to be made as to whether to turn right using the offside to offside, or nearside to nearside method.

Make sure that your learners understand the principles involved and that they can make sound decisions based on the size of the junction, its layout and the position of any oncoming, right-turning drivers.

For all types of crossroads, make sure that:

- the M S M routine is correctly applied, particularly when turning right for the first few attempts;
- signals are timed correctly;
- the learner responds safely to road signs and markings;
- observations are made all around no matter what direction is being taken;
- learners are fully aware of pedestrians who are about to cross side roads;
- there is a correct response to other drivers, cyclists and motorcyclists.

At the end of the lesson, make sure that your learner is fully aware of any weak areas of skill or understanding, but balance this against any good points and confirm where improvement has taken place. As with all lessons, allow time for the learner to ask questions.

Look forward to the next few lessons, confirming that you will be introducing more complex junctions, busier crossroads, dual carriageways and roundabouts.

Meeting and dealing with other traffic

The objectives are to encourage learners to respond safely to other drivers when:

- travelling on narrow roads;
- there are obstructions on either or both sides of the road;
- passing parked vehicles;
- turning right across the path of others.

Because of the design of roads in built-up and rural areas, the volume of parked vehicles, and the need to keep traffic flowing, learners should understand how to deal safely with these subjects from quite early on in their learning.

Meeting other traffic

The most common 'meet' situation is where there are vehicles parked at the side of the road. If these are on the nearside, using a visual aid, you could ask your learner: 'Where are you going to have to drive to pass the parked car?'; 'Who should have the priority then?'

If the obstruction is on the other side of the road, similarly you could ask:

- 'Who will have priority then, when the obstruction is on the other side of the road?'
- 'What if the other driver doesn't wait, though?'
- 'Do you think it might be appropriate to be ready to give way, just in case they keep coming?'
- 'So, it really doesn't matter whose priority it is, does it? You should consider that you never really know what the other driver is going to do. Be prepared to give way.'

Clearances

To encourage the development of sensible and safe attitudes your learners will need plenty of practice. In the early stages this should be in quiet areas with the occasional parked vehicle, progressing to busier areas where there are vehicles parked on both sides and oncoming traffic to deal with.

Initially, when dealing with cars parked on the nearside, the learner needs to understand how to give enough clearance to allow for:

- car doors opening and drivers stepping out;
- pedestrians, particularly children, or animals wandering into the road from between the parked vehicles;
- drivers moving off without signalling.

Any discussion should include:

- forward planning and applying the M S M routine for approaching the hazards;
- deciding on whose priority it is and whether to give way;
- the ideal clearance – give a demonstration of this by getting your learner to check the road and then open their door to see exactly how far into the road it goes;
- at busier times of the day the need to keep the traffic flowing by creeping slowly through some of these gaps – the reduction in speed compensating for the lack of clearance and creating more time to respond should a door open;
- being prepared to move into passing places on the left to allow oncoming drivers through.

Crossing the path of other vehicles

Our drivers need to be courteous in all situations and not make any other road user have to take avoiding action. The key points to cover are when: turning right – encourage learners to work out whether they have enough time to turn, that they have checked on what's happening in the new road and that they won't make any oncoming road user slow down; driving in lanes – ensure the learner checks what's happening all around them before deciding to change lanes.

Practice

Use routes that have varying amounts of parked and moving traffic and encourage the learner to use early planning and 'holding back' to allow time for hazards to clear and to try to keep the car moving.

Some of the more common faults include:

- lack of planning and response to oncoming vehicles;
- not giving way to oncoming vehicles;
- arriving at hazards at too high a speed and having to stop at the last moment;
- steering in towards the kerb instead of keeping out towards the centre of the road;
- steering out too far for passing;
- driving too close to vehicles parked on the left;
- driving too far out and getting too close to those parked on the right;
- failing to anticipate doors opening;
- lack of response to pedestrians waiting in between parked vehicles.

Feedback

Feedback should always be used to encourage positive improvement. Confirm where the learner has learnt and shown improvement and discuss where there is room for improvement.

Look forward

Confirm that during all future lessons you will be encouraging your learner to develop their planning and decision-making skills. The next lesson will deal specifically with how to anticipate and make allowances for the actions of other road users, including drivers, cyclists, motorcyclists and pedestrians.

Overtaking

During normal lessons, you will find that very few opportunities will present themselves for teaching how to overtake. However, it will be your responsibility to ensure that your learners know about the dangers involved and how to carry it out safely. When driving along dual carriageways opportunities will occur when there are vehicles driving at speeds much lower than the legal limits. In this situation overtaking is much safer as there won't (hopefully) be any oncoming traffic. First you need to stress the following important questions:

Is it safe? Is it legal? Is it NECESSARY?

Points you then need to cover include:

- keeping back from the vehicle to be overtaken;
- looking ahead and working out the speed and distance of any oncoming vehicles;
- checking to see that it's safe by looking for bends, junctions, dead ground, etc;
- checking the mirrors to see what's happening to the rear and sides;
- moving to get a view along the nearside of the vehicle ahead;
- checking the mirrors again and moving out to get a view ahead and deciding on whether anyone (including the driver to be overtaken) will benefit from a signal;
- adjusting the speed, including selecting a lower gear to give sustained power;
- moving out to pass, giving plenty of clearance;
- checking the mirrors and in some circumstances deciding on whether or not a signal will be beneficial (for example on dual carriageways when a driver is approaching from behind at high speed);
- moving back to the left without cutting in;
- accelerating away and changing gear as normal.

Manoeuvres

The driving test syllabus includes:

- reverse parking at the side of the road (parallel park);
- reversing into bays (left and right);
- driving into a bay and reversing out (left and right);
- pull over to the right, reverse about two car lengths and then rejoin traffic.

These manoeuvres are now included in the driving test because they are seen to be more realistic and appropriate for today's driving conditions. However, your learner may still benefit from learning how to carry out a turn in the road and reverse around a corner.

Before starting to teach any manoeuvres, it is worth making sure that the learner is completely skilled and confident with uphill and downhill starts and stops. Experience is also needed in angled starts on up and down gradients, so that the learner has complete control of the car in all of these circumstances.

For example, moving away straight ahead downhill is relatively easy because you don't need too much coordination between the foot controls and the steering – as soon as the handbrake is released the car is on its way! With an angled start, though, there is a need to introduce the use of the footbrake and coordination between that and the clutch to avoid the car running away too quickly and to allow enough time for steering round the obstruction (or to turn into the main road). This exercise is often neglected by some instructors. The result of this is that their learners are not properly prepared for similar situations when careful control is needed for stopping and starting uphill and downhill.

The manoeuvres do not necessarily need to be taught in any particular order, but there is a certain amount of logic in dealing with basic reversing before introducing some of the other complicating features of the reversing exercises. A lot of the time it will depend on the availability of suitable parking facilities and corners in your own locality.

Introducing the subject

As always, at the start of the lesson establish previous knowledge. Find out if the learner:

- has done any reversing while they have been practising;
- understands about low speed control, for example when creeping forwards at junctions;
- appreciates that it is important to make effective all-round observations;
- knows why the normal rules about steering do not necessarily apply.

If the learner has no previous experience of reversing, you could give an explanation using a visual aid.

Demonstration

A demonstration combined with an explanation could be helpful in allowing the learner to see what's required. The demonstration may be appropriate if, for instance, the learner is particularly nervous about the manoeuvre, or they obviously do not understand the requirements from your explanations.

In keeping with a client-centred approach, some learners benefit from seeing a demonstration before attempting a task themselves. You should consider offering a demonstration to help the learner understand what is required and build their confidence before they practise the skill.

Talk yourself through each element, carrying out the manoeuvre a little more slowly than normal. This will allow the learner time to take note. Be able, if necessary, to carry out certain parts in slow motion. You may sometimes need to replicate the way in which a learner has carried out a manoeuvre so that they can compare the two.

Keep any demonstration simple and carry it out at a slower than normal speed.

Key teaching/learning points

- The speed of the car should be kept as slow as possible by effective clutch control.
- Pull/push is not always the most effective or comfortable steering method when reversing at slow speed.
- Explain that there is a delayed action with the steering, because the rear wheels are now being used to steer with.
- Look across the rear corner of the car – not at the side – to judge the amount of steering.
- Avoid 'over-steering' – think about how you only have to make small adjustments to the steering when going forwards. Remember, though, the delayed action on the steering.

Observations

A constant check should be made throughout the manoeuvre, looking all around for traffic. Learners should be encouraged to watch carefully for pedestrians. Remember that there's a blind area to the right when they're looking over the left shoulder.

Make sure that you emphasize the need to be able to manoeuvre the car as part of a driver's everyday requirements, rather than just 'because it's part of the test'. If the learner persists with raising the question of the driving test, make it clear that we are dealing with driving safely and manoeuvring for convenience and that test procedures will be outlined in future lessons.

With all of the manoeuvres, it's important to recap on what the learner has covered on previous lessons by asking a few appropriate questions. For example:

- 'As this is the first manoeuvre you'll be carrying out and good clutch control is required, tell me how you would creep forwards at a junction to get a better view.'
- 'What would you do if your car started to creep forwards before you wanted to move?'
- 'Why is it important to keep the speed very low when you're moving out from behind a parked car?'

With any manoeuvre, always get the learner to consider – is it safe? Is it legal? Is it convenient?

Confirm that, because they are part of normal everyday driving requirements, the manoeuvres are included in the training programme. This is so that new drivers will have the ability to control and manoeuvre the car in confined areas, including car parks and driveways, and when parking at the roadside.

Practice

Don't expect perfection first time!

For learners' first attempts use an appropriate amount of 'talk-through' so that a reasonable degree of success is achieved, and they are not put off or demoralized by getting it completely wrong.

Watch for, and correct right from the start, any basic errors of control or observations. However, you should make allowances for the fact that the learner has not done a particular manoeuvre previously and several elements are being combined. These are: car control skills, observations and accuracy.

On subsequent attempts, transfer some of the responsibility by reducing the amount of 'talk-through'. When a reasonable amount of consistency is achieved, introduce slightly more complex situations.

At the end of the lesson

Use effective questions to obtain some verbal feedback from learners and to find out how they feel about the lesson.

Give feedback, balancing any discussion on areas of weakness with comments on the good points.

Summarize the overall content of the current lesson, emphasize the reasons for each particular manoeuvre and confirm how to make sure they are legally carried out.

Look forward to the next lesson by discussing what will be covered, confirming any preparation work that you require the learner to do.

During the latter stages of the learner's training you will need to point out that they will be tested on some of the specified manoeuvres. These test exercises are included as a means of assessing the learner's ability to handle the car in confined spaces. This means that, to a certain extent, they are slightly contrived 'test exercises'. It is helpful to focus on the skills needed for any manoeuvre rather than the specific requirements of the subject.

For example, we would not normally reverse into a parking space at the side of a busy road unless the existing parked vehicles were close together – we would simply drive forwards into the gap. When using a car park, rather than reversing in, we might prefer to drive forwards into the space to allow us to load shopping into the boot on our return.

In all these respects, the manoeuvres are included in the driving test to assess, in a controlled environment, the candidate's ability, observations and responses. They are also intended to be realistic examples of everyday driving situations we are likely to encounter.

Emergency stop

Objective

To stop the car promptly, safely and under complete control.

Introducing the subject

Using effective questions, confirm that your learner has stopped in various types of situation on previous lessons, for example at junctions, at the side of the road and in specific places such as 'by the second lamppost'.

Emphasize that an 'emergency stop' is only an extension of what they have done before. The main difference is that the brakes will need to be applied more firmly.

Ask questions to confirm previous knowledge and understanding, for example:

'Why is it necessary to apply progressive braking?'

'Do we need a gear change when stopping?'

'Why is it important to keep both hands on the wheel when we are braking firmly?'

'Do we need a signal?'

'What about the handbrake?'

Discuss possible situations where an emergency stop might be needed, for example if a child ran out from a gateway into the road. Relate this to the learner's previous hazard perception understanding when they will have been responding mainly to things they could see.

Your initial discussions should include information on:

- the fact that there may not be enough time to check on what's happening behind, because of the need to stop quickly;
- prompt reaction in moving from gas pedal to footbrake;
- use of the footbrake – progressive, firmly;
- maintaining steering control because the weight of the car is thrown onto the front wheels;
- avoiding locking wheels;
- having the clutch down just before stopping;
- securing the car after stopping;
- all-round observations before moving away.

Emphasize the need for both hands to remain on the wheel to keep the car on a straight course, and for controlled braking. Confirm this by giving an example such as, 'There's no point in avoiding the child who's run out if we then slide across the road and hit other pedestrians.'

Confirm the learner's understanding of braking distances. For example:

'What is the thinking distance if you're travelling at 30 mph?'

'At 70 mph how far would we travel before starting to brake?'

'How does that relate to a number of car lengths?'

'How far do you think it takes to stop from 20 mph?' (Or any other speed.)

'Tell me how far that is in terms of the distance from here.'

In preparation for their theory test learners should be doing some homework on reaction times, thinking distances and braking distances. Make sure they realize that there is a straightforward means of calculating the distances and that they are not random figures. For example: the thinking distance is based on an average reaction time of two-thirds of a second, which equates to about 60 feet (or 18 metres) when travelling at 60 mph (88 ft per second); the braking distance at 20 mph is 20 feet (6 metres) and it increases with the square of the speed, which means that if you travel at twice the speed, the braking distance is multiplied four times.

Confirm that on future lessons, thinking, braking and stopping distances will be discussed and related to practical situations.

Practice

Find an area where it's going to be safe to practise and make sure your learner understands that you will check there's no following traffic before giving the signal to stop. Explain how you will give the instruction and signal for stopping.

On the first few attempts at an emergency stop, check on the learner's:

- slow reactions to respond;
- prompt movement from accelerator to brake;
- harsh or too gentle use of the footbrake;
- left hand off the steering wheel before stopping;
- clutch being pushed down too early or too late;
- lack of adequate precautions after a stall;
- failure to secure the car when stopped;
- lack of all-round observations before moving off.

Look forward to future lessons by indicating that this exercise will be repeated at different speeds and in varying situations, unless, of course, real emergencies crop up.

Pedestrian crossings

The point at which you introduce learners to pedestrian crossings will depend, to a large extent, on the area in which they live and where the nearest crossings are situated. However, they should have reached a stage at which they can consistently apply the M S M routine to hazards and be able to cope with more traffic and pedestrian activity.

Objectives

As pedestrians, your learners will have used most types of crossing. Avoid patronizing them by treating the subject as if they know nothing about it.

Indeed, the lesson objective will be to build on this existing knowledge by introducing the differences between how, as pedestrians, they will have used crossings and how drivers should deal with them.

First, recap on the learner's previous progress, using effective questions to confirm that the learner fully understands the M S M routine. Find out what they understand about the different types of crossing and then set your base line according to their responses. The following are a few sample questions:

- 'When should you apply the M S M routine?'
- 'Can you name three different types of pedestrian crossing?'
- 'How would you recognize a zebra crossing?'
- 'How would you claim priority at a zebra crossing?'

As always, listen carefully to your learners' responses and vary the discussion according to their level of knowledge and understanding. In any case you need to ensure that the basic principles in dealing with the different types of crossing are covered.

A discussion with the learner should include:

- the different types of crossing, ie: zebra, pelican, toucan, puffin and equestrian;
- why these differences are in place;
- signs and markings and what they mean, including the rules relating to waiting, overtaking, parking;
- the sequence of the different traffic lights;
- how to look and plan well ahead, applying the M S M routine in good time to stop safely when necessary, and securing the car;
- the use of arm signals when appropriate.

As this subject is very wide-ranging, and so that the lesson doesn't become a one-way lecture, keep your learner involved by asking the occasional question. For example:

- 'What do the zigzag lines on approach to crossings mean?'
- 'What's the sequence of lights at a pelican crossing?'
- 'What does the flashing amber light mean?'

- 'What's the difference between a pelican and a toucan crossing?'
- 'What would you do if you saw someone waiting at a zebra crossing?'

Level of instruction

To avoid over-instruction, give your learners an opportunity to demonstrate their skill in subjects learnt previously. For example, by this stage their car control skills should be reasonably well developed, so they should be able to deal virtually unaided with simple junctions.

When you approach the new situations, and to ensure the learner is able to deal safely with the crossings, use prompts where appropriate to help with the correct routines and procedures.

Practice

Depending on your area, try to incorporate as many types of crossing as you can so that your learner will see what the main differences are. Ensure that all the basic routines are carried out, particularly in relation to planning ahead and approaching them at a safe speed.

Initially, as you will be giving some prompted instruction, there should be few faults. However, as the learner's skill improves, and you start transferring to them the responsibility for making decisions, errors are bound to occur.

Watch carefully for these mistakes and give positive correction. Analyse what happened and explain what should have been done to deal with the situations safely.

Feedback/recap/summary

At the end of the lesson give positive feedback and praise where the learner improved on skills previously covered and has learnt how to deal with the new topics.

Recap on the most important points that arose and give an overall summary on applying the M S M routine to dealing with crossings.

Look forward

Advise your learner on which reference materials to study. Confirm that you will be asking a few questions on crossings and getting in some more practice on approaching them during the next lesson.

Roundabouts and dual carriageways

Whichever topic you are dealing with, your lessons should all follow the pattern described previously:

- recap, using questions, to establish prior knowledge and understanding;
- agree the objectives;
- set the baseline;
- work from the known to the unknown;
- feedback;
- look forward to the next session.

It is normal to deal with two-way roads, T-junctions and crossroads in order to build up learners' confidence in applying the basic driving routines before introducing more complex road systems. However, depending on the area you are working in, or where each learner lives, you may need to be flexible with the introduction of roundabouts and dual carriageways. In any case, in some quieter areas where most basic training should be carried out, there may be mini roundabouts to be dealt with.

In most areas, you will need to deal with roundabouts in combination with driving on dual carriageways.

Mini roundabouts

These are usually sited in reasonably busy areas where the minor roads used to have 'give way' or 'stop' signs. They provide for better traffic flow by allowing drivers in the minor roads to merge more easily. The following are a few sample questions you could use to establish learners' understanding:

- 'Which routine do you need to apply when you're approaching junctions?'
- 'What does the "give way" sign mean at a T-junction?'
- 'Who will you have to give way to at a roundabout?'

Following on from these questions you will need to transfer learners' prior knowledge and develop it to include the different rules to be followed. For example:

- looking and planning ahead for signs and markings;
- applying the M S M routine;
- selecting the appropriate position (lane) in the road;

- making full all-round observations;
- giving way to traffic from the right;
- maintaining the correct position through the roundabout;
- checking the mirrors;
- signalling for leaving if appropriate and where it won't affect the steering.

Create plenty of opportunities for practice at as many different mini roundabouts as the training area will allow. Begin with straightforward left turns and then approach from different directions, explaining about the need to adapt road positioning to suit each individual roundabout.

For learners' first few attempts, you might need to give talk-through instruction on the unfamiliar aspects. The learner will probably need some guidance and/or prompting when traffic is arriving at the junction from all directions at the same time.

Depending on how quickly they pick up the new routines, gradually transfer the responsibility of decision making when you feel you can.

Some of the common faults to watch for at mini roundabouts are:

- lack of application of the M S M routine;
- failure to respond to signs and markings;
- incorrect lane selection;
- emerging in front of other drivers;
- missing opportunities to proceed;
- not signalling when required;
- signalling when not required or when it interferes with steering;
- not maintaining lane discipline.

Roundabouts

If the training area you are working in dictates that you have to deal with mini roundabouts first, then you will be able to transfer this knowledge and introduce the differences that apply to the larger ones.

To deal with larger roundabouts first, you will need to give a full explanation of all the items listed under mini roundabouts, but more information will be required on signs, markings, lane selection and discipline.

Using a visual aid, explain how to deal with a straightforward four-exit roundabout, beginning with turning left. Use effective questions to confirm learners' prior knowledge of applying the M S M routine as you talk your way through your diagram. For example:

- 'Who has priority at a roundabout?'
- 'Will you need a signal for turning left at a roundabout?'
- 'Do you always need to stop at a roundabout?'
- 'What does the broken white line mean?'
- 'Where should you be looking?'

Remember that questions should be used to get some feedback and not as an interrogation tool. Learners often become anxious when faced with new and complex situations, so respond to body language, be prepared to back off and give more help if necessary.

Explain the procedures the learner will not yet be familiar with and then continue by describing the procedures for going ahead and turning right. No matter which direction is to be taken, emphasis needs to be placed on:

- looking ahead for signs and markings;
- application of the M S M routine and maintaining full control of the car;
- looking early for gaps in the traffic from the right;
- watching for traffic coming around the roundabout from other roads – these often create gaps by preventing the traffic directly to our right from emerging;
- continual observations in all directions so that we know what's happening to the right and in front, and to help maintain our position;
- maintaining position and lane discipline throughout the roundabout;
- signalling for leaving so as not to hold up those waiting to merge into the roundabout.

Practice

Each learner will have their own individual rate of learning, ability and aptitude. This means that the amount of training each one needs will also vary.

Roundabouts also come in many varieties. As the learner's competence and confidence improve, plan your routes to cover as many different types as possible, including roundabouts with more than four exits.

Your questions might include: 'How do think you should signal if you were taking the second exit?'; 'Where should you position on approach for taking the third exit that is just beyond the 12 o'clock position?'

As learners' ability improves in applying the basic routines, you will need to focus on their skills at looking and planning ahead, making good progress and taking safe opportunities to proceed.

Errors will generally be similar to those listed under the heading 'Mini roundabouts'. However, the larger roundabouts are generally busier and carry traffic that's often travelling much quicker. You will need to watch for learners:

- failing to read and respond to signs and markings;
- approaching too fast to allow themselves sufficient time to start looking;
- making unnecessary gear changes;
- looking only at the traffic in the roundabout and not at the gaps;
- not preparing the car in time to move into suitable gaps;
- failing to take opportunities to move;
- concentrating on making observations to the right – this often results in them not keeping to the left as they move into the roundabout and not being aware of what the driver ahead is doing;
- straddling lanes;
- not checking mirrors before signalling or changing lanes;
- leaving in the incorrect lane.

Recap

Some of the questions you could use to further develop learners' understanding include:

- 'Why is it important to be planning ahead and looking for signs and markings?'
- 'Who has priority at roundabouts?'
- 'If you were going to travel straight ahead at a roundabout would you need to signal on the approach?'
- 'Which signal should you use for leaving a roundabout and when should you put it on?'
- 'Where should you check before moving across into the left lane?'
- 'Why do you think it's important to keep looking both ways at a roundabout?'
- 'What might happen if you wander across into another lane on a roundabout?'
- 'What might happen if you fail to move into safe gaps in the traffic?'

Develop your own questions and adapt each one to suit the circumstances.

As with all lessons, give positive feedback on areas of improvement and advice on where more practice is needed. Use effective questions and encourage your learners to ask questions if there are any aspects they don't quite understand.

Look forward

Confirm two main points:

- To become consistently skilful in dealing with these busier junctions, lots of practice will be needed.
- During the rest of their training you will help them become confident and able to cope in as wide a variety of circumstances as the area allows.

Dual carriageways

Before introducing dual carriageways, a recap on driving on two-way roads could include the following questions:

- 'Where do you normally drive on a two-way road?'
- 'What is the most dangerous manoeuvre on a two-way road?'
- 'What's the speed limit in built-up areas and on other roads?'
- 'What routine should you always apply when dealing with hazards?'

Objectives

The objective is to teach your learners how to join, drive along and leave dual carriageways safely and efficiently. Because there are numerous types of dual carriageway you will not be able to achieve this in one lesson – it will be a gradual process over a series of lessons up to and beyond the driving test.

You will need to confirm that dual carriageways come in lots of different designs and layouts. Some of the variations are the:

- number of lanes;
- speed limit;
- methods of joining – ie roundabouts, T-junctions, slip roads;
- volume of traffic;
- parked vehicles.

The following are some questions you could use to confirm what the learner knows about dual carriageways:

- 'What's the speed limit on dual carriageways where the national limit applies?'
- 'What's the speed limit in built-up areas?'
- 'Tell me what a "repeater" sign means.'
- 'Where should you normally drive on a dual carriageway?'
- 'What's the right-hand lane for?'
- 'Why do you think it might be important to plan further ahead and use all of the mirrors more frequently?'

It might be useful to use visual aids to help the learner 'see' what you mean, particularly when you're describing how to turn right onto dual carriageways from side roads. You will need to explain the differences that apply where the width of the central reserve varies. The most important key elements you should include in your explanation are:

- joining from roundabouts;
- turning left onto dual carriageways from T-junctions;
- turning right onto dual carriageways through narrow and wider central reserves;
- driving in the left lane unless passing parked vehicles, overtaking or turning right;
- planning further ahead – for parked vehicles or slower-moving traffic;
- using the mirrors more frequently;
- positioning in the centre of the lane;
- planning for junctions and applying the M S M routine early;
- changing lanes safely;
- keeping up with the traffic flow.

The following are some of the questions you might use to coach the learner:

- 'Why do you think you might have to look and plan further ahead on dual carriageways?'
- 'How often should you use the mirrors?'
- 'Why do you think you have to start the M S M routine earlier than on normal roads?'

- 'How would you turn right if the central reserve is narrow?'
- 'What would you do if the central reserve is very wide?'

As with any other complex subject, the list of questions is endless; you will have to devise questions that suit each set of circumstances.

Demonstrations

Unless your learner has difficulty in understanding, 'hands on' experience is the most effective way of learning to apply the different rules. You may, in some particularly difficult situations, decide that a demonstration would be the safest way to initially explain how to deal with them.

Practice

For the first few outings on dual carriageways, practice will need to be guided. Although your learner should by now have good car control skills and can apply the M S M rules on normal two-way roads and at junctions, you may need to offer a certain amount of prompting in these new situations.

Make sure, at this stage, that your talk-through is restricted to the unfamiliar procedures. If you're not careful, it's very easy to revert to giving basic instructions in those skills the learner has already mastered.

Depending on the road systems in your area, practice should be given on all the procedures listed under the explanation section.

Some of the problems that arise during the early development of skills in driving on dual carriageways are very similar to those listed under roundabouts. Other faults include:

- failing to look ahead and respond in time to parked vehicles – this can often result in the learner either becoming boxed in or signalling and pulling out in front of another driver;
- not keeping up with the traffic flow and causing problems for others;
- keeping up when the other traffic is breaking the speed limit;
- not planning early enough for junctions;
- blocking a carriageway by failing to work out the width of the central reserve before pulling across;
- moving onto a dual carriageway and failing to build up the speed effectively.

Feedback, recap and look forward

Following the normal lesson format, give positive feedback and advice on aspects that need more attention, recapping on the strengths and areas of weakness.

Formulate questions like those listed under other subjects in order to coach your learner and develop better understanding and attitude.

Confirm that, as with roundabouts, driving on dual carriageways requires lots of practice and experience in order to build confidence.

Making progress and road positioning

When you have covered most of the syllabus, you will need to cover some important points:

- how to maintain the correct position on the road;
- how to respond positively;
- taking safe opportunities to merge into traffic at all types of junction;
- driving at appropriate speeds to keep the traffic moving.

The agreed objectives could be something like:

> 'During your next few lessons we will be driving in more congested areas to build up your confidence and improve your personal driving skills. We will be focusing on:

- road positioning and lane discipline;
- how to judge safe gaps in the traffic to emerge into;
- driving on higher speed and multi-lane roads so that you learn how to keep up with the flow of the traffic.'

By this stage learners should be able to apply the basic driving routines to most situations. The following are a few examples of questions to confirm understanding:

- 'What's the speed limit in a built-up area?'
- 'Give me a few examples of when and where it wouldn't be safe to drive up to the speed limit.'
- 'At what speed would you drive past a school around lunchtime?'

- 'What's the normal driving position on a two-way road?'
- 'When do you think it might be safer to drive a little further out in the road?'
- 'What's the national speed limit on a two-way road?'
- 'What might a following driver be tempted to do if you're driving too slowly for the conditions?'
- 'When you're waiting at a roundabout, why is it important to look to the left as well as to the right?'
- 'What do you think might happen if you miss a suitable gap in the traffic at a roundabout?'
- 'Where should you position the car when you're driving on multi-lane roads?'

Using effective questions at this stage should help establish in your learners an awareness of the need to remain alert to the all-round traffic situation.

Through discussion on these points, you should be able to explain to your learners what is required in order to become a good and confident driver. Listen carefully to their responses and guide them towards the correct answers, giving added information as necessary.

Level of instruction

At this stage, learners' driving skills should be fairly well developed. Give them the responsibility for making decisions in the types of situation they have previously experienced.

You may need to give some prompted assistance at the busier junctions in order to encourage them to take suitable opportunities to emerge and make good progress along the road.

Practice

By selecting appropriate routes, create as many opportunities as you can to cover as wide a variety of road and junction type as is possible within each session.

As you see confidence growing, back off and transfer the responsibility to the learner. Obviously, how long this will take will vary from learner to learner and you may sometimes have to adapt your teaching to suit their progress.

Fault identification and analysis

As with all other subjects, use your learners' mistakes as opportunities to coach them into being better drivers. You need to ensure they can:

- move off promptly when safe;
- build up speed and change through the gears positively;
- apply the M S M routine effectively at all types of junction;
- take opportunities to emerge safely into traffic;
- travel at speeds appropriate for the road type and traffic conditions and drive in the correct position;
- look and plan well ahead to minimize unnecessary stops at hazards.

Feedback/recap/summary

This is another area where the use of questions and guided discussion on what occurred during each session can help improve learners' understanding of the principles involved in becoming effective drivers.

Remember to give praise where learners demonstrate good decision-making skills and use any incidents that arise as discussion points.

Look forward

At the end of each lesson, confirm to the learner that on the next lesson you will be introducing even more complex situations in order to build up their experience.

Refer them to any specific reading material that may help in their development.

Anticipating the actions of other road users

Today's roads are really congested, with everyone trying to get from A to B as quickly as possible, often with little thought given to those around them. All your learners will have been passengers and will probably have observed some of the unsafe actions that have from time to time put them at risk.

Objectives

Teaching anticipation cannot be done in one lesson; it is an ongoing process. Try to use all opportunities that present themselves to encourage the learner to drive defensively by anticipating what others may do and to work out the safest way to avoid conflict.

By applying coaching techniques, you can use learners' previous experiences to develop their awareness and anticipation and hopefully, by encouraging them to come to their own conclusions, you will influence safer attitudes.

Using the client-centred skills described earlier in this book and in the lesson plans contained in this chapter, make sure that your learners are able to deal safely with the following:

- Other car drivers. They may pull out from side roads or turn across their path, push their way through spaces between parked vehicles, overtake unsafely or follow too closely.
- Cyclists and motorcyclists. Be aware of them overtaking on either side of your car, particularly between lanes of slow-moving traffic. Remember that they are less easy to see at junctions. Recognize that cyclists may ride off the pavement onto the road.
- Drivers of larger vehicles, for example anticipating that they may straddle lanes in roundabouts and will require more room when turning into and out of junctions.
- Emergency vehicles. Listen for sirens and watch for flashing lights; encourage learners to be prepared to make room for them to pass.
- Pedestrians. Expect children to step into the road, to mess around with their friends around school time, to misuse crossings, etc. Expect older people to misjudge speed and distance, to be hesitant and to take longer to cross the road.
- Animals. In both urban and rural areas they are unpredictable. Allow plenty of time and clearance.
- Differing road, light and weather conditions. These influence the driver's needs, for example, being dazzled by the headlights of oncoming or following drivers.

Independent driving and use of sat nav

The driving test includes about 20 minutes of 'independent' driving where the learner follows a predetermined route. This is done by a set of instructions from the examiner or by use of a sat nav.

It is important you give your learners plenty of opportunities to take control of the route. This could happen right in the early stages where you discuss what would be a safe road to practise moving off and stopping; or ask them to find their own way home when you know they can control the car reasonably safely; or ask them to pick a route that lasts around five minutes and includes left and right turns. Later on, you can ask them to drive following signs and road markings; or nominate a particular road or area, pick a road and ask them to take you there; or pull them up at the side of the road and give them three or four directions to see if they can remember them and still plan their approach to hazards and junctions.

A part of the independent drive on the driving test may include the use of sat nav (satellite navigation).

The examiner provides the sat nav and sets it up using a stored route. The candidate doesn't need to touch it.

It doesn't matter which sat nav you use for practice. It could be a built-in sat nav, a mobile phone or stand-alone sat nav. The learner is not being tested on their ability to set a route in a sat nav – just the ability to follow directions from one.

The examiner will make sure that the sat nav is positioned appropriately and safely.

In most cases, the sat nav will not be fixed to the windscreen – it will be on a special dash-mat so it doesn't move or fall off. However, because of the design of some vehicles, there will be some cases where it will need to be mounted on the windscreen.

Managing technology and distractions

Modern vehicles place increasing demands on a driver's attention. Sat nav, driver assistance systems, infotainment screens and mobile devices can all support driving – but they can also distract from it. As an instructor, your role is to help learners develop disciplined habits so that technology is used safely, deliberately and only when appropriate.

Learners should understand that the primary task is always observation, planning and control. Any interaction with technology should be secondary and should never compromise this. Encourage them to set up sat nav routes, music or vehicle settings before moving off, and to avoid making adjustments whilst the car is moving unless it is safe to do so. If a change is needed, the safest option is to find a suitable place to stop.

Build awareness of different types of distraction:

- Visual (eyes off the road)
- Manual (hands off the wheel)
- Cognitive (mind off the task).

Even hands-free systems can create significant cognitive distraction, reducing a driver's ability to anticipate hazards. Help learners recognize this in themselves – for example, noticing when they miss a sign or react late whilst engaged in conversation or using in-car systems.

You should also introduce strategies to manage distraction. These include pausing or limiting conversations in complex situations, reducing in-car noise and prioritizing driving tasks during busy or unfamiliar routes. Where vehicles are equipped with ADAS features, ensure learners understand both their benefits and their limitations, so they do not become over-reliant or complacent.

Ultimately, safe use of technology comes down to judgement and self-awareness. By encouraging learners to take responsibility for how and when they use it, you are helping them develop the focus and discipline needed to drive independently and safely in an increasingly complex driving environment.

Advanced Driver Assistance Systems (ADAS) and how to teach

Modern cars increasingly come with Advanced Driver Assistance Systems (ADAS) which are designed to help drivers, reduce risk and make driving easier – but they are not a replacement for the driver. Understanding how to use them safely and how to teach learners to do the same is essential in today's driver training. For more information on ADAS features, see *The Driving Instructor's Handbook*.

Feature	Purpose	Instructor Tip
Lane Keeping Assist / Lane Departure Warning	Helps maintain lane position	Demonstrate on a quiet road; ask learner to notice alerts and correct gently
Adaptive Cruise Control / Intelligent Speed Assistance	Manages speed and distance	Let learners experience following traffic; discuss when to override
Blind Spot Monitoring / Rear Cross-Traffic Alert	Alerts to unseen hazards	Practise lane changes and reversing when alerts are active
Automatic Emergency Braking / Forward Collision Warning	Prevents or mitigates collisions	Use controlled practice to show system activation and proper response
Parking Assistance / Sensors / Cameras	Assists in low-speed manoeuvres	Show when to trust sensors vs. eyes; supervise practice in a car park

Teaching approach

Consider using the Explanation, Demonstration and Practice (EDP) approach. Giving the learner the opportunity to see and hear how to operate ADAS safely can be a powerful learning tool, particularly when it matches their preferred learning style. Demonstrations can help learners build confidence, understand system limitations and develop the skills needed to use ADAS safely and effectively.

Lesson planning integration

- Start simple
  Teach one feature at a time
- Scaffold learning
  Move from quiet roads to busier roads as confidence grows
- Use simulators
  If available, simulators can be used to safely practise emergency braking or collision scenarios

- Combine features
  Only once individual functions are understood.

Common learner errors and correction

- Over-reliance on ADAS: remind learners they remain in control.
- Ignoring or mis-reading alerts: demonstrate correct responses repeatedly.
- Unintentionally switching features off: check activation before each lesson.

Correct errors by identifying, analysing and remedying, keeping feedback practical and supportive.

Reinforcing safe habits

- ADAS reduces cognitive load, but situational awareness is still vital.
- Build habits: consistent mirror checks, alert recognitions, and conscious control
- Encourage learners to see ADAS as a tool, not a crutch.

ADAS mini-lessons: step-by-step teaching

1. Lane Keeping Assist (LKA) / Lane Departure Warning (LDW)

Lesson aim: Learners understand how the system supports lane maintenance and respond correctly to alerts.

- Explain
  'This system gives a gentle nudge or alert if you drift from your lane. It's a reminder, not a replacement for steering.'
- Demonstrate
  Drive slowly on a quiet road and let the system engage. Comment on alerts:

  'Notice the vibration or sound – this is the car telling you you're drifting.'
- Practice
  Ask the learner to drive and respond to alerts. Observe reactions.

- Reflect
  Discuss: 'When did the alert help you?' 'How did you correct your steering?'

Common errors: Over-correction, ignoring alerts, assuming the car will steer fully.

Instructor tips: Encourage calm, measured responses and repeated practice.

2. Adaptive Cruise Control (ACC) / Intelligent Speed Assistance (ISA)

Lesson aim: Learners maintain safe following distance and understand when to override the system.

- Explain

  'This system adjusts your speed automatically to keep a safe distance. You remain responsible for braking and steering.'

- Demonstrate
  Engage on a quiet dual carriageway or motorway. Explain system behaviour when traffic slows.
- Practice
  Learner uses ACC while you observe: 'Notice how the car slows down automatically – when would you need to intervene?'
- Reflect
  'How did it feel to have the system adjust speed?' Were there moments when you overrode it? Why?'

Common errors: Assuming the car will stop for everything, delayed reaction in dense traffic.

Instructor tip: Reinforce that ACC is an aid, not a substitute for attention.

3. Blind Spot Monitoring (BSM) / Rear Cross-Traffic Alert

Lesson aim: Learners understand the system's alert during lane changes and reversing.

- Explain
  'Sensors alert you to cars or cyclists you might not see. Always check mirrors and look over your shoulder.'
- Demonstrate
  Show alerts during lane changes or reversing in a quiet area.

- Practice
  Learner performs manoeuvres with alerts active.
- Reflect
  'Did you notice the alert before or after you checked manually?' 'How did the alert change your actions?'

Common errors: Ignoring alerts or over-trusting sensors.
Instructor tip: Reinforce the system as a secondary check – not a primary.

4. Automatic Emergency Braking (AEB) / Forward Collision Warning (FCW)

Lesson aim: Learners recognize system activation and react appropriately.

- Explain
  'The car can brake automatically if it detects a likely collision. You still need to monitor traffic and react early.'
- Demonstrate
  Use controlled settings, eg empty car park with cones or a simulator.
- Practice
  Learner experiences system activation under supervision.
- Reflect
  'Did you feel the car braking? How did you react?' 'Would you respond differently next time?'

Common errors: Relying solely on the car to prevent collisions.
Instructor tip: Reinforce that anticipation and attention remain critical.

5. Parking Assistance / Sensors / Cameras

Lesson aim: Learners learn when to rely on cameras and sensors and when to use their own observation.

- Explain
  'Sensors and cameras help you judge space, but your eyes are still the best guide.'
- Demonstrate
  Use a quiet car park. Show correct use of visual checks vs. sensor alerts.
- Practice
  Learner performs parking with system active.
- Reflect
  'Which cues did you trust most?' 'How did the sensors help or mislead?'

Common errors: Looking only at screens, ignoring surroundings.

Instructor tip: Stress balanced use of all inputs.

Here are four general coaching prompts for ADAS lessons:

- 'What did you notice when the system activated?'
- 'How would you respond if it didn't alert?'
- 'Which situations do you think the system helps most with?'
- 'Are there times you feel it could mislead you?'

Eco-driving and electric vehicles (EVs)

Driving today isn't just about safety – it's also about efficiency, environmental responsibility and understanding the technology at your fingertips. Eco-driving encourages smoother, more thoughtful control of the vehicle, which reduces fuel or energy use, lowers emissions and improves safety.

Key principles of eco-driving

1. Smooth acceleration and braking
   - Avoid sudden starts and stops; anticipate traffic flow.
   - ADAS can assist here. Adaptive Cruise Control, for example, naturally encourages smoother driving.
2. Maintain steady speeds
   - Use gears efficiently in conventional vehicles; in EVs, make the most of regenerative braking.
   - On motorways or dual carriageways, small speed adjustments can significantly reduce energy consumption.
3. Plan ahead
   - Anticipate junctions, traffic lights and roundabouts to reduce unnecessary braking or acceleration.
   - Route planning in EVs also helps avoid range anxiety and allows for efficient charging stops.
4. Minimize idle time
   - Switch engine off if stopped for long periods in conventional vehicles.
   - EVs consume less energy at standstill, but unnecessary use of climate control or accessories still drain the battery.

5 Check tyre pressure and vehicle load

- Correctly inflated tyres reduce rolling resistance saving fuel or battery energy.
- Avoid carrying unnecessary weight – especially important in EVs where every kilogram affects range.

Driving electric vehicles (EVs)

EVs introduce a few unique considerations for eco-driving:

- Regenerative braking
  EVs can capture energy when slowing down. Encourage learners to ease off the accelerator early rather than brake sharply.
- Range awareness
  Teach learners to monitor battery levels and understand how speed, temperature and accessories affect range.
- Efficient charging habits
  Charging to 100% isn't always necessary; partial charges are faster and better for battery longevity.
- Instant torque
  EVs accelerate quickly, so learners need to modulate pressure on the accelerator to avoid wasting energy or startling passengers.

Eco-driving as a teaching tool

- Reinforce eco-driving alongside ADAS and distraction management: smooth, thoughtful driving complements all modern vehicle technologies.
- Encourage reflection after lessons:
  - 'Which eco-driving habits came naturally?'
  - 'Where would you improve efficiency without compromising safety?'
- Frame eco-driving as part of developing skilful, responsible drivers, not just as an environmental concern.

Summary

This section helps you teach learners to understand that technology, safety and efficiency are interconnected – whether it is ADAS aiding control or EV features influencing how we drive. Teaching eco-driving is an opportunity to combine practical skill, awareness and responsible driving habits in a single lesson.

06

The ADI Standards Check

The ADI Standards Check is a legal requirement for all ADIs. To maintain your ADI qualification you are required to take at least one Standards Check in each four-year period of registration.

You must provide the learner and a suitable car. The car you use for the Standards Check must be roadworthy, safe and reliable; it must also have a valid MoT certificate if it is more than three years old. A soft-top convertible is not acceptable, nor is a car with limited rear seating for the examiner. 'L' plates (or 'D' plates in Wales) must be displayed if the driver is a provisional licence holder. You must make sure that all seatbelts (both front and rear) are in good working order. Your learner can be either a learner driver or a full licence holder, but they must not be another ADI or someone who is preparing for the ADI Part 3 Test.

You are assessed on your delivery of instruction to the learner, based on the criteria set out in the National Standard for Driver and Rider Training. The Standard sets out the skills, knowledge and understanding you need to be an effective driver trainer. The Standards Check assesses how well you meet the standard. This allows the DVSA to assess an ADI's ability to instruct and whether their instruction helps a person to learn in an effective way. The Standards Check is conducted with a DVSA examiner observing the ADI delivering a normal one-hour lesson. You can take the Standards Check in either English or Welsh.

The Standards Check looks at whether your instruction helps the learner to learn effectively. It is designed to help ADIs to understand, demonstrate and develop the competences in the national standards and allows you to demonstrate to the examiner what you do in your normal daily work.

The National Standard covers training for drivers or riders of all types of cars, light vans, motorcycles and mopeds, and describes the requirements for delivering successful learning. It talks about instructors delivering agreed syllabuses using a 'client-centred' approach. The Standard deals mainly with the skills, knowledge and understanding required to work 'in-car' but also acknowledges that some driver/rider training organizations may opt to deliver part of any given syllabus to a classroom group. The knowledge, skills and understanding that apply in the classroom have therefore been included, but not all instructors will choose to train in this way. As a National Standard, it should be used by all instructors as a basis for any programme of driver training.

The main elements of the Standard include:

- Prepare to train learner driver/riders – meet all legal requirements.
- Design learning programmes.
- Enable safe and responsible driving/riding.
- Manage risk to instructor, learner and third parties.
- Evaluate and develop your knowledge, understanding and skills in the driver/rider training industry.

There are several points worth highlighting in the Standard, including:

- Instructors deliver agreed syllabuses using a 'client-centred' approach.
- Using a client-centred learning approach is about maximizing learning by taking into account the status, prior experience and particular needs of the learner.
- A learner-centred instructor is able to adjust an outline programme to meet the needs of the learner by taking account of prior learning and identifying issues as the training progresses.
- Use best-practice tools, techniques and exercises to support transfer of ownership of the learning process.
- Plan routes for on-road training sessions that provide safe, legal and effective learning opportunities.
- 'Client-centred' is taken to mean, broadly, the same as 'student-centred' or 'learner-centred'.
- Client-centred learning is not about the learner taking charge of the learning process and deciding what is going to happen. It is about creating a conversation.
- Within the learner-centred approach there is a legitimate role for well-delivered explanation and demonstration.

- Frequent explanations and demonstrations can be supportive for some learners; for others this may be demotivating.
- Transfer the balance of responsibility for their learning process to the learner as soon as they are ready to take it.

The Standard can be downloaded at www.gov.uk/national-standard-for-driver-and-rider-training and should be used in conjunction with the National Standard for Driving Cars and Light Vans and the Car and Light Van Driving Syllabus.

Assessment

During the Standards Check you will be assessed and marked on 17 areas of competence that are grouped into three categories:

- lesson planning
- risk management
- teaching and learning skills

Lesson planning

Did the trainer identify the learner's learning goals and needs?

Was the agreed lesson structure appropriate for the learner's experience and ability?

Were the practice areas appropriate?

Was the lesson plan adapted, when appropriate, to help the learner work towards their learning goals?

Risk management

Did the trainer ensure that the learner fully understood how the responsibility for risk would be shared?

Were the directions and instructions given to the learner clear and given in good time?

Was the trainer aware of the surroundings and the learner's actions?

Was any verbal or physical intervention by the trainer timely and appropriate?

Was sufficient feedback given to help the learner understand any potential safety-critical incidents?

Teaching and learning strategies

Was the teaching and learning style suited for the learner's level of ability?

Was the learner encouraged to analyse problems and take responsibility for their learning?

Were opportunities and examples used to clarify learning outcomes?

Was the technical information given comprehensive, appropriate and accurate?

Was the learner given appropriate and timely feedback during the session?

Were the learner's queries followed up and answered?

Did the trainer maintain an appropriate non-discriminatory manner throughout the session?

At the end of the session was the learner encouraged to reflect on their own performance?

Marking

For each of these competences a mark is given on a scale of 0–3:

3 – Competence demonstrated in all elements

2 – Competence demonstrated in most elements

1 – Competence demonstrated in a few elements

0 – No evidence of competence

Score description

3 Keep up the good work

2 Acceptable – there are clear areas of improvement

1 Not acceptable – more work needed

0 Completely unacceptable

These marks are added together to give an overall mark and they will also provide a profile of the areas where you have any strengths and where you might need to do some more development work.

If you get a total score of 43 or more you will be given a Grade A. With a total score of between 31 and 42 you will be given a Grade B. You will fail the Standards Check if:

- you get a score of 7 or less for the 'risk management' category;
- the examiner stops the lesson because you have put yourself or someone else in danger; or
- you have a total score of 30 or less (out of a possible 51).

It is important to remember that the Standards Check is simply a way of assessing what you are doing in your day-to-day business and therefore these competences should be part of your everyday driver training. The Standards Check will be straightforward if you are practising these competences on a regular basis.

The key thing to understand is that the lower-level competences can themselves be broken down into elements. You will have to use a range of skills to ensure each of these elements is in place.

Total score	Grade	Description
0 to 30	Fail	Your performance is unsatisfactory
31 to 42	Grade B	You will be added to the register of ADIs or remain on it
43 to 51	Grade A	You have shown a high standard of instruction, and will be added to the register or remain on it

Note: If you do not reach an acceptable standard in three consecutive Standards Checks, the ADI Registrar can start the process of removing you from the register.

For example, the first lower-level competence, in the lesson-planning section, is 'Did the ADI identify the learner's learning goals and needs?'

To fully satisfy this requirement you must:

- actively recognize the need to understand the learner's experience and background;
- ask suitable questions;
- encourage the learner to talk about their goals, concerns, etc, and actively listen to what the learner has to say;

- understand the significance of what the learner says; and
- recognize other indications, for example body language, that the learner is trying to express something but perhaps cannot find the right words.

Competence standards examples

An ADI who grasps the importance of understanding the learner's needs and makes a real effort to do so, but who finds it difficult to frame suitable questions, would be demonstrating competence in most elements and would be marked 2. Your performance is regarded as acceptable but there are clear areas where you could improve.

An ADI who makes an attempt, asks a few questions, but doesn't really listen and then goes ahead and does what they intended to do regardless, would be demonstrating a few elements of competence and would be marked 1. This is indicating that your performance is not acceptable and that you may need to do a lot more work, even though you have given evidence of knowing what you are supposed to be doing.

An ADI who makes no attempt to understand their learner's needs would be demonstrating no evidence of competence and be marked 0.

If the examiner gives a score of 3 they are effectively saying that this is an area where you do not need to do any further work, apart from continuously reflecting on your performance.

The maximum mark is 51 and the score achieved will dictate the final grade. Whatever the overall marks, you will automatically fail if:

- you achieve a score of 7 or less on the 'risk management' section; or
- at any point in the lesson, you behave in a way which puts you, the examiner, the learner or any third party in immediate danger so that the lesson has to be stopped.

REAL-WORLD EXAMPLE

The Road Traffic Act 1988 (as amended) states that continued registration as an ADI is subject to the condition that they will undergo a test of 'continued ability and fitness to give instruction', known as a standards check, as and when required by the Registrar. The Standards Check allows one of the Agency's examiners to check that your instruction is up to the required standard, by accompanying you while you conduct a normal lesson.

Standards Check Form SC1

Driver & Vehicle Standards Agency

INFORMATION

Trainer Name ☐

PRN ☐☐☐☐☐☐

Valid Certificate Yes ☐ No ☐

Location ☐

Date ☐☐ / ☐☐ / ☐☐

Dual Controls Yes ☐ No ☐

Reg No. ☐

Accompanied? QA ☐ Trainer ☐ Other ☐

Outcome ☐

ASSESSMENT

Learner: Beginner ☐ Partly Trained ☐ Trained ☐ FLH New ☐ FLH Experienced ☐

Lesson theme: Junctions ☐ Town & city driving ☐ Interacting with other road users ☐ Dual carriageway/faster moving roads ☐ Defensive driving ☐ Effective use of mirrors ☐ Independent driving ☐ Rural roads ☐ Motorways ☐ Eco-safe driving ☐ Recap a manoeuvre ☐ Commentary ☐ Recap emergency stop ☐ Other ☐

	Score	Competence 0: No evidence	1: Demonstrated in a few elements	2: Demonstrated in most elements	3: Demonstrated in all elements
LESSON PLANNING					
Did the trainer identify the learner's learning goals and needs?					
Was the agreed lesson structure appropriate for the learner's experience and ability?					
Were the practice areas suitable?					
Was the lesson plan adapted, when appropriate, to help the learner work towards their learning goals?					
Score for lesson planning	☐	☐	☐	☐	☐
RISK MANAGEMENT					
Did the trainer ensure that the learner fully understood how the responsibility for risk would be shared?					
Were directions and instructions given to the learner clear and given in good time?					
Was the trainer aware of the surroundings and the learner's actions?					
Was any verbal or physical intervention by the trainer timely and appropriate?					
Was sufficient feedback given to help the learner understand any potential safety critical incidents?					
Score for risk management	☐	☐	☐	☐	☐
TEACHING & LEARNING STRATEGIES					
Was the teaching style suited to the learner's learning style and current ability?					
Was the learner encouraged to analyse problems and take responsibility for their learning?					
Were opportunities and examples used to clarify learning outcomes?					
Was the technical information given comprehensive, appropriate and accurate?					
Was the learner given appropriate and timely feedback during the session?					
Were the learner's queries followed up and answered?					
Did the trainer maintain an appropriate non-discriminatory manner throughout the session?					
At the end of the session – was the learner encouraged to reflect on their own performance?					
Score for teaching and learning strategies	☐	☐	☐	☐	☐
Overall score	☐				

REVIEW	YES	NO
Did the trainer score 7 or less on Risk Management? (A 'Yes' response to this question will result in an automatic Fail)		
At any point in the lesson, did the trainer behave in a way which put you, the learner or any third party in immediate danger, so that you had to stop the lesson? (A 'Yes' response to this question will result in an automatic Fail)		
Was advice given to seek further development?		

Feedback offered to trainer ☐

Examiner Name ☐ Signature ☐

C 1/2014

Assessment notes

This form is designed to identify the strengths in your instructional ability and to highlight any areas which you may need to develop. The form is provided in conjunction with verbal feedback with the aim of helping you improve your instructional ability.

Criteria for scoring

Assessment is against three broad areas of competence:

- lesson planning;
- risk management;
- teaching and learning strategies.

A full description regarding the assessment can be found in the 'National standard for driver and rider training', available at www.gov.uk/government/publications/national-standard-for-driver-and-rider-training

ADI grades

Assessing the lower competencies will represent a 'profile' of Instructional Competence.

Score	Description	Grade
0 – 30	Unsatisfactory performance	Fail
31 – 42	Sufficient competence demonstrated to permit or retain entry on the Register of Approved Driving Instructors	Grade B
43 – 51	A high overall standard of instruction demonstrated	Grade A

Note: If you score 7 or less in the Risk Management section the Standards Check will be deemed substandard and a fail. Also, if the examiner believes your behaviour is placing you, the learner or any third party in immediate danger they may stop the lesson and record an immediate fail.

Appeals

You cannot appeal against the examiner's decision. You may appeal to a Magistrate's Court, or in Scotland the Sheriffs Office, if you consider that your test was not conducted properly.

Before you consider making any appeal you may wish to seek legal advice.

The examiner will assess your competence to deliver effective driving instruction. The 'National standard for driver training' is expressed in terms of learning outcomes and there may be more than one way for you to achieve those outcomes. Of course, if you do something or say something that is clearly wrong this will be picked up, especially where it could lead to a safety issue. However, the overall approach by the examiner is focused on recognizing achievement and promoting improvement and development – rather than purely identifying faults. Your task is to provide an effective learning experience for the learner. This is judged to be one in which the learner is supported to take as much responsibility as possible for their learning process.

Where it is correct and safe to do so, feel free to introduce wider issues from the driving standard into the lesson. This could include assessing the learner's personal fitness to drive, the use of alcohol or drugs, or dealing with aggression. If, for example, a learner offers an inappropriate comment about the use of alcohol it would be appropriate for you to challenge this.

Similarly, it would be appropriate for you to encourage the learner to think through what might happen, in particular situations, if the conditions were different. For example, after negotiating a particularly difficult junction it might be helpful to discuss how different it would be at night or in bad weather. The important thing to remember here is that the most effective learning takes place when the learner finds the answers for themselves.

If opportunities arise for discussion of issues between you and the learner while on the move, these can be used, but this needs to be tailored to the learner's ability and should not create distraction. Too many unnecessary instructions can both demotivate the learner and create a real hazard. You may be given more detailed feedback by the examiner relating to the competences against which you have been assessed:

- lesson planning;
- risk management; and
- teaching and learning strategies.

The purpose of feedback from the examiner is to help you understand where you might have failed to demonstrate full competence and where you might need to focus your efforts when undertaking further development.

The Standards Check form shows a 'profile' of your performance, against the individual competences. This will help you to see where you have given a strong performance as well as where you may need development.

Typical lessons

Partly trained inexperienced learner

Drivers at this stage of their career are likely to want/need experience of a steadily increasing variety of road and traffic conditions to enable them to develop their basic skills. They may have areas where they are uncomfortable or not yet competent, such as complex junctions or roundabouts, heavy or fast-moving traffic. They may not have a good understanding of theory, for example, of road signs and markings.

In this context the key objectives of the 'National standard for driver and rider training' include being able to:

- create a climate that promotes learning (element 6.3.1);
- explain and demonstrate skills and techniques (element 6.3.2);
- transfer the balance of responsibility for their learning process to the learner as soon as they are ready to take it.

You should be working to understand where the learner is having difficulties and how you can help them develop sound basic skills. If you are not making the effort to understand, you are not demonstrating competence. By asking questions or staying silent and listening and watching you are clearly making the effort to understand and demonstrate competence. It doesn't matter if you don't achieve full understanding by the end of the lesson.

In the same way, learners at this level should not feel they are being patronized or talked down to as this will make them unreceptive. They do not all learn in the same way.

Consequently, there is no single, correct way to transfer responsibility to them and, in any case, this is not going to take place instantly. In this context, just as it is unreasonable to expect a learner to get it right instantly, so it is unreasonable to expect the instructor to transfer responsibility instantly. The key thing that you must demonstrate is that you understand the need to transfer responsibility and make the effort to do so.

It is important to understand that, at this level, a learner will not always 'get it right' as soon as the instructor gives them some direction or coaches them around a problem. You should understand the issue, at least in principle, and what you need to do in theory. Be willing to try to overcome weaknesses, but remember that your efforts may not always be successful. During the Standards Check the examiner will not penalize you if you do not immediately 'solve the problem'.

Use a variety of tools to encourage the learner to analyse their own performance and to find solutions to problems. Be supportive and give suitable and technically correct instructions or demonstrations where appropriate. Of course, where a learner cannot come up with a way forward you may decide to provide suitable input – especially if failure to do so might result in a risk to anyone else.

Experienced learner – about ready to take their test

At this stage the key objective of the 'National standard for driver and rider training' is 'to work with the learner to agree when they are ready to undertake formal assessment of driving competence' (element 6.3.3).

Evidence suggests that, by this stage, some learners may:

- be technically skilful;
- be able to complete manoeuvres competently;
- have experience of driving on a wide range of roads and in a range of conditions.

They may be confident and feel that they are at the stage of refining their competence around 'what they need to do to pass the test'. On the other hand, they may have:

- already developed bad habits, especially if they have been taught by a relative or friend;
- an inflated opinion of their competence;
- a poor understanding of risk;
- not developed the skills of scanning and planning that will help them to cope when they drive independently;
- not developed the skills of reflection that will help them to be life-long learners.

They may not be used to being challenged to analyse and come up with solutions. They could be impatient and resistant to correction if they do demonstrate 'bad habits'. They may well have forgotten a lot of what they learnt when they did their theory test. Responses at this level could vary from enthusiastic acceptance of the information they need, to real resistance to being told things they do not think are relevant.

During the Standards Check you must demonstrate that you understand the key issues that need to be addressed to try to reduce the numbers of newly qualified drivers who crash in the first six months. You should:

- develop a realistic understanding of ability and an enhanced understanding of risk;
- be checking, developing and reinforcing systematic scanning and planning tools;
- strongly encourage reflection;
- be supportive;
- not over-instruct; and
- give suitable and technically correct instructions or demonstrations where necessary.

However, the emphasis is likely to be on the use of tools, such as practical examples, to develop a more joined-up and outward-looking approach.

New full licence holder

This type of learner will have demonstrated 'competence' against those elements of the national standards for driving that are tested in the theory and practical tests. Remember, however, that these tests are limited in scope. They do not require the learner to drive on all classes of roads and they do not test understanding of that part of the national standards for driving which calls on learners to reflect on their competence as they go through their driving career. At this stage your objective is to develop the learner's competence across the full range of driving environments and to support and reinforce their commitment to life-long learning around driving.

Reasons why an individual might come to an ADI for lessons at this stage include the following:

- Wanting to refresh their skills if they haven't driven since they took their test
- Moving on to a bigger or technologically different vehicle
- Starting to drive for work
- Starting a family and wanting to improve their skills
- Moving from an urban to a rural environment, or vice versa
- Starting to use motorways
- A simple desire to become a better-developed driver
- Preparation for an advanced driving test

This learner is likely to be enthusiastic and, in theory at least, open to learning if they have chosen to take training. If, on the other hand, they have been told to take it, perhaps by an employer, they might be resentful and resistant. They may well have already lost the disciplines of the mirror–signal–manoeuvre routine and forward-planning skills. They may not be used to driving in an 'eco-safe' way and may not even understand the term. They may be nervous about increased responsibility and accountability.

During the Standards Check the key thing that you must demonstrate is that you are able to find out exactly what it is the learner wants from the lesson and put together a plan to deliver that. You must of course identify and deal with bad habits that might have been acquired. However, if all you do is go over what the learner should have learnt prior to their test you are unlikely to reinforce the commitment to life-long learning.

Experienced full licence holder

At this stage this type of learner should be more confident and competent than they were immediately after passing their test. They should have gained experience across all or most of the possible classes of roads, at night and in bad weather. They may already be driving for work and are likely to regard themselves as capable drivers, even though their application of safety routines and forward-planning skills may show they are not quite as competent as they think.

Reasons why an individual might come to an ADI at this stage include:

- being required by employers to undertake additional training to keep insurance costs down;
- wanting to drive more economically to reduce business costs;
- having had an accident or near miss that has shaken their confidence;
- returning to driving after a period of ill-health, injury or loss of licence;
- recognizing that their driving skills are deteriorating through age or ill-health.

The learner may be an overseas driver who has significant experience but, having been in the UK beyond the statutory period, is now required to take the tests to qualify for a UK licence.

Depending on their reasons for undertaking training, these learners could be enthusiastic or very nervous, willing or very resistant. Older learners may find it harder to learn new skills or to get out of bad habits. They may have developed unsafe habits such as not leaving large enough separation distances and failing to carry out systematic observation routines.

Reflecting on today's lesson	
Please consider filling in this reflective log – it's yours to keep and your comments may help you identify where you can make improvements in your performance.	
What went well today?	
What did not go as well today?	
What could I do to improve?	
Notes	

In assessment the key thing is that you must demonstrate you can find out exactly what it is the learner wants from the lesson and put together a plan to deliver that. You should, of course, spot and deal with bad habits that might have been acquired. However, the lesson must take the learner forward in their learning. If it does not deliver what the learner is looking for they will not engage with the learning process.

This is not an exhaustive list of possible scenarios, but it should give some indication of the sorts of things that should be considered.

Interpreting the assessment criteria

Lesson planning

The purpose of all driver training is to assess and develop the learner's skill, knowledge and understanding in relation to the contents of the National Standard for Driver Training. Research indicates that this is best achieved by placing the client at the centre of the learning process. In this context the assessment criteria will be interpreted as follows.

Did the trainer identify the learner's learning goals and needs?

Usually this process will take place at the beginning of a lesson. However, where you and the learner have been working together for some time prior to the Standards Check, you may have already laid down the basic structure of the learner's learning goals. This is considered by the examiner when assessing this element.

If you have not worked with the learner before it is perfectly OK for you to ask the learner to undertake a demonstration/assessment drive. This should give a good idea of the learner's level of competence and provide a basis for a discussion of the learner's needs.

As the examiner observes the lesson they will be looking for indications that the elements which go to make up the low-level competence are being demonstrated. In this case the sorts of things that would show an indication of competence include:

- encouraging the learner to say what they want from the lesson;
- asking questions to ensure understanding;
- checking understanding as the lesson progresses;
- listening to what the learner is saying;
- taking note of body language.

During the assessment it's important that you:

- encourage the learner to say what they want;
- ask questions to check understanding at the beginning and as the lesson progresses;
- listen to what the learner is saying; and
- pick up on body language.

If you deal with all these topics you are likely to get a 3. If, on the other hand, you do all the listening bits but fail to spot the learner getting very tense and nervous in a particular situation you would probably get a 2. You would have demonstrated your understanding of the need to listen, etc, but have not yet developed the ability to spot non-verbal clues. Indications of a lack of competence could include:

- making assumptions about understanding or experience;
- failing to note negative or concerned comments or body language that show discomfort;
- undermining the learner's confidence by continually asking questions clearly beyond the learner's knowledge or understanding;
- pushing the learner to address issues that they are not happy to talk about, unless there is a clear need, such as an identified risk or a safety-critical issue.

This is all about goal-setting. The goal needs to be agreed with the learner. This is done in the belief that the learner knows best what they need to learn and achieve in each lesson. This might sound a strange thing to say if you are focused on technical skills and control of the vehicle. However, our behaviour is always motivated by our thoughts and feelings and individually we all think and feel very differently from the next person. The learner might be reluctant initially to state their goals for a lesson because they may not know what they want to get out of a lesson. However, this is part of the learning curve every learner is on – it is not just about learning how to control the vehicle, it is also about learning how their thoughts and feelings impact on their behaviour and learning how to regulate and manage their thoughts and feelings so that their behaviour is safe. One of the important first steps in this process is making choices.

Instructors often express reservations about allowing the learner to choose what they want to do in a lesson because it interferes with what they are used to doing and the syllabus they want to work through. If you are focused on the driving test, then you will find this process difficult. However, while you are practising goal-setting it is okay to stick with your syllabus and work on getting the learner to define what they 'want to achieve by the end of the lesson' or 'how they want to feel' or 'what they most want to improve'. You could, for example, say, 'OK, so today we are going to look at the reverse park, so what would you like to achieve by the end of the lesson?'

Was the agreed lesson structure appropriate for the learner's experience and ability?

The lesson structure should allow the learner to progress at a manageable rate; stretching them without overwhelming them. For example, a learner who is concerned about entering roundabouts should not be asked to tackle a fast-flowing multi-lane, multi-exit junction as their first attempt. Neither should they be restricted to very quiet junctions, unless you identify a potential risk issue that they want to check out first.

Indications that all the elements of competence are in place could include:

- ensuring the learner understands what they plan to do and agrees with that plan;
- a lesson that reflects the information given by the learner and the learning goals they want to tackle;
- building in opportunities to check the statements made by the learner before moving to more challenging situations;
- checking theoretical understanding.

Indications of lack of competence include: delivering a pre-planned, standard lesson that doesn't consider the learner's expressed needs or concerns; failing to build in a suitable balance of practice and theory.

This competence is closely tied in with the previous one about setting a goal for the session. Having asked, 'What would you like to achieve by the end of the lesson?' the next question might be, 'How do you want to do this?' It is important that, having started to give the learner responsibility for their learning, you don't take it back from them by assuming they need a briefing. It is often inappropriate for the learner's experience and ability anyway to give a briefing. Many people already know everything they need in order to reverse into a parking space – and it depends on the goal they set for themselves. For example, if the learner says that they simply want to be able to park accurately there may be no need to give a briefing that includes observations and control. They may simply want to have a go and see how they get on. This is then matched to their experience and ability.

Were the practice areas suitable?

You should use an area or route that allows the learner to practise safely and helps them to achieve their goals. It should provide some stretch and challenge, but without taking them out of their comfort zone.

Indications that all the elements of competence are in place could include choosing a practice area/route that provides a range of opportunities to address the agreed learning objectives, and which challenges, but is realistic, in terms of the learner's capabilities and confidence.

Indications of lack of competence include taking the learner into an area that takes them outside of their competence zone – so that they spend all their time 'surviving' and have no space left to look at learning issues – or exposes them to risks they cannot manage.

This is where you rely on your experience and expertise. It is important that you ensure the practice areas are appropriate and you may have to guide the learner in this so that if they want to choose the area themselves you decide if it will be appropriate for their experience and ability.

The conversation might go like this:

ADI: 'What would you like to do today?'

Learner: 'Could I try reversing into a parking space?'

ADI: 'Do you have a reason for saying that?'

Learner: 'Yes, I was watching my brother parking the other day and thought I would like to have a go at that.'

ADI: 'What would you like to achieve by the end of the lesson?'

Learner: 'I would just like to get the car parked reasonably accurately.'

ADI: 'Okay, how do you want to do this?'

Learner: 'Well, do you think I could just have a go? I could show you what my brother did.'

ADI: 'Yes, that's fine. Do you want me to give you directions to a suitable area because it's too busy here to do it?'

Learner: 'Yes please.'

ADI: 'There will be a couple of roundabouts to deal with on the way. Would you like some help from me to deal with these?'

Learner: 'Yes please.'

Was the lesson plan adapted, when appropriate, to help the learner work towards their learning goals?

You should be willing and able to adapt if your learner:

- appears to be uncomfortable or unable to deal with the learning experience that you have set up; or
- suggests that it is not providing what they were looking for.

If the learner's inability is creating a possible risk situation you must adapt quickly. This might require a few extra questions to clarify what is out of line. It may be that the problem is because of the teaching and learning style being used rather than because the overall plan is wrong. Whatever the reason for adapting the plan, you must make sure the learner understands what they are doing and why.

Indications that all the elements of competence are in place could include:

- comparing the actual performance of the learner with their claims and clarifying any differences;
- responding to any faults or weaknesses that undermine the original plan for the session;
- responding to any concerns or issues raised by the learner;
- picking up on non-verbal signs of discomfort or confusion.

Indications of lack of competence include:

- persisting with a plan despite the learner being clearly out of their depth;
- persisting with a plan despite the learner demonstrating faults or weaknesses that should lead to a rethink of the plan;
- changing the plan without reason;
- failing to explain to the learner why the plan has been changed.

Risk management

It is vital that all parties in any on-road training situation understand and are clear about where the responsibility lies for the safety of themselves, others in the vehicle and other road users.

There are two aspects to the management of risk in any training situation:

> At all times you are responsible for your own safety, the safety of the learner and the safety of other road users. In some circumstances this can extend to taking physical control of the vehicle to manage a safety-critical incident. If you fail in this basic responsibility at any time, you will fail the Standards Check.
>
> From a training point of view, you are also responsible for developing the learner's awareness of and ability to manage risk (as the driver, the learner also has responsibilities).

These are the aspects being assessed in this section.

Did the ADI make sure that the learner fully understood how the responsibility for risk would be shared?

The 'balance of responsibility', between the learner and the ADI, will inevitably vary in different circumstances. For example, compare the following two scenarios:

A learner in the very early stages of their training, in a car fitted with dual controls. In this situation it might be reasonable for you to start a lesson by saying something like:

> At all times I expect you to drive as carefully and responsibly as possible. I will expect you to be aware of other road users and to control the car. However, I do have the ability to take control of the car in an emergency. I will only use these controls when I feel that you are not dealing with the situation yourself. If that happens we will take some time to talk about what happened so that you understand for next time.

A learner who has passed their driving test but has asked you to give them some additional training in their own car, which is much bigger and more technically advanced than the one they learnt in. In this situation you might say something like:

> You have passed your test and I will therefore assume that you are taking full responsibility for our safety. I will be talking to you from time to time, but I will try to keep that to a minimum so that I don't distract you. If I am quiet don't worry; that just means I am comfortable with what you are doing. I will, of course, let you know if I see any risk that you appear to have missed.

However, such opening statements are not all that is involved in meeting this criterion. You should be managing this process throughout the lesson. So, for example, if the learner makes some sort of mistake carrying out a manoeuvre you should, ideally, find an opportunity to analyse that mistake with the learner. Having achieved an understanding of what went wrong you might then ask the learner to try the manoeuvre again. At that point you should provide the learner with clear information about what is required of them.

So, for example, you might say:

> Let's try that manoeuvre again. I won't say anything. Just try to remember what we have just been talking about.

On the other hand, you may want to take back a bit of control and might say:

> Let's try that again. I will talk you through it this time. Just follow my instructions.

You should work with the learner to decide the best way of tackling the problem and that might mean a temporary change in the 'balance of responsibility'. The important thing is that the learner knows what is expected of them.

Under test conditions there are no circumstances in which you can assume that the issue of risk management has been dealt with. Even if you and the learner have had discussions about risk before the observed lesson, you must show that you are actively managing the issue for assessment purposes.

Indications that all the elements of competence are in place could include:

- asking the learner what is meant by risk;
- asking the learner what sorts of issues create risk, such as the use of alcohol or drugs;
- explaining clearly what is expected of the learner and what the learner can reasonably expect of you;

- checking that the learner understands what is required of them when there is a change of plan or they are asked to repeat an exercise.

Indications of lack of competence include:

- failing to address the issue of risk management;
- giving incorrect guidance about where responsibility lies for management of risk;
- failing to explain how dual controls will be used;
- undermining the learner's commitment to being safe and responsible, for example, by agreeing with risky attitudes to alcohol use;
- asking the learner to repeat a manoeuvre or carry out a particular exercise without making sure that they understand what role you are going to play.

Once the goal has been agreed you must consider how to share the responsibility for risk. If the learner has said they would like to practise something on their own, you might simply state that you will keep the car safe. In this instance, for example, the learner may have agreed they would like to practise emerging from junctions on a route that might last a few minutes and involve three or four different junctions in a reasonably quiet area. The learner has said that they would like to drive this route with no help from you, their instructor, so that they can concentrate on approaching the junctions, assessing their speed and visibility and choosing a safe gap. You must allow the learner to do this and, at the same time, be prepared to step in with instruction or the use of dual controls where necessary to keep the car safe. Similarly, if the learner has agreed that the goal for the lesson is the reverse park and that they will have achieved their goal if they can get the car manoeuvred into the space reasonably accurately, then it might be that you do the observations. This is sharing the responsibility for risk. The learner will be able to focus on the accuracy and control part of the manoeuvre, while you look after the observations.

In both examples, the risk is shared to ensure that the learner has the best possible chance of achieving the agreed goal.

Were directions and instructions given to the learner clear and given in good time?

'Directions' should be taken to mean any instruction, such as 'turn left at the next junction' or 'try changing gear a little later'. Any input from you must be sufficient, timely and appropriate. It is important that you take account of the ability of your learners when giving directions. Directions given late, or in a confusing or misleading way, do not allow the learner to respond and can make weaknesses worse.

Too many unnecessary instructions can both demotivate the learner and create a real hazard. Remember it is an offence to use a mobile phone while driving because this is known to create a level of risk equivalent to or, in some cases, greater than driving while drunk. It cannot, therefore, be good practice to constantly bombard the learner with unnecessary questions.

Indications that all the elements of competence are in place could include:

- clear, concise directions;
- ensuring the learner understands what they plan to do and agrees with that plan;
- directions given at a suitable time so that the learner can respond.

Indications of lack of competence include:

- giving confused directions;
- giving directions too late;
- giving unnecessary directions; and
- failing to recognize when your input is causing overload or confusion.

If directions and instructions are given clearly and in good time, then you are managing the risk effectively and enabling the learner to focus on achieving the agreed goal. It might be that the learner has decided they want to choose the route or drive on a previous route without directions. This is perfectly acceptable and, in this case, you would not be expected to give directions. However, you may still need to give instruction if this is what has been agreed, or if a safety-critical incident occurs. In these situations you must ensure that you are giving your instructions clearly and in good time.

'Right, turn left here' is a confusing direction where the trainer should have clearly stated, 'At the end of the road turn left' to avoid the learner turning right into someone's driveway. Similarly, the timing of instructions and directions can be very distracting, especially if the trainer barks them out late. This can actually increase the risk of being involved in a crash simply because the learner becomes distracted and confused and may make mistakes.

Was the trainer aware of the surroundings and the learner's actions?

This question lies at the heart of the ADI's professional skill. You should be able to:

- take in the outside world;
- observe the actions of the learner, including comments and body language;
- judge whether those actions are suitable in any given situation; and
- respond accordingly.

Any serious lapses in this area are likely to lead to a zero marking.

Being able to observe the road ahead and behind as well as the learner's eyes, hands and feet is a vital part of risk management. It is your responsibility to ensure that the learner is going to be able to cope safely with whatever presents itself on the road and to do this you have to be constantly assessing the whole of the environment.

Was any verbal or physical intervention by the trainer timely and appropriate?

The overall approach should be client-centred. Remember that there is a fine balance between giving enough input and giving too much.

When stationary it would be expected that inputs and interventions would take the form of a dialogue with the learner. In the moving-car environment, you remaining silent and signalling your confidence in the learner through your body language, is just as much a coaching input as asking a stream of questions. Clearly the most important 'interventions' are those that manage risk in a moving car. You would be expected to point out situations in which a risk or hazard might arise to your learner. However, direct intervention to prevent a situation escalating may be needed. This criterion is primarily about your response in those situations.

Indications that all the elements of competence are in place could include:

- intervening in a way that actively supports the learner's learning process and safety during the session;
- allowing the learner to deal with situations appropriately;
- taking control of situations where the learner is clearly out of their depth.

Indications of lack of competence include:

- ignoring a developing situation and leaving the learner to flounder;
- taking control of a situation the learner is clearly dealing with appropriately;
- constantly intervening when unnecessary;
- intervening inappropriately and creating distractions;
- undermining the learner's confidence;
- reinforcing the instructor as the person who is in sole control of the lesson.

Say, for example, the learner has agreed that they would like to focus on adequate clearance to parked vehicles along the high street. At the start of the session you have looked at the responsibility for risk and agreed that you will share the risk by ensuring that the learner can focus on their goal while you manage any other hazards. On the route there is a pelican crossing, which, at first glance, looks safe. There is no need to mention the pelican crossing because the learner's goal is, specifically, adequate clearance to parked cars.

It wouldn't be appropriate to talk about the pelican crossing if the learner appears to be dealing with it OK and there is clearly no risk – unless pedestrian crossings are part of the goal for the session, or the learner has clearly said that they want to be alerted to other hazards outside of their goal. This is to do with understanding how people learn and very often driving instructors disrupt the learner's learning by giving partly trained instruction. In many situations the learner will achieve far more understanding about how to practically apply their skills and assess the risk involved if they can carry out the task in silence. This raises their awareness of their personal strengths and limitations and therefore builds their responsibility. Constant verbal instruction while the car is moving can lead to a bombardment of the senses and a task overload where something has to give.

Nevertheless, if you need to intervene to keep the car safe then it really doesn't matter if there is a sensory overload. So, in the example shown earlier let's now imagine that a pedestrian approaches the crossing. You must now assess whether you will need to step in and take control in some way. There are four possible options to choose from:

- Option 1: There is no need to do anything. The learner has already checked their mirror and eased off the gas in case the lights change.

- Option 2: The learner has made no response and the lights are now starting to change. It is necessary to say something, and a question will keep the responsibility sitting with the learner for longer. You could ask: 'Do you think you need to slow down for the lights ahead?' This is a leading question with an implicit call for action.
- Option 3: You decided to wait a little longer to see if the learner was going to respond. You don't want to interfere too early with their achievement of the goal – adequate clearance to parked vehicles. However, it is clear that the learner is not responding so a direct instruction is necessary: 'Slow down for the lights.'
- Option 4: You decided not to give a verbal instruction and must now take physical action as the learner is not responding, the lights are on red and the pedestrian is crossing the road. You use the dual brake.

Was sufficient feedback given to help the learner understand any potential safety-critical incidents?

If a safety-critical, or potentially critical, incident does occur it is vital that the learner fully understands what happened and how they could have avoided or dealt with it better. Ideally the learner should be supported to analyse the situation for themselves. However, it may be necessary for you to provide feedback if, for example, the learner simply did not see a problem. That feedback should be given as soon as is practical after the incident.

Indications that all the elements of competence are in place could include:

- finding a safe place to stop and examine the critical incident;
- allowing the learner time to express any fears or concerns the incident might have caused;
- supporting the learner to reflect clearly about what happened;
- providing input to clarify aspects of the incident that the learner does not understand;
- supporting the learner to identify strategies for future situations;
- providing input where the learner does not understand what they should do differently;
- checking that the learner feels able to put the strategy in place;
- agreeing ways of developing that competence if the learner feels the need.

Indications of lack of competence include:

- failing to examine the incident;
- taking too long to address issues generated by an incident;
- not allowing the learner to explore their own understanding;
- telling the learner what the solution is and not checking their understanding;
- failing to check the learner's ability to put in place the agreed strategy.

Teaching and learning strategies

The important thing to remember when considering teaching and learning strategies is that it is about client-centred learning. The examiner's assessment is about whether you have been able to help the learner to learn in an active way.

There will be many times when it is useful to use a coaching technique. The principle that underpins coaching is that an engaged learner is likely to achieve a higher level of understanding and that self-directed solutions will seem far more relevant. This applies in every situation, including instruction. Direct instruction is useful in helping a learner in the early stages cope with new situations or supporting a learner who is clearly struggling in a certain situation. Good coaching will use the correct technique at the correct time, matching the learner's needs. In some cases you may need to give direct instruction through a particularly difficult situation. That instruction forms part of a coaching process if you then encourage the learner to analyse the problem and take responsibility for learning from it. A good ADI will take every opportunity to reinforce learning.

Was the teaching style suited to the learner's learning style and current ability?

You should take into account all that you understand about the learner. Recognize that different learners will have different preferred approaches to learning, although these may only emerge fully over a number of lessons. Some learners may be very willing to learn actively, while others may want opportunities to reflect before they make the next step in their learning. You should at least be able to give evidence of their sensitivity to these issues. In a one-off session this will probably be best demonstrated by offering a range of options. Be prepared to adjust your approach if evidence emerges of a different preferred style.

It is impossible to force learning on a learner. Progress is always determined by what the learner is comfortable with. The skill is in recognizing when the learner stops learning. The pace of a session should be set by the learner. On the other hand, a learner should not be talked out of experimenting, if this is within safe bounds.

When coaching, you should ensure that the tools used are suitable. If a question and answer technique is used this should match the learner's level of ability and encourage them to use a higher level of thinking to give a response. Asking closed questions of a learner who is demonstrating a high level of ability, unless this is to check knowledge, is of little use. Asking open questions to a learner of limited ability who is finding it difficult to achieve the task they have set for themselves may be very confusing. These are not hard and fast rules. The effectiveness of any question is assessed given the circumstances at the time.

Indications that all the elements of competence are in place could include:

- Actively working to understand how you can best support the learner's learning process. (You might not achieve a full understanding in the session – it is the attempt that demonstrates competence.)
- Modifying your teaching style when or if you realize there is a need to do so.
- Providing accurate and technically correct demonstration, instruction or information. Giving technically incorrect instruction or information is an automatic fail if that input might lead to a safety-critical situation.
- Using practical examples and other similar tools to provide different ways of looking at a particular subject.
- Linking learning in theory to learning in practice.
- Encouraging and helping the learner to take ownership of the learning process.
- Responding to faults in a timely manner.
- Providing enough uninterrupted time to practise new skills.
- Providing the learner with clear guidance about how they might practise outside the session.

Indications of lack of competence include:

- adopting a teaching style clearly at odds with the learner's learning style;
- failing to check with the learner whether the approach they are taking is acceptable;

- failing to explore other ways of addressing a particular learning point;
- concentrating on delivering teaching tools rather than looking for learning outcomes;
- ignoring safety issues.

If you are in the habit of giving briefings to every one of your customers then you may be slowing down the learning of some of them, particularly if they have a more kinaesthetic learning preference. It is not necessarily true that the most effective way to learn is following the 'explain–demonstrate–practice' (EDP) route. Unfortunately, for many of us, training to become a driving instructor was all about passing the Part 3 test with very little emphasis – if any – on how people learn; and now we have become conditioned to believe that this is therefore the way things should be.

Consider how you got on at school. Did you have teachers you preferred over others, or favourite subjects? Did everyone in your class share your preferences? 'Yes' and 'No' respectively is probably how you answered those two questions because everyone is different and each of us is unique in how we absorb and process information and therefore how we learn new things. Our interpretation of the world and our individual set of experiences, existing knowledge and understanding influence how we gain new knowledge and experiences.

When you are teaching someone to drive you need to adapt the way you teach to suit the way someone learns most effectively. This is not a hard and fast science and most people process information through several different channels. However, consider a situation where your customer is yawning while you are giving them a briefing. It is not necessarily because they were out partying the night before; it is far more likely to be because they are bored by your lengthy briefing and you need to change your method of communication.

Was the learner encouraged to analyse problems and take responsibility for their learning?

A key part of the client-centred approach is development of active problem solving in the learner. This means that you should provide time for this to happen and you have to stop talking for long enough for the learner to do the work. The main point to remember, however, is that different learners will respond to this invitation in different ways. Some may be able to do it instantly, in a discussion. Others may need to go away and reflect upon a particular problem. They may need to be pointed at readings or other inputs to help them get a handle on the issue. Pushing a learner to come up with answers on the spot may be unproductive for some.

Indications that all the elements of competence are in place could include:

- providing time, in a suitable location, to explore any problems or issues that arose during the lesson or that were raised by the learner;
- providing timely opportunities for analysis, promptly in the case of risk-critical incidents;
- taking time and using suitable techniques to understand any problems the learner had with understanding an issue;
- suggesting suitable strategies to help the learner develop their understanding, such as using practical examples or pointing them at further reading;
- giving clear and accurate information to fill gaps in the learner's knowledge or understanding;
- leaving the learner feeling that they had responsibility for their learning in the situation.

Indications of lack of competence include:

- leaving the learner feeling that you were in control of the teaching process;
- failing to explore alternative ways of addressing a problem – in response to evidence of different learning preferences;
- providing unsuitable or incorrect inputs.

There is no need to jump in with the answer every time a fault occurs. If your customer stalls the car, for example, ask them if they know what just happened. This develops their ability to analyse problems, which is a crucial skill when they are driving independently. It might be obvious to you that the reason they stalled is because they have just tried to pull away in third gear, or that they brought the clutch up too quickly, or they forgot to release the handbrake, or they didn't have enough gas. But is it obvious to them? No one gets things right all the time and, particularly in driving, it is easy to make mistakes. However, the ability to analyse why something is not working and put it right is very important and could easily mean the difference between a crash occurring or not.

Were opportunities and examples used to clarify learning outcomes?

While training in technique is core to the learning process it is important to reinforce this input and to link it with theory. The best way to do this is to use real-world situations during the lesson. The use of practical examples and scenarios on a lesson gives the learner a better understanding of when, how and why to use a particular technique.

This can be done, for example, by asking the learner to think about why mirrors are important when changing direction.

Indications that all the elements of competence are in place could include:

- using examples identified on a lesson in a suitable way and at a suitable time to confirm or reinforce understanding;
- exploring different ways to use examples to respond to differences in preferred learning style;
- using examples that are within the learner's range of experience and ability to understand; and
- recognizing that some learners will be able to respond instantly while others will want to think about the issue.

Indications of lack of competence include:

- using examples the learner cannot really understand through lack of experience;
- using complex examples that the learner doesn't have the ability to respond to;
- failing to give the learner time to think through the issues and come to their own conclusion; or
- imposing an interpretation.

Learning outcomes are the same as goals and these were established at the beginning of the session. This links back to the lesson planning competence and is about taking advantage of the environment and recognizing that there are plenty of opportunities that can be drawn on during the session that will help ensure the goals are achieved. For example, the skills involved in planning and anticipation can be developed on a number of different occasions; for example, a goal that has been set around deciding whether to give way or continue in meeting situations could be developed when judging a safe gap on the approach to a roundabout or anticipating whether to give way at a pedestrian crossing.

Was the technical information given comprehensive, appropriate and accurate?

As noted above, giving incorrect or insufficient information, with the result that a safety-critical situation might occur, will result in an automatic fail.

Remember that good information is:

- accurate;
- relevant; and
- timely.

Failure to meet any one of these criteria makes the others redundant.

Most sessions will require some technical input from you to help the learner solve problems or to fill a gap in their knowledge. This input must be accurate and appropriate.

Information given must be comprehensive when associated with a recurring weakness in the learner's driving. Simply telling the learner that they have done something wrong is unlikely to help them overcome the problem.

Any practical demonstration of technique must be clear and suitable. The learner should be engaged and given the opportunity to explore their understanding of what they are being shown.

Information given unnecessarily may not be helpful, for example, continually telling the learner what to do and not allowing them to take responsibility.

Unclear or misleading advice should also be avoided. Comments such as 'You're a bit close to these parked cars' could be used to introduce coaching on a weakness but are of little use on their own as they are unclear. How close is 'a bit' and is it significant?

Indications that all the elements of competence are in place could include:

- giving clear, timely and technically accurate demonstrations or explanations;
- checking understanding and, if necessary, repeating the demonstration or explanation; and
- finding a different way to demonstrate or explain if the learner still does not understand.

Indications of lack of competence include:

- providing inaccurate or unclear information, too late or too early in the learning process;
- failing to check understanding; or
- failing to explore alternative ways of presenting information where the learner does not understand the first offering.

Taking a client-centred approach to learning does not mean that you cannot give information where relevant. Your expertise as an ADI is of vital importance when teaching people to drive safely for life. Some people seem to think that coaching is all about asking questions and nothing to do with giving information. This is an inaccurate interpretation of coaching or client-centred learning. Your role as a driving instructor is to teach someone safe driving skills that they will be able to apply and develop throughout their lives. Using a client-centred learning approach ensures that you engage with them in the way that is most conducive to their learning because research shows that this kind of learning sticks. Telling people how to behave/drive does not necessarily stay with them beyond the driving test. You have to determine when it is necessary to give technical information and when it would be more effective for the learner to go away and research it. Nevertheless, when you give technical information you do need to be certain that it is comprehensive, appropriate and accurate.

Was the learner given appropriate and timely feedback during the session?

Feedback is an essential part of learning but the process must be balanced. A learner needs to have a clear picture of how they are doing, against their learning objectives, throughout the lesson. They should be encouraged when performing well and coached when a problem or learning opportunity occurs. However, a constant stream of words, however technically accurate, given at an unsuitable time may be demotivating or actually dangerous. Sitting quietly and saying nothing can also be a very powerful form of feedback in some situations.

All feedback should be relevant, positive and honest. It is not helpful if the learner is given unrealistic feedback which creates a false sense of their own ability. Where possible, feedback should not be negative. Rather than saying somebody has a weakness, consider expressing it as a learning opportunity. However, if they need to be told something is wrong or dangerous there is no point in waffling. The learner should have a realistic sense of their own performance.

Feedback is a two-way street. It should, ideally, be prompted by the learner with you responding to the learner's questions or comments. The learner's feedback should never be overlooked or disregarded.

Indications that all the elements of competence are in place could include:

- providing feedback in response to questions from the learner;
- seeking appropriate opportunities to provide feedback that reinforces understanding or confirms achievement of learning objectives;

- providing feedback about failure to achieve learning objectives that helps the learner achieve an understanding of what they need to do to improve;
- providing feedback that the learner can understand;
- providing consistent feedback that is reinforced by body language.

Indications of lack of competence include:

- providing feedback a long time after an incident so that the learner cannot link the feedback to what happened;
- providing feedback that overlooks a safety-critical incident;
- continuously providing feedback when this may be distracting the learner;
- failing to check the learner's understanding of feedback;
- providing feedback that is irrelevant to the learner's learning objectives, for example commenting on their personal appearance;
- refusing to hear reasonable feedback about your own performance.

Giving appropriate and timely feedback is about ensuring the goals agreed for the session will be met within the timescales and lesson plan already discussed. This particular competence indicator is not necessarily about dealing with faults because the overall competence is aimed at assessing your teaching and learning strategies. The use of feedback is a strategy that will enhance the learner's learning and therefore will be solution focused, taking strengths (as well as weaknesses) into consideration. In this respect, this indicator is linked to the others under this competence heading and, perhaps especially, the one about drawing on opportunities and examples to clarify learning outcomes.

Were the learner's queries followed up and answered?

Direct questions or queries from the learner should be dealt with as soon as possible. The response may involve providing information or directing the learner to a suitable source.

Remember that, wherever possible, the learner should be encouraged to discover answers themselves. However, if you do need to provide information you must ensure that the learner completely understands the information given.

Learners may not always have the confidence to ask direct questions. You should be able to pick up comments or body language that indicate uncertainty or confusion and use suitable techniques to explore possible issues.

Indications that all the elements of competence are in place could include:

- responding openly and readily to queries;
- providing helpful answers or directing the learner to suitable sources of information;
- actively checking with learners if their comments or body language suggest they may have a question;
- encouraging the learner to explore possible solutions for themselves.

Indications of lack of competence include:

- refusing to respond to queries;
- providing inaccurate information in response to queries;
- avoiding the question or denying responsibility for answering it.

With good rapport any driving lesson becomes a two-way exchange of information, ideas and opinions. If the learner is fully engaged in their learning then they may need to ask questions to check their understanding and assess their progress towards achieving their goal. It is important that you attend to their queries and ensure you are listening and remaining focused on their learning more so than your teaching. This does not mean that learners' queries should be answered immediately because sometimes this would simply not be safe or appropriate. Deflecting a question until a more appropriate time – pulled up at the side of the road – is all about you applying appropriate teaching strategies to maximize their learning. You might, for example, say, 'Good question – let's deal with this situation first and then we can discuss it in more detail when we are parked.'

Did the trainer maintain an appropriate, non-discriminatory manner throughout the session?

You should maintain an atmosphere in which the learner feels comfortable to express their opinions. You should create an open, friendly environment for learning, regardless of the learner's age, gender, sexual orientation, ethnic background, religion, physical abilities or any other irrelevant factor. This implies active respect for the learner, their values and what constitutes appropriate behaviour in their culture.

You must not display inappropriate attitudes or behaviours towards other road users and should challenge your learner if they display these behaviours.

Indications that all the elements of competence are in place could include:

- keeping a respectful distance and not invading the learner's personal space;
- asking the learner how they wish to be addressed;
- asking a disabled driver to explain what you need to know about their condition;
- adopting an appropriate position in the car;
- using language about other road users that is not derogatory and that does not invite the learner to collude with any discriminatory attitude.

Indications of lack of competence include:

- invading somebody's physical space;
- touching the learner, including trying to shake hands, unless it is necessary for safety reasons;
- using somebody's first name unless they have said that this is acceptable;
- commenting on the learner's appearance or any other personal attribute unless it has a direct impact on their ability to drive safely, such as wearing shoes that make it difficult for them to operate the vehicle's pedals.

There are two aspects to being non-discriminatory. One is ensuring that your attitude and approach to your customer is consistently non-judgemental. The other is not expressing what might be construed as judgemental views about other road users.

You might find yourself feeling frustrated or impatient with your customer because they don't seem able to grasp the skills you are teaching. Remaining non-discriminatory or non-judgemental encourages you to consider different methods of engaging with them. It might be that the teaching strategy you are using does not suit their learning preferences and therefore they are really struggling to meet your expectations. Learners are neither thick nor stupid – they simply need a different approach.

Commenting on other road users – whether the appearance of pedestrians or the way someone is driving – does little to accelerate the learner's learning or achievement of the goal set for the lesson. However, using the way someone is driving, or the potential outcomes of distraction caused by focusing on a particular type of pedestrian, as discussion points can be valid and constructive.

At the end of the session – was the learner encouraged to reflect on their own performance?

At the end of the session the learner should be encouraged to reflect on their performance and discuss their feelings. You should encourage honest self-appraisal and use client-centred techniques to highlight areas that need development if the learner has not recognized them. Once development areas have been identified the learner should be encouraged to make them part of future development.

Reflection is a necessary part of learning. Reflecting on one's own performance helps embed the learning that has taken place and determine whether or not the goal has been achieved. Reflection also develops self-evaluation skills and the ability to recognize strengths, limitations and development needs. This is crucial in ensuring your customer has the best chance of reducing their risk when driving on their own. At the end of the session you could ask your learner to name three things they were particularly pleased with in their driving and discuss these with them so that they are able to articulate what it is that pleased them about each of these three things and whether there is anything they would want to improve on and develop further. This is an ideal opportunity for your learner to consider what goals they would like to set for next lesson.

Review

In most situations you will maintain your awareness of what is going on around you, give reasonably clear and timely directions and intervene in an appropriate and timely way to ensure that no safety-critical incidents occur.

However, from time to time, situations will arise in which your actions or instruction are of such poor quality that the examiner may decide that they are putting themselves, the learner or any third party in immediate danger.

Example: the learner is approaching a closed junction. They ask the instructor whether they should stop at the 'give way' line. The instructor is completely unable to see down the joining roads but tells the learner to 'go, go, go'.

In these circumstances the examiner would be entitled to stop the lesson and mark it as an immediate fail.

07 Goal-setting and risk management

This chapter introduces the Model for Goal-Setting and Risk Management. The model can be used in all driver training and ensures that a great lesson is being delivered where learning is taking place and value for money is given. The model works for your Standards Check or Part 3 because it is a simplified representation of the Standards Check marking sheet.

A Model for Goal-Setting and Risk Management

Over- and under-instruction

Driving instructors often come back from a Standards Check or Part 3 saying the examiner commented that they had over-instructed or under-instructed. This is a difficult comment to understand if it is taken as a broad, sweeping statement. There is no such thing as over- or under-instruction on its own. The comment means that the driving instructor has used the wrong amount of instruction in a given situation or at a given time. It will boil down to the fact that either the goal was not being achieved, or the risk was not being managed because the instructor was saying too much or too little at particular points in the lesson.

If a driving instructor is accused of over-instructing, they may think that the solution is to talk less during their lessons. But you can guarantee that the instructor will then end up not giving the learner enough help where it is needed because the instructor hasn't identified where they were over-instructing. Of course, the instructor may simply talk too much throughout the lesson and this is where the model is really helpful because it helps identify how much 'talk' or 'input' is needed at each stage of the lesson in order to achieve the goal and manage the risk.

Context

Over-instruction or under-instruction can happen in two distinct areas:

- whilst helping the learner to achieve the goal;
- whilst managing the risk.

It is important to know the precise context the instructor has been over- or under-instructing in:

- Was it whilst helping the learner achieve the goal?
- Was the instructor giving full talk-through when the learner clearly needed to have a go on their own – and, in fact, had asked to have a go on their own?
- Or, did the instructor sit back and say nothing when the learner clearly needed help?
- Or, was it whilst managing the risk so that the learner could achieve the goal?

It might be that the learner has said they want to have a go on their own in terms of the goal they want to achieve, and the instructor has sat back and said nothing. This is okay but what about the risk? For example, if the goal is something to do with emerging from junctions and it has been agreed that the learner will have a go on their own and practise emerging from three or four junctions before pulling over to review progress, the instructor still needs to manage the risk. This means that if there are meeting situations on the route, for example, the instructor has to consider what support, if any, the learner needs to manage these. There is a possibility of both over- or under-instruction around the risk – in this example, meeting situations – even if the instructor sticks to the agreed level of support around the goal.

Instructor's input

To deliver a lesson that will ensure learning takes place and value for money is being given, be clear on the level of input needed. Input means, quite simply, what you need to say (or do). This is where the Model for Goal-Setting and Risk Management comes in:

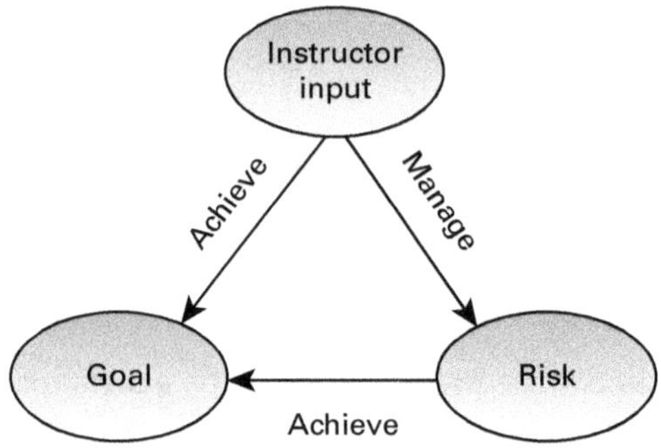

You have two opportunities for input:

- firstly, to ensure the learner achieves the goal;
- and secondly, to manage the risk, so that the learner will achieve the goal.

Let's look at each of these in turn.

Goal-setting

Going down the left-hand side of the model first, your main priority is to ensure the learner achieves the goal.

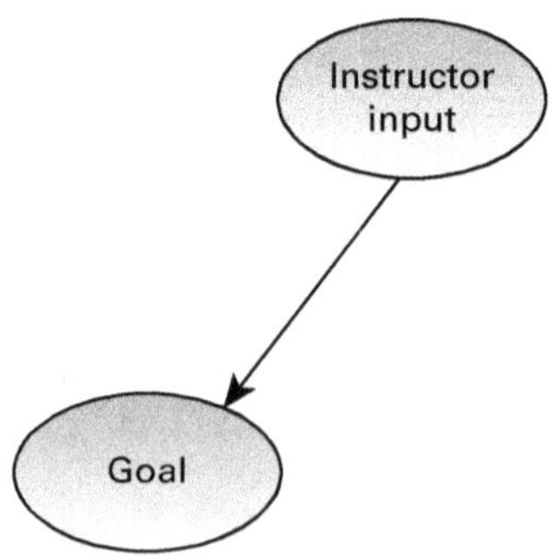

Learning takes place when people achieve goals and how well you plan the lesson will determine how effective the learning is. Lesson planning is the first heading on the Standards Check and Part 3 marking sheet and there are four competences underneath this:

- Did the trainer identify the learner's learning goals and needs?
- Was the agreed lesson structure appropriate for the learner's experience and ability?
- Were the practice areas suitable?
- Was the lesson plan adapted, when appropriate, to help the learner work towards their learning goals?

The goal for the session needs to be SMART:

- specific;
- measurable;
- achievable;
- realistic;
- timed.

It is not always practical to set the goal completely at the start of the session and you may well find that some elements of SMART fall into place later into the session. For example, the measurable, achievable, realistic and timed aspects of SMART may become apparent as you agree the lesson structure, practice areas and get the car on the move.

Here's an example.

You: *Today we're going to look at roundabouts. What would you like to focus on first?* (SPECIFIC)

Learner: *The approach to roundabouts.* (SPECIFIC)

You: *Okay and what do you want to achieve by the end of the session?* (ACHIEVABLE)

Learner: *I want to feel confident about the approach to roundabouts.* (ACHIEVABLE)

You: *So, on a scale of 0 to 10 where 0 is 'I don't feel at all confident about approaching roundabouts' and 10 is 'I am totally confident about approaching roundabouts' where are you now?* (REALISTIC)

Learner: *About a 3.* (REALISTIC)

You: *Where would you like to be by the end of the session?* (MEASURABLE)

Learner: *A 6 would be good.* (MEASURABLE)

You: *So, what is in the 3?* (REALISTIC)

Learner: *Well, I've done junctions and understand how to deal with these. I'm okay with the MSPSL on the approach to junctions – whether I'm turning into side roads or emerging. I can see that roundabouts are similar but I'm concerned about the speed on approach because I know that I should aim to keep the car moving if I can, whereas at junctions I'm more likely to come almost to a stop because the visibility is closed on the approach.* (REALISTIC)

You: *That's great. You've told me your main concern is the speed on the approach because roundabouts tend to be open and are designed to keep the flow of traffic moving. So, what help do you need from me to get you up to a 6 and how long do you want to spend on this?* (TIMED)

Learner: *If I could go and practise a few and you could just help me where you think I need it, that would be good. Could we just spend half an hour and then look at something else?* (TIMED)

You: *Okay, I have a circuit in mind. There are four roundabouts on it. We go left at the first one, straight ahead at the second, right at the third and right at the fourth, finishing back here. How about if we practise that now? I will aim to let you get on with the approach to each of these on your own because that's what we have just agreed – the goal is the approach each time. When we pull up again, we can review how you have got on and decide what to do next to improve. We will just spend half an hour on this and then move onto something else. How does that sound?*

Learner: *Great.*

The above example is somewhat contrived to make the point about SMART goals but what you notice is that a SMART goal often will address the first three bullet points in lesson planning:

- identifying the learner's goal(s);
- agreeing the structure;
- confirming suitable practice areas.

As the instructor, you are now clear on what needs to happen in terms of your 'input' once the car gets moving, to achieve the goal. The learner wants to move from a 3 to a 6 in terms of confidence about approaching roundabouts. You know that they may well struggle with the speed on approach because they have expressed this as a concern. You have selected a route with four roundabouts and the learner wants to have a go approaching these on their own.

Risk management

Now, you need to work your way down the right-hand side of the model and ensure that the risk is managed so that the learner can achieve the goal.

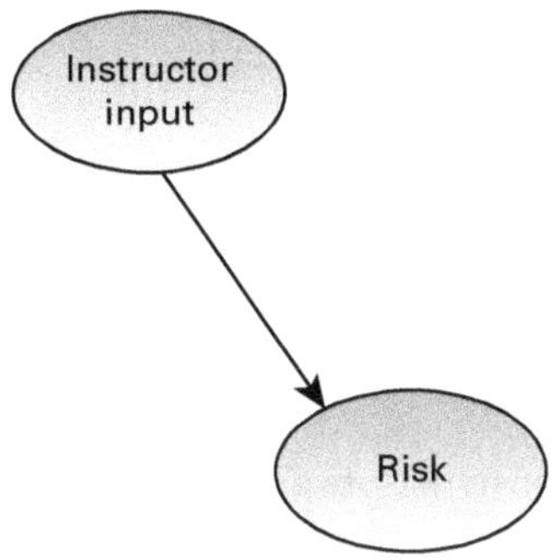

You cannot judge what input to have into the risk management until you have confirmed the goal. If the goal is too vague and not specific enough, you will not understand how to manage the risk and, therefore, the learner will not be able to achieve the goal. This is key. The model shows how the two aspects go together – goal-setting and managing the risk.

To do this, you need to visualize the route you will be driving on – the four roundabouts – and consider what else is on this route that could interfere with your learner's ability to achieve the goal. The learner's goal is to gain confidence approaching roundabouts. This will happen most effectively if you encourage the learner to experiment and work things out for themselves. In terms of the roundabouts, the learner does not need to focus on anything other than the approach and it is down to you, the instructor, to break the learning down sufficiently so that the learner can do just this. The learner might not deal with the emerge, going around or exiting of the roundabout but these are not part of the goal and it is your job to manage the risk and keep the car safe. It doesn't matter if the learner has previously been emerging, going around and exiting the roundabout on their own. It is possible that because they are focusing on the approach the rest goes to pieces. However, if it is a complete disaster and you are struggling to manage the risk and keep the car safe, you might have agreed a goal and chosen a route that is too demanding for both of you. You might need to adapt the lesson plan because the learner is not going to be able to achieve the goal and all you are doing is managing the risk, which will feel a bit like firefighting, where you are basically dealing with faults. In this situation, learning will not be taking place because of your input.

Once the goal is agreed and you both know how the learner wants to practise and learn, you need to manage the risk.

The learner wants to have a go at this on their own so that they can then evaluate their progress and determine what they need to further do each time to improve. We know that people learn best when they can experiment in a safe environment and work out for themselves what they need to do to improve. This is why you need to manage the risk to create the safe environment. Having agreed the goal, the next thing you need to state is how the responsibility for risk will be shared. This is the first competence under the heading 'risk management'. There are five competences on the marking sheet:

- Did the trainer ensure the learner fully understood how the responsibility for risk would be shared?
- Were directions and instruction given to the learner clear and given in good time?
- Was the trainer aware of the surroundings and the learner's actions?
- Was any verbal or physical intervention by the trainer timely and appropriate?
- Was sufficient feedback given to help the learner understand any potential safety-critical incidents?

You might say:

'You're going to concentrate on the goal, which is to improve your confidence in approaching roundabouts. I will let you have a go at this on your own and will step in if I need to help keep us safe. I will also help you with everything else – you know I've got the dual controls so I can use these if I need to.'

Imagine your learner is now on the circuit dealing with the four roundabouts. To manage the risk after you have made your statement about sharing responsibility, you need to be able to:

- give clear and well-timed directions and instructions;
- observe the learner and the surroundings;
- step in verbally or physically appropriately;
- give sufficient feedback for any safety-critical incidents.

If you are in any doubt about your learner's ability to deal with something safely, you will need to intervene but note that the word here is 'safely'. The learner might get it wrong and make mistakes but with you managing the risk, they will be better able to achieve the goal because they are learning from their own mistakes. In other words, you should let your learner make mistakes in a safe environment because this is how learning takes place and it is your job to create the safe environment by managing the risk.

It can be helpful to see the risk as two-fold – within the goal and outside of the goal.

Risk within the goal

Let's look at two examples.

1 You have agreed that the learner will complete four roundabouts before pulling over to review progress around the goal. The learner wants to be able to get on and have a go on their own. You have stated that you will manage the risk and help them where necessary with other things but let them get on with the approaches. The learner approaches the first roundabout too fast.

   You consider the risk and judge that the approach speed, whilst too fast, is not going to cause a problem on this occasion. It will be a great discussion point when you pull over and, if they can recognize this for themselves and take steps to prevent it from happening on the next practice, they will be well on their way to achieving the goal.

   You decide to say nothing but keep an eye on it to make sure that if the speed on the approach is too fast on the second, third or fourth roundabout and safety is in any way compromised, you will step in.

   When you pull up after the fourth roundabout, you will discuss with the learner:

   - what went well;
   - what didn't go so well; and
   - what needs improving?

2 This is all around the goal. In the 'what didn't go so well' or the 'what needs improving' part of the evaluation, the speed on the approach will come up. It doesn't matter whether you bring it up or the learner does but at this point, your input is to make sure the learner achieves an appropriate speed on the approach to the roundabouts and, therefore, goes on to achieve the goal – to grow their confidence with the approach from a 3 to a 6.

   This example is the same as previously, except that when the learner approaches the first roundabout too fast, you judge that this is a definite risk and needs managing. It is important, here, to recognize that you still need to leave the learning with the learner about how to achieve the goal. Your job is to manage the risk, so you are not aiming to get the approach speed perfect, you just want it to be safe. You might, therefore, say, 'How's your speed?'

Of course, you have other options as well. If the learner doesn't respond, or you have left it a little late, you might need a direct command, like, 'Brake, you're a bit too fast.' Your final resort is the dual brake. If you have intervened either verbally or physically, you will need to consider what the learner needs to know in order to understand the risk and why you intervened – what would have happened if you hadn't stepped in.

The second, third and fourth roundabouts will need to be prompted as far as the speed on the approach is concerned. You cannot allow the problem to occur again because, by stepping in, you judged it was safety critical. In other words, if you intervene verbally or physically, it is because an incident would have occurred otherwise. Again, you don't have to get the speed on the approach perfect. It just has to be safe.

Pull over after the circuit is completed and ask the reflective questions:

- What went well?
- What didn't go so well?
- What needs improving?

This time you need to ensure that sufficient feedback is used to help the learner understand any potential safety-critical incidents because you had to intervene to keep the car safe by telling the learner to slow down more on the approach to the first roundabout. As this is part of the goal, you would need to agree with the learner what they are going to do next time to ensure they do not need your intervention again, and also, what they need to do to get the approach speed right.

Risk outside of the goal

It is highly likely that there will be potential risk outside of the goal that needs managing. This is because you are teaching the learner to drive in a safety-critical environment where there are plenty of hazards and risks that will get in the way of the learner being able to concentrate on achieving the goal. If we could teach someone to drive in a simulator there would be minimal other risks, but we are teaching people to drive in a dangerous environment.

The goal is to do with roundabouts and there are four opportunities for the learner to practise their approach to roundabouts but what else is there that has the potential of getting in the way? Here are some examples of the kind of things that might get in the way of the learner easily being able to remain focused on the goal:

- Everything else to do with roundabouts that is not to do with the approach, such as:
  - Identifying the roundabout
  - Emerging onto the roundabout
  - Going around the roundabout
  - Exiting the roundabout
- Ordinary junctions
- Pedestrian crossings
- Meeting situations
- Changing gears smoothly
- General positioning
- Use of mirrors
- Use of signals
- Use of speed.

The final part of the model is about the teaching and learning strategies that are applied so that the goal is achieved and the risk is managed. On the Standards Check and Part 3 marking sheets there are eight competences under the heading 'teaching and learning strategies':

- Was the teaching and learning style suited to the learner's level of ability?
- Was the learner encouraged to analyse problems and take responsibility for their learning?
- Were opportunities and examples used to clarify learning outcomes?
- Was the technical information given comprehensive, appropriate and accurate?
- Was the learner given appropriate and timely feedback during the session?
- Were the learner's queries followed up and answered?
- Did the trainer maintain an appropriate non-discriminatory manner throughout the session?
- At the end of the session was the learner encouraged to reflect on their own performance?

Your own learning takes place through reflection and self-evaluation. Reflect on the model after a lesson and consider the amount of input you had in the lesson.

> Did I have enough input into the lesson so that the learner achieved the goal, and did I manage the risk sufficiently for the learner to achieve the goal?

What follow are some practical examples of how you might use the Model for Goal-Setting and Risk Management to deliver a great driving lesson where value for money is given, learning takes place and the car is kept safe. The examples are outlines and do not reflect the whole of the conversation you might have with your learner. However, they do show how the model helps you address the competences on the Standards Check and Part 3 marking sheets.

The first lesson – lesson planning

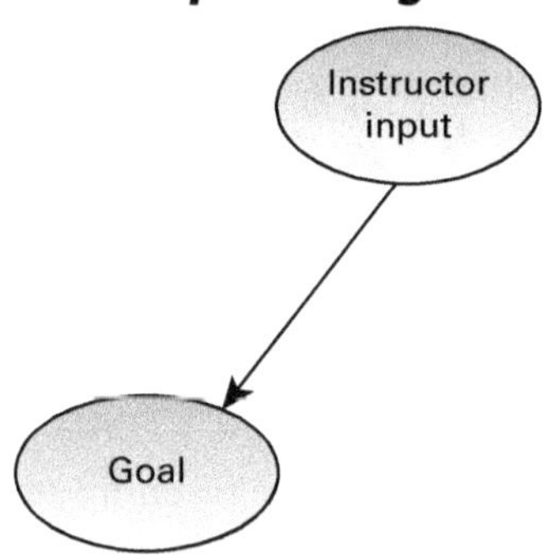

Traditionally, driving instructors have been encouraged to run through the cockpit drill and the controls of the car before the learner moves away and stops for the first time. If we apply the model to this and go down the left-hand side of the model first to see what instructor input is needed to ensure the learner achieves the goal, we can simplify the whole process.

The conversation might go like this:

Instructor: *What needs to happen today for you to feel you have really achieved something?*

This is a goal-setting question and addresses the first competence on the marking sheet – identifying the learner's learning goals and needs.

Learner: *If I could get the car moving, that would be great.*

Instructor: *And how would you like to learn this?*

This question addresses the second competence on the marking sheet – agreeing the lesson structure appropriate for the learner's experience and ability. The learner could answer this in any number of ways, and you need to be able to adapt your methods to suit the way the learner wants to learn. You also may need additional questions to prompt the learner – you won't necessarily get the answer straightaway.

Learner: *I'd like to just have a go.*

Instructor: *That's great. Do you want any help from me?*

Learner: *I'm not sure.*

You need to consider your practice area – especially as the learner wants to have a go straightaway. It needs to be a wide, straight road, ideally with very few, if any, parked cars. You also need to be aware of how you might adapt the lesson plan to help the learner work towards their learning goals. This is often about the amount of help you give, so even though the learner has said they want to have a go, you can vary the amount of help you give. You might sit in silence whilst they experiment with the controls at the start, but, as soon as they actually move the car, you might need to step in and give a lot of support and encouragement.

The first lesson – risk management

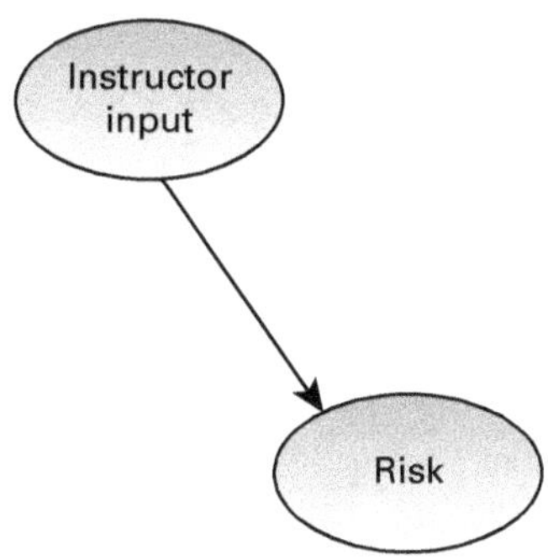

Now, you go down the right-hand side of the model to manage the risk.

Instructor: *Okay, so the goal is to move the car away and you would like to just have a go at doing this. I will support you as necessary and also I will keep you safe. I have the dual controls and I can step in at any time, so you can feel confident about that.*

This addresses the first competence under risk management. Whatever the learner doesn't do, you will do for them. For example, if they move the car away without checking their mirrors or blindspot, it is your job to make sure it is safe. If there is a car coming, you would step in and say, 'Is it safe?' or, 'Wait a moment' or, 'Fraction clutch down.'

The first lesson – teaching and learning strategies

This is where the model closes and the input you need is around ensuring the learner achieves the goal by utilizing the teaching and learning strategies.

Imagine the learner has had their first go and you and they are beaming with excitement. They are really pleased with their achievement and you have discussed all the things that went well. You know, however, that they did not take effective observation before moving away, and you judge that they would be able to do this next time.

Instructor: *You're going to have another go at this. This time, I would like you to include some observations so that you can decide if it is safe to move off, and then, if it is safe to pull in.*

You have just set a mini goal and could imagine yourself going down the left-hand side of the model again. You could ask the learner how they would like to learn this and, again, be prepared to adapt the way you teach to suit the way they learn. This meets the first competence under the heading 'teaching and learning strategies': Was the teaching style suited to the learner's learning style and current ability? There are a number of options you could consider:

- Explain when and where to look, including discussing M S M.
- Show a diagram whilst you are explaining.
- Ask the learner to draw a car and identify where they think they should look and when.
- Swap seats and demonstrate when and where to look – make sure the learner knows to watch your head and eye movements.
- Talk the learner through as they have a go for the first time.
- Let the learner move away again and work it out for themselves – be careful with this one, because there is no point in the learner doing exactly what they did the first time they had a go, ie, not check their mirrors nor their blindspot. You would have to be prepared to risk manage this and step in if the learner is going to miss something.

What about the cockpit drill and the controls?

If you use the model and think about the goal and the risk, you can start to see where everything else fits. Much of the information that would be in a traditional first driving lesson is not needed in a client-centred lesson where the focus is on the goal that needs achieving, whilst you manage the risk. And this information can be added as and when it is necessary as the lessons progress.

If the learner's seat is clearly not set up correctly for them, you can decide when to deal with this by considering how likely the learner is to achieve their goal. For example, if they are stretching for the pedals but can reach them, it might be good for them to move away and stop and, during the feedback, realize that their seat needs adjusting. If they need an explanation of what to look for when adjusting their seat, this would be a good time to give it.

If they don't put their seatbelt on, you would need to remind them to do so as part of managing the risk. It is illegal to drive without wearing a seatbelt, unless exempt, and therefore, the goal could not be achieved.

Most people have grown up watching other people drive and they have a good idea of what the controls are called and what they do. However, if someone needs this kind of input from the start then there is nothing wrong with that. The important thing to remember is that everyone learns differently, and your job is to adapt the way you teach to meet each individual's needs. Using the model helps you do this, in terms of understanding what your input needs to be.

Left and right turns major to minor

Let's start this example by making some assumptions about the type of junctions you are going to be teaching and the learner's development around these junctions.

In order to teach moving off and stopping, and then to go on to teach gear changes, it is possible that you have needed to turn left already. So, pick a circuit of left turns that will take you around the block and allow you to pull up in the same place each time, whilst you are practising gear changes. If the goal was to do with gear changes (left-hand side of the model), then your input around these junctions would have come under risk management (right-hand side of the model).

As soon as the learner has practised moving off and stopping, and changing gears a few times, they can focus on left turns. This shifts the left turns to the left-hand side of the model where there is a focus on the goal. Moving off and stopping, gear changes and emerging left all come under risk management (right-hand side of the model). The conversation might go like this:

Instructor: *Now that you have practised moving off and stopping and then some gear changes, we are going to focus on turning left. Did you notice that we were doing some left turns whilst you were practising changing gear?*

Learner: *Yes, I did notice. I found it really awkward to steer – I didn't know when to steer or how much.*

Instructor: *So, would you like to make that your new goal? To learn to judge when to steer and how much?*

Learner: *Yes, that would be good.*

Instructor: *Great! How would you like to learn this?*

Learner: *Could I just have a go again?*

Instructor: *Absolutely, you can. So, first of all let's see what you noticed about turning left apart from the steering.*

It's worth noting here that the instructor has decided to intervene in the learner's desired structure of the session. There is no point in them just having a go because they have already been having a go whilst practising gear changes. Here, you, the instructor, could get out a diagram and discuss the approach to the corner, showing the learner when they changed gear as part of a structured approach. This would give a new context to the gear change – to prepare for a left turn. You could also tell the learner about the MSPSL sequence on the approach. However, remember that the learner's goal is to judge when and how much to steer. The rest of the left turn comes under risk management for the time being and is therefore your responsibility.

You need to let the learner know about the practice area. It is always best to 'chunk' your lessons. In other words, allow the learner to complete three or four left turns in one circuit, each time focusing on the timing and amount of steering.

Imagine the learner is now driving around the agreed circuit of left turns. It is important that you keep the goal in mind – to learn how to judge when to steer and how much. This is the most important part of this exercise. It is your job to manage the risk on the approach to the left turn and afterwards. Be careful not to overload the learner. It doesn't matter if they do not check their mirrors or give a signal – you can use your understanding of levels of instruction to talk this part through or prompt it. However, if you feel it is too much for your learner to process, just be encouraging. You might say something like this:

> *'Take the next road on the left. It's safe so give a signal. Start to brake. Brake more. (Now steer. Now steer back.)'*

Notice in the example above that the instructor chooses to leave out the mirrors and the position parts of the MSPSL routine. This is because the instructor manages the risk here and has checked their mirror before saying, *'It's safe so give a signal.'* Equally, the position is okay and therefore does not need mentioning. However, to achieve the goal, the learner is likely to need help with the speed. On this first practice, where the focus is on the timing and amount of steering needed to get around the corner, it is probably a good idea to just have the learner change into second gear and stay in this gear.

The learner said they would like to have a go on their own at the steering so you would judge whether the instructions in brackets are needed to keep the car safe. *How* the learner steers does not matter because this will be addressed in feedback around the goal once the agreed practice area has been completed.

Now imagine that the learner has pulled up, as agreed, after completing three or four left turns. You have assessed their steering and know exactly what they need to do to improve it. Your job now is to use your questioning skills around feedback to help the learner identify what they need to do to improve next time they go around. In other words, you are working with the learner to set another mini goal. The conversation might go like this:

Instructor: *Okay, so what was the goal?*

Learner: *I was focusing on when and how much to steer.*

Instructor: *Great. How do you think that went?*

Learner: *(Laughing) It was a bit of a shambles and I was all over the place.*

Instructor: *(Also laughing) What were you pleased about?*

Learner: *I loved the whole feel of it! I think the speed was okay but I just couldn't get my hands moving quickly enough.*

Instructor: *That's great that you loved the feel of it and that you think the speed was okay – I agree. So, let's focus on your hands. What stopped you from moving your hands quickly enough?*

Learner: *I'm not sure.*

Instructor: *Do you think it's about moving your hands more quickly and making shuffling movements around the wheel – or, do you think you could make bigger movements with the wheel?*

Learner: *The idea of letting go of the wheel to make bigger movements scares me.*

Instructor: *So, how about if you just slid your hands around the wheel without losing contact and tried to make bigger turns on the wheel? When we go and practise this, I will remind you. How did you feel about the timing of the steering – in other words, did you know when to start steering and when to start steering back?*

Learner: *I think I can improve on this, but felt it was okay.*

Instructor: *Okay, so let's go round again and you are still focusing on the timing and amount of steering as your goal. In particular, notice when you start to steer and when you start to straighten up. Also, I am going to prompt you to slide your hands around the wheel. As before, I will keep the car safe in every other respect.*

In this conversation, the instructor stays focused on the goal. This makes the lesson so much easier because both you and the learner are totally clear on what each of you needs to do to ensure the learner achieves the goal. You are clear on your job of managing the risk. And, most importantly, learning is taking place. You might end up going around this block of left turns several times and after each lap pulling up at the side of the road and eliciting the feedback from the learner.

You will also understand how to adapt the lesson plan to help the learner achieve the goal (the fourth competence under 'lesson planning'). This might mean you can introduce more of the MSPSL routine and encourage the learner to take greater responsibility for each part of the routine, whilst still focusing on the goal. You also can vary the approach by getting the learner to change up into third gear and then back down into second on the approach to the corner.

At some point, you will decide it is time to set another goal, around right turns major to minor. The learner is still developing the same skills but transferring them to a slightly different situation. The decision about when to move the learner onto another goal is based on the conversation you had at the start of the session when you set a SMART goal and asked the learner how much time they wanted to spend on this. The learner may have said they only want to spend 15 minutes on left turns.

The more you are able to visualize the Model for Goal-Setting and Risk Management, the more you will find it straightforward to address the 17 competences on the Standards Check and Part 3 marking sheets.

Dual carriageways

In this final example, let's take a look at how the Model for Goal-Setting and Risk Management can be applied to a lesson on dual carriageways.

Regardless of whether you have decided to set the topic, or the learner has chosen this topic, you will still need to have a conversation where you go down the left-hand side of the model to discuss the lesson planning aspect; and then down the right-hand side of the model to address the risk management.

If it is the first time you are teaching dual carriageways to the learner, you will probably find it best to start with joining and leaving a dual carriageway. (The learner may have driven on dual carriageways before but perhaps you were just giving them a chance to drive at speed and were helping them all the way). The conversation might go like this:

Instructor: *So, today we are going to look at dual carriageways. We will start by focusing on joining and leaving a dual carriageway. What would you like to achieve by the end of this session?*

Learner: *I want to be able to understand how to join and leave a dual carriageway and have a chance to practise this.*

Instructor: *Great. How would you like to do this?*

At this point, the learner could say any number of things (with or without you prompting them). They might want to listen to you explaining how to join and leave a dual carriageway, or look at some diagrams, or have you demonstrate joining and leaving, or dive straight in and have a go. This part of the conversation addresses two of the 17 competences:

Lesson planning: Was the agreed lesson structure appropriate for the learner's experience and ability?

Teaching and learning strategies: Was the teaching and learning style suitable for the learner's level of ability?

When it comes to the third competence under 'lesson planning' – Were the practice areas suitable? – you will need to choose a route that allows the learner to join and leave a dual carriageway two or three times in a circuit. This means you cannot have huge lengths of dual carriageway in between junctions. Choose a route where you can join a dual carriageway, drive for a short distance (ideally no more than a mile), leave the dual carriageway, re-join immediately, drive back the same stretch and leave again, and pull in and park to discuss.

Remember, that the goal focuses on joining and leaving, so any conversation on the move needs to help the learner prepare for the next part of the goal – either to join or leave. In the meantime, you are managing the risk for everything else, so if there is a need to overtake or change lanes, be prepared to talk the learner through this.

The fourth competence under 'lesson planning' is: Was the lesson plan adapted when appropriate to help the learner work towards their learning goals? This means you need to constantly assess whether learning is taking place and the learner is going to achieve their goal. For example, if the learner is struggling to match their speed to the speed of the traffic on the carriageway, whilst accelerating on the slip road, you may need to step in and give them some full instruction. Equally, this competence means that if the learner has done everything really well, you will need to move the goal post further away.

For example, you might say, '*You are doing this really well. I have still been giving you some support, so next time we go around, imagine I am not here. Let's say, you have passed your driving test and are going to a friend's house for the first time on your own. Of course, I will still keep the car safe and step in with the dual controls if necessary. However, I want you to try this as if you were completely on your own.*'

Creating a scenario like this for the learner helps you assess to what extent learning is taking place. The learner is encouraged to take responsibility for the driving task. It doesn't matter if they make mistakes (so long as it is safe, of course) – what matters is that the learner is experiencing what it would be like driving on their own once they have passed their test. This gives the learner a real sense of achievement.

Applying the Model for Goal-Setting and Risk Management to all driving lessons

In summary, the model is a simple way of ensuring you are delivering great driving lessons every time and, in doing so, you will be developing your knowledge and understanding of the 17 competences that make up a great driving lesson. Remember, a great driving lesson is one where:

- Learning takes place
- Value for money is given
- The car is kept safe.

08 Professional development

After passing the exams and qualifying as an ADI, the only continuing check on your professional ability is the Standards Check conducted at intervals by the DVSA. This periodic test is an assessment of your ability to deliver a lesson to a specific learner on the specified date. In other words, it's only a snapshot of your overall ability as a professional trainer.

Within this regime many of the other skills required to offer an efficient service to the public and to run a small business effectively and legally are not formally tested or monitored in any way. For example, customer care skills and business administration are generally not part of an instructor's initial training. This leads to a situation where many instructors feel that the only ongoing training they should concern themselves with is in preparation for their periodic Standards Check. This is clearly not how it should be. To be an effective all-round professional driver trainer and to keep up to date with modern methods of coaching and business skills, you need to continually maintain and develop various areas of skill and knowledge.

As part of your Continuing Professional Development (CPD) you should be regularly:

- improving your instructional/coaching skills to deal with learners and trainees at all levels;
- improving your driving skills by taking regular courses or exams such as the Cardington special test (for details, see page 257);
- using your driving skills to full advantage by keeping an open mind and not being dogmatic about trends in terms of lane discipline (for progress), signalling, steering, fuel economy and environmental issues;
- improving your customer care skills and your business skills, including legal issues, cash flow, insurance responsibilities and public liability.

CPD has been described formally as specific and planned activities that serve to enhance our performance in our work role; that is, how we:

- carry out our job;
- manage our related administrative and business responsibilities;
- deal with others to whom our job relates, including particularly our employees and customers.

You should have your own complaints procedure and give customers the opportunity to use it first.

If the person remains dissatisfied after completing your complaints process, direct them to www.gov.uk/complain-about-a-driving-instructor.

You must follow the ADI Code of Conduct. If your behaviour falls below the standards set out in the Code, DVSA may take action against your instructor registration.

CPD can be both formal and informal professional development, based on the individual person's needs.

To maximize your individual potential, it is important that you maintain a high level of professional competence. You can get involved in CPD in various ways, for example by:

- updating your practical coaching or driving skills;
- attending local or national seminars;
- spending time in developing your business skills;
- networking with other instructors and local business people.

Benefits of CPD

An effective programme of CPD will enhance your job satisfaction, improve your overall performance and maintain or improve your credibility within the profession.

Many instructors are perfectly happy to devote their careers to teaching learner drivers, while others feel that they need to broaden their work to give themselves a wider range of customers. Either way, there is a need for all of us to continually look for ways of developing and improving our instructing and coaching skills and level of professionalism. After all, 'Nothing stays the same forever – it either gets better or it gets worse.' It means that you can't afford to stand still – if you think you are standing still, you will in fact be going backwards!

If you are looking for more variety in your work you could think of developing your practical teaching skills in order not only to improve your levels of driving and instruction, but also to expand your potential market. This applies even if your work is entirely related to teaching learners. Because the driving school market has traditionally focused on the training of learners in preparation for the driving test, many ADIs allow themselves to be limited by this – even to the extent of feeling that anything outside the learner driver market is, by definition, not for them. Instructors in this category are often reluctant to work within a group or to cooperate with other instructors, preferring to do their own thing, remaining completely independent in their own working environment. Many do not even join any of the professional associations. It is probable that one of the reasons this type of person chose to be an instructor in the first place was that they preferred to work alone, at their own pace and in their own way.

This approach may have been acceptable in the past, but nowadays it is not realistic. To be an effective instructor, there is a need to develop all of the required skills, but in particular those relating to instructional and coaching ability – and not forgetting the importance of business skills and your own driving skills.

The general trend in most other professions is for CPD to be much more widely undertaken and indeed is an expectation for most people. For example, in the road transport industry there is a requirement for all lorry drivers to take a minimum amount of refresher training every few years and to hold a Certificate of Competence alongside their vocational driving licence.

There is clearly a need for more development for instructors but, as always, it is uncertain how any CPD courses or initiatives will be funded because it is extremely unlikely that the majority of instructors will take training or extra qualifications unless they are obliged to, or are motivated in some way. Nevertheless, it can be shown that CPD is now even more important in a world that is very competitive.

Providers of CPD training are encouraged to focus on the range of topics covered in the 'driver trainer competence framework' (for details see below). It is for you to decide what type of CPD to take and which training provider to use.

CPD usually has a cost attached to it, although some courses may be available through grants. If you are self-employed you may find that at least some of the cost could be off-set against tax, but always check with your accountant or your local tax office.

Your CPD should always be compatible with the items outlined in the framework.

Driver trainer competence framework

Monitoring and assessment

- Evaluation of road and traffic conditions to drive the trainee's actions
- Supervision of trainee's driving
- Directing trainee in specific actions and manoeuvres
- Monitoring of trainee's progress
- Provision of feedback to trainee
- Recording of trainee's achievement
- Supervision of trainee through assessment
- Directing trainee's future development and training

Strategy and planning

- Lesson delivery
- Instructor development

Instruction delivery

- Demonstration of driving skills and methods
- Coaching of driving skills and methods

Driving knowledge

- Road and traffic knowledge
- Vehicle knowledge

Driving skills

- Vehicle handling ability
- Awareness of driving situation

Driving abilities

- Sensory perception
- Cognitive abilities
- Physical movement and coordination

Communication skills

- Appropriateness
- Watching
- Speaking
- Listening
- Writing and drawing
- Non-verbal communication
- Special needs training

Personal characteristics

- Attitude
- Awareness
- Instruction

Business practice

- Monitoring and controlling resources
- Record keeping
- Health and safety, welfare
- Relationships with trainees, customers and the general public

Business development

- Sales and marketing
- Staff recruitment
- Vehicle selection

In their advice to instructors the DVSA suggests that you can take CPD in different ways, such as:

- updating your teaching or driving skills
- attending local or national meetings or seminars
- researching new vehicles for your business
- spending time developing your business skills
- going on formal courses
- spending time on the internet carrying out research
- networking with other driver trainers

The documentation includes a 'development plan' covering the following areas:

- What do you want to learn/develop?
- Which competencies does it relate to?
- Who will you need to contact to achieve this?
- Target dates for review and/or completion.

By carrying out at least seven hours of CPD your commitment can be highlighted to learner drivers using the 'find your nearest driving instructor' service offered by the DVSA. Through this database, which is part of the DVSA's integrated register of driver trainers, prospective learners can access details of their local ADIs and see at a glance whether someone has signed up for CPD. Being involved with CPD shows the potential learner that you are being professional and are keeping up to date.

Note: The situation is slightly different in Northern Ireland. You can still take CPD, but you can't register your commitment to it.

Any properly prepared programme of CPD should include an element of business and customer care skills as well as the personal and instructional skills that were discussed in previous chapters.

Business skills and customer care

Both sets of skills can be important elements in your programme of CPD, as they can enhance your business and maintain professionalism and credibility with your customers.

Business skills

Financial management and planning

- Keeping proper business records
- Organizing budgets and cash flow
- Overheads
- Holidays and sickness
- Pension planning
- Financing assets

Business administration

- Bookkeeping and accounts
- Income tax and National Insurance
- VAT
- Banking

Insurance

- Vehicle, premises, personal and public liabilities
- Professional indemnity

Legal responsibilities

- Health and safety matters
- Equal opportunities

Sales and marketing

- Lesson pricing
- Advertising

Customer care skills

- Dealing with enquiries
- New customers
- Follow-up procedures
- Personal contact

Customer services

- Customer records
- Feedback
- Communication
- Handling complaints

There are several useful books on running a small business, including *Start Up and Run Your Own Business* by Jonathan Reuvid, published by Kogan Page. For details of this and other books, see Appendix 2.

Customer care

Customer care is an important element of CPD for anyone running their own business or franchise and training for it can be used as a legitimate element of qualification for CPD.

Customers (and, more importantly, potential customers) have a great deal of freedom of choice between suppliers – particularly in the service industry. Furthermore, their expectations of efficient service are greater than previously. Your instruction skills may be top-grade, but if you let your customers down in any way your business and your reputation will suffer.

As well as offering good-quality instruction, think of other areas of your business – personal appearance, punctuality and timekeeping during lessons. Avoid short-changing the learner: give a little extra rather than a little less time.

Customers' expectations – quite rightly – include:

Efficiency. Be on time for all lesson appointments. A wait of two to three minutes can seem a long time to a waiting learner – five minutes is unacceptable.

Honesty. Carry out your business and instruction honestly and professionally, but tactfully.

Politeness. Maintain the instructor–learner relationship in a friendly, but not overfamiliar manner.

Respect. The learner can rightly expect to be treated as an individual person, and does not want to be patronized or treated dismissively.

Dress code. You are not necessarily expected to wear formal clothing or a traditional business suit, but at least you should be neat, clean and tidy – whatever style of dress you choose.

Be professional, but at the same time be friendly and approachable.

Handling complaints

Complaints from customers can be dealt with in a positive manner. The important issue is to try to ensure that any minor problems are tackled before they become major problems.

Your complaints procedure should be clear, stating that in the first instance clients should approach you with their grievance. If you cannot come to an amicable agreement, clients should be advised to refer to the DVSA to consider and give advice on the matter. See www.gov.uk/complain-about-a-driving-instructor.

You – or your franchiser – should have an effective procedure in place for dealing with complaints. Dealing with complaints properly and fairly can help to maintain good customer relations. The important thing, though, is to try to deal with minor queries before they turn into complaints.

To keep up to date with CPD it is worth joining a local and/or national association to keep fully informed on developments in the industry. All national ADI organizations offer CPD courses.

ADI national organizations

Approved Driving Instructors National Joint Council (ADINJC)

The ADINJC (Approved Driving Instructors National Council) is the leading association of its kind, established in 1973 by a body of driving instructors who set out to create a supportive space for ADIs and PDIs. A not-for-profit association, the ADINJC unites driving instructors, local associations and businesses and presents our collective voices and views to the DVSA and other relevant bodies.

Freephone enquiry line: 0800 8202 444

Email: Secretary@adinjc.org.uk

Driving Instructors Association (DIA)

Formed in 1978, the Driving Instructors Association (DIA) is the UK's largest membership body for driver and rider trainers, representing over 10,000 working members delivering training across every licence and vehicle class – from trainee instructors to experienced ADIs, Fleet and Rider Trainers.

DIA is a professional membership body, with a full-time team able to prioritize delivering quality services and support to its membership, without being distracted or conflicted by operating our own driving school.

Telephone: 020 8686 8010

Email: help@driving.org

Motor Schools Association of GB (MSA)

The Motor Schools Association was formed in 1935, about the time the driving test was introduced. Full membership is available only to fully qualified ADIs, but trainee instructors may join as temporary members. The Association's main aims are:

- to represent members at all levels of government;
- to provide services that will be of benefit to members;
- to set standards of professional and ethical behaviour for professional driver trainers.

The MSA offers a wide range of services, including professional indemnity insurance, a monthly newsletter, vehicle equipment and special discounts on trainer-related products and services.

Membership enquiries: 01787 221020

www.msagb.com

Email: info@mssagb.com

Local associations

As well as joining one (or more) of the national associations, you should consider getting involved with your local association. This is a good way of keeping up to date with what is happening in your local area and of networking with other instructors, both of which can be part of a programme of CPD.

For details of local associations, check in your test centre or contact one of the main national associations who will be able to provide details.

Driving standards

Each year about 2,000 people are killed on our roads. Over the past 15 years or so the figure has been reduced from about 5,000 and the government has indicated its intention to reduce it by a further 40 per cent over the next few years.

As part of the government strategy, there is a commitment to a programme of improvements in driver training and testing. These measures include:

- Instilling in young people the correct attitudes to safe driving by providing presentations in schools and to youth associations.

- Encouraging learner drivers to take a more structured approach to learning and by emphasizing the need for it as a lifetime skill, not just a means of passing the test. The main focus of this is on the introduction of the Driver's Record.
- Raising the standard of driver training offered by instructors through improvements to the ADI exams and the periodic Standards Check.
- Focusing on the immediate post-test period for newly qualified drivers. This has been partly addressed by encouraging a greater awareness of the 'Pass Plus' scheme. Over the past four or five years the take-up for these courses has increased from 7 per cent to around 14 per cent.
- An enhancement of the various advanced motoring qualifications. The DVSA has recently agreed national minimum standards with the organizations that offer advanced tests. These tests are now regularly monitored by the DVSA to ensure that the standards are maintained.

Advanced driving tests

To make sure that your own driving skills are up to date, consider taking one (or more!) of the advanced driving tests that are widely available.

Special Cardington Driving Test

The Cardington test is specially designed and operated by the DVSA for ADIs who – as part of their ongoing CPD – want to demonstrate that they have a high standard of driving competency.

The test is conducted in your own car and is carried out by a specially trained staff member at the DVSA Training and Development Centre at Cardington, Bedfordshire. It involves about 90 minutes of practical driving on all types of road, including motorways, and in a variety of traffic conditions. To pass the test, you have to show a positive, courteous attitude and the ability to control the position and speed of the vehicle safely, systematically and smoothly. In particular you are assessed on your:

- expert handling of the controls;
- use of correct road position;
- anticipation of the actions of other road users and taking appropriate action;
- sound judgement of distance, speed and timing;
- consideration for the convenience and safety of other road users.

There is no element of theory testing and a commentary drive is not required.

More detail about the Cardington test is available from the DVSA on 0300 200 1122 or at www.gov.uk/dvsa-special-tests-for-instructors

Institute of Advanced Motorists (IAM)

The IAM's advanced driving test has been operating since 1956 using Metropolitan Police principles of advanced driving.

You can take the test at various locations around the country. It lasts about 90 minutes and usually covers 30 to 40 miles on all types of road, including motorways if available.

The examiners are holders of the Police Advanced Drivers certificate and all have considerable experience in police driving methods. IAM examiners are not looking for driving faults alone; they are trained to check for positive aspects of the driving as well as any negative points.

For more information, contact the IAM on 0300 303 1134 or at www.iamroadsmart.com

Royal Society for the Prevention of Accidents (RoSPA)

The RoSPA Advanced Driving Test normally lasts about 1¼ hours and is based on the principles in *Roadcraft*, the Police Driver's Manual. RoSPA advanced tests are conducted at locations throughout the UK.

One unique feature of this test is that there is a grading system. At the end of the test the examiner discusses any points that have arisen and allocates a grade according to the overall driving performance of the candidate.

Application forms and further details about the test can be obtained from RoSPA on 021 248 2046 or at www.rospa.com

During advanced driving courses, and in preparation for a test, you should develop a better understanding of some of the issues relating to driving, such as:

- the importance of fatigue – we all tend to use the roads for much longer periods;
- fuel economy driving – to lessen the impact of our use of world resources;
- the different types of fuel available;
- the growing importance of 'dual-fuel' vehicles.

In our approach to our personal skills, and when teaching our learners to drive, we need to be much more flexible in today's road and traffic conditions, especially in terms of:

- lane selection;

- selective signalling;
- roundabout procedures;
- right-turn positioning;
- use of steering;
- appropriate use of gears;
- other procedures that might have been regarded as correct when we took our own driving test, but which we now must reconsider in relation to the current conditions on the roads.

Taking one of the advanced tests will not necessarily provide all the answers, but your preparation for it will provoke and stimulate you into possibly re-evaluating your style of driving.

Driving instructor training

After you have gained some experience as an ADI, have regularly achieved a good Standards Check grading and have a consistently high success rate in the driving test, you might consider becoming a tutor or trainer of instructors. This could be as part of your ongoing CPD or supplementary to your ADI work. To prepare for this change, you will need to:

- have a thorough knowledge of the syllabus for the ADI theory and hazard perception test and be able to provide your students with the relevant study materials and necessary support;
- always drive to a consistently high standard;
- have a thorough knowledge and understanding of the official syllabus for learning to drive and of the ADI Part 3 syllabus;
- be able to deliver appropriate practical training;
- adapt your practical teaching skills to suit drivers who will have much more experience than learners;
- be competent in the skills required to train people to teach, including coaching skills;
- acquire and develop your role-play skills;
- undertake training with a specialist organization.

While preparing for your own ADI exams, you should have become fully aware of the in-depth knowledge required for the theory test and the high standard of personal driving skills required for the Part 2 test. However, training to instruct is very different from teaching people to drive. You will need to develop more of your practical teaching skills to progress into the field of instructor training.

Some of the skills discussed in previous chapters will certainly be beneficial, but one of the most important parts of the tutor's job is having the ability to stimulate and motivate trainees with varying aptitudes, attitudes and personalities. Role play takes up a large percentage of the time spent in training new instructors and you will need to develop this skill so that your simulation of the learner driver becomes credible.

Before making the decision to take a course in the tutoring of ADIs, you should already be able to confidently and effectively apply all the essential practical teaching skills in your everyday work with learners. Prior to committing yourself and embarking on this more challenging aspect of the driving instruction world, you should seek advice and assessment from a recognized tutor. You will find a list of specialized training establishments in ORDIT – the Official Register of Driving Instructor Training – on the DVSA's website (www.gov.uk/guidance/become-a-driving-instructor-ordit-trainer).

Driving instructor qualifications

Pearson SRF BTEC level 4 Professional Award in Coaching for Driver Development

The course consists of four one-day classroom sessions backed up by a self-development project or assignment. There is also a one-day in-car session.

City and Guilds

Various courses and qualifications are available including:

- introduction to trainer skills;
- personal and professional development qualification; and
- learning and development.

For more detail contact City and Guilds on 0207 294 2468 or at www.cityandguilds.com, email: general.enquiries@cityandguilds.com

Royal Society for the Prevention of Accidents (RoSPA)

Advanced Driving Instructor Diploma.

A five-day course for ADIs to 'reach the next level'.

For more detail contact RoSPA on 0844 543 0033 or www.rospa.com

Business opportunities

Various business opportunities are available to supplement your learner driver training, and which can be regarded as part of your ongoing professional development.

Although most driving instructors concentrate solely on teaching learner drivers, there are many other opportunities for increasing your scope of work. As well as adding variety to your daily work in driver training, these other activities will offer the opportunity for additional revenue and income streams for your business.

Some of the areas you might consider include:

- pre-driver training;
- Pass Plus training;
- learning materials;
- training for people who have a disability;
- defensive and advanced driver training;
- taxi driver assessment;
- company and fleet driver training;
- light van driver training;
- trailer and caravan towing;
- assessments for older drivers;
- driver training schemes for local authorities;
- speed awareness courses;
- corrective and driver rehabilitation courses.

Which (if any) of these you decide to offer will depend on your individual interests, experience, qualifications or expertise.

Pre-driver training

If you have access to any off-road facility such as a large private car park, school grounds or a disused airfield, you may be able to offer pre-driver training for under-17s. Training would normally be more cost-effective for groups of learners rather than one-to-one instruction, so target your local youth groups and schools – through the head teacher or direct with the education authority. If you have a local road safety group, it would be worthwhile liaising with them for course content and for marketing or promotion purposes. It is often beneficial to work with one or more other instructors in your area and to organize the course as part theory and part practical. This has the added benefit of working on attitudes in addition to practical vehicle control skills at an early age. Even if you only have a relatively small training area available, it is still possible to organize the course programme with an emphasis on lower-speed manoeuvring.

Training for people who have a disability

Teaching learners who have a disability can be extremely rewarding. They are usually very motivated and keen to gain independence with their driving. Training courses for instructors are available at www.drivingmobility.org.uk and www.disabilitydrivinginstructors.com. A three-day course for instructors costs £450 plus VAT and covers the skills needed to teach people to drive, including:

- disability awareness
- considering physical conditions
- effects of cognitive impairments
- medical conditions
- teaching techniques – physical disabilities, learning difficulties, hearing impairment
- car controls
- visual problems and testing vision
- wheelchair seating, loading, management and stowage
- driving tests and licences
- information services
- interaction with volunteers with differing disabilities.

Disabilities and impairments are dealt with in detail in *The Driving Instructor's Handbook*.

Intensive 'L' driver course

Offering intensive courses can be a useful way of generating business – particularly if you are based in an area that people would like to visit.

Before considering this business opportunity, you need to be aware of a few important points:

- If you offer a one-week intensive course with the practical driving test on the final day, the learner must have already passed the theory test.
- The customer should be made aware that they may not be ready to take the test – in which case, the driving test fee would be lost. What is your policy on refunds?
- Full payment should be taken in advance as you will not want to risk having an empty diary for the whole week.
- Intensive courses are, by their nature, hard work for both the learner and the instructor. Not everyone responds to them effectively – many learners would be better off with a less concentrated programme of training consisting of two or three hours of instruction each day over a longer period.
- Intensive or concentrated courses involve having the same customer with you for an extended period – possibly all day, every day for a week or more. You will need to deal with this situation – even with a client who you do not particularly like, or who may have personal hygiene problems.

Pass Plus

If you are going to offer Pass Plus as an extra course of post-test training, make sure that you educate your learners (and their parents) at an early stage. There is little point in introducing the subject once the learner has passed the driving test. Make it clear from the start of the training that Pass Plus is regarded as an important and integral part of the whole process of learning to drive.

Pass Plus was originally set up by the DVSA to encourage new drivers to take further training rather than regarding the driving test as the end of the learning process. The intention was (and still is) for the learner to be trained in a wider range of road and traffic conditions than those that are tested in the ordinary driving test. The course builds on the learner's existing skills and knowledge and so should be tailored to individual requirements. Although there is no exam at the end of the course, the learner is assessed by the instructor in each of the modules and must reach an acceptable standard.

Learners can be encouraged to take the extra training by making sure that they realize the benefit of the extra training and the financial benefit of substantial discounts that many insurance companies offer.

Anyone who holds a full UK licence can take part, but it is usual for learners to take the course shortly after passing the driving test. By doing this, the new driver can qualify for the special insurance rates.

Your fees for Pass Plus should be more than your normal hourly rate. This is because you will be using more fuel, travelling longer distances and will have an element of office work and DVSA fees to cover. As well as this, there is the probability that the night driving element of the course will involve out-of-hours work.

Pass Plus Syllabus

- town driving
- all-weather driving
- driving out of town
- night driving
- dual carriageways
- motorways

The course takes a minimum of six hours, but more sessions might be needed for some learners to attain a satisfactory standard.

For details of the complete syllabus for Pass Plus, see *The Driving Instructor's Handbook*.

The Pass Plus course can be taken at any time up to 12 months after passing the practical 'L' test and any insurance discount can be deferred for a further two years if the new driver is driving on another person's insurance.

Although the number of drivers taking Pass Plus is gradually increasing, it is still a market where a minority of instructors take advantage of the potential for extra business.

Instructors who are actively involved and are successful emphasize the need to:

- mention Pass Plus and the benefits when learners first enquire about lessons;

- involve parents at an early stage, getting them to understand the added reassurance that Pass Plus offers;
- remind learners about the scheme before and after they take the 'L' test;
- inform learners and parents of the statistics of newly qualified drivers being involved in a disproportional number of accidents.

To register as a Pass Plus instructor, you need to apply to the DVSA (www.gov.uk/pass-plus) for a starter pack.

Vocational driver training

If you have held the appropriate driving licence for a minimum period of three years and if you have sufficient expertise or experience, there are several areas of vocational training for widening the scope of your business.

Minibuses

Anyone who held a full driving licence before 1 January 1997 has entitlement to drive minibuses with up to 16 passenger seats if the vehicle is not used for hire or reward. Drivers who have passed their 'L' test since January 1997 can drive vehicles with up to eight passenger seats. Many minibuses belonging to schools, youth groups and community groups have vehicles with more seats and these can all be potential customers. Instruction can usually be carried out in the customer's own vehicle but be particularly careful of any insurance issues.

Remember, you must have held a licence for that type of vehicle for at least three years.

Car and caravan or trailer

Drivers who passed the car-driving test before 1 January 1997 are allowed to drive a vehicle and trailer combination up to 8.25 tonnes maximum authorized mass (MAM).

For licences issued after 1 January 1997, the driver is restricted in the type of trailer or combination used:

Most caravans and small trailers towed by cars on a category B licence should be within the threshold, but if not, a separate licence for category B+E must be obtained. This entails higher medical standards and a separate driving test with the car and trailer needs to be taken.

For details of the car and trailer requirements, see www.gov.uk/driving-licence-categories .

Fleet driver training

For anyone wanting to expand his or her business opportunities, fleet training is a particularly interesting and rewarding area of driver training. The Fleet Driver Training Register is operated in conjunction with the ADI Register, but with emphasis on coaching and assessment.

Full details of fleet training are available from Fleet Driver Training, DVSA, 112 Upper Parliament Street, Nottingham NG1 6LP.

As well as formal fleet training, there is also the possibility of offering training individually to local companies, education departments and health authorities as in-service, ongoing training or as pre-employment assessments.

Taxi driver assessments

The driving assessment for taxi drivers usually consists of a practical drive lasting about 35–40 minutes. Some of the skills that are assessed are specific to taxi driving, such as making a U-turn and not stopping anywhere that would be dangerous for the passenger.

The driver is tested on his or her knowledge of *The Highway Code* and is also asked to identify several road signs and markings.

During the assessment, the driver is checked on:

- awareness and anticipation;
- effective planning of the prevailing road and traffic conditions;
- correct use of speed;
- emergency stop;
- a manoeuvre involving reversing;
- passenger comfort and safety.

If the taxi is suitably fitted there will be an assessment of wheelchair usage.

The driver needs to complete the assessment with no more than nine minor faults and with no serious or dangerous faults.

Many local authorities are now using this special assessment and you may well find that there is scope in your area for carrying out training, assessments or appraisals.

LGV training

An ordinary driving licence nowadays covers the driver for vehicles up to three tonnes gross weight. For any vehicle over that weight, a special category of licence and a separate test are required.

Vehicles over three tonnes fall into different categories of licence:

C1 medium-sized goods vehicle

C1E medium-sized vehicle with trailer

C rigid goods vehicle

CE articulated goods vehicle or rigid LGV with trailer

The only statutory requirement for instructing in lorries is to have held a licence for that category of vehicle for at least three years.

A register of LGV instructors is operated by the DVSA, but it is purely voluntary at the present time. Compulsory training and re-training of LGV drivers was introduced as part of the Driver Certificate of Competence regulations and this has had an impact on the demand for driver training for this category of driver – both for initial instruction in preparation for the driving test and for refresher training for full licence holders.

Joining a Register

ADIs can contact one of the these if they wish to enquire about joining one of the Registers:

- National Vocational Driving Instructors Register: https://www.lgvregister.org.uk/registered-lgv-training-centres
- National Register of LGV Instructors: https://lgvinstructorregister.com/find-an-exam-centre
- Register of Logistics Instructors: www.rli.org.uk

You can apply for inclusion on the Register if you hold a full category C1 licence (medium goods vehicle), category C1+E (medium-sized goods vehicle with trailer), category C (rigid goods vehicle) or a full category C+E (articulated large goods vehicle or large goods vehicle with trailer).

To qualify for the Register you must hold a full, unrestricted licence for the category of vehicle in which you intend to instruct. You must not have been disqualified from driving at any time in the previous four years, must have held the appropriate licence for at least three years and must be over 21.

As with the ADI exam, there are three parts to the qualifying exams:

- theory test and hazard perception test;
- practical test of your own driving ability;
- practical test of instructional ability.

For more details contact the National LGV Instructor Register, c/o RTITB, Access House, Halesfield 17, Telford, TF7 4PW (telephone 01952 520210 or at www.lgvinstructorregister.com

Summary

CPD can include the development of communication skills, eco-friendly driving, special needs training and business development. You do not necessarily have to attend a formal training course; your involvement can be through informal training or by way of home study.

It is up to you as an individual to decide what type of CPD is most appropriate to your needs and the way you want to undertake it. However, bear in mind that CPD is an ongoing activity and that the DVSA recommend that you should have a minimum of seven hours of CPD training each year.

Apart from formal training courses, continuing professional development can be undertaken in a variety of different ways, including:

- attendance at local or national meetings and seminars;
- spending time developing business skills;
- updating teaching, coaching or driving skills;
- attending formal training courses;
- networking with other instructors.

APPENDIX 1
Useful contacts

Driver and Vehicle Standards Agency (DVSA)

DVSA customer support

Twitter/X and Facebook: dvsagovuk

email: customerservices@dvsa.gov.uk
telephone: 0300 200 1122
Monday to Friday, 8am to 5pm

Driving and Vehicle Licensing Agency (DVLA)

Longview Road
Swansea
SA6 7JL
www.gov.uk/dvla

Drivers' enquiries

Drivers' Customer Services
DVLA
Swansea
SA6 7JL
telephone: 0300 790 6801

Vehicle enquiries

Vehicles Customer Services
DVLA
Swansea
SA6 7SL
telephone: 0300 790 6802

ADI consultative organisations

Approved Driving Instructors National Joint Council (ADINJC)

Freephone enquiry line: 0800 8202 444
Email: secretary@adinjc.org.uk
www.adinjc.rg.uk

Driving Instructors Association (DIA)

telephone: 020 8686 8010
email: help@driving.org
www.driving.org

Motor Schools Association GB Ltd (MSA)

Membership enquiries: 01787 221020
fax: 0161 429 9779
email: info@msagb.com
www.msagb.com

APPENDIX 2
Reference books

DVSA/TSO books:

The Official DVSA Guide to Driving: The essential skills

The Official DVSA Guide to Learning to Drive

The Official DVSA Theory Test for Car Drivers

Know Your Traffic Signs

The Highway Code

Published by Kogan Page:

The Driving Instructor's Handbook, 23rd edition

by John Miller and Su McCormack

Practical Teaching Skills, 13th edition

By John Miller and Su McCormack

INDEX

Note: Page numbers in *italic* refer to figures or tables.

Abrams, Creighton 96
ACC. *See* Adaptive Cruise Control (ACC)
accelerator 27, 42, 127, 172
  emergency stop 150–151
acronyms 49
active listening 48, 61, 62, 89
  basic principles 77
  coaching 64–65
  as key feature for communication 76–77
  nodding and smiling 68
  rapport and 71, 117
  see also effective questions
Adaptive Cruise Control (ACC) 169, 171
ADAS. *See* advanced driver assistance systems (ADAS)
ADHD 29, 31, 33
ADI Examiner (ADIE) 93
ADI exams
  DVSA criteria 34
  Part 1 (theory test) 17, 111–114, 124, 132–133, 150–151, 184, 242, 245, 250, 251
  Part 2 (practical test) 79, 250, 251
  Part 3 (instructional ability test) 124, 176–209, 250
  skills requirement 242
  see also driver training; instructors
ADI NJC 237, 252
ADI Register 248
ADI Standard Check 2, 3, 30, 174–209
  accuracy of technical information 203–205
  appropriate, non-discriminatory manners 207–208
  assessment criteria 187–209
  competence standards 179–182, *180*, *181*
  core elements 32
  development of active problem solving 201–202
  directions and instructions 194–195
  feedback for safety-critical incidents 198–199
  importance of reflection 209
  inputs and interventions 196–198
  introduction 174–176
  learning goals and needs identification 187–189
  lesson planning 176–179
  lesson structure 189–190
  marking 177–179, *178*
  observation skills 196
  practice areas 190–191
  response to queries 206–207
  risk management 176–177, 192–194
  Road Traffic Act (1988) 179–181, *180*, *181*
  significance of timely feedback 205–206
  teaching and learning strategies 177, 199–209
  teaching style vs preferred style 199–201
  typical lessons 183–187, *187*
  use of opportunities and practical examples 202–203
  see also Model for Goal-Setting and Risk Management
advanced driver assistance systems (ADAS) 1–2, 166–171, 173
  Adaptive Cruise Control/Intelligent Speed Assistance 169
  Automatic Emergency Braking/Forward Collision Warning 170
  Blind Spot Monitoring/Rear Cross-Traffic Alert 169–170
  coaching approach 167
  common errors and corrections 168
  key principles of Eco-Driving 171
  Lane Keeping Assist/Lane Departure Warning 168–169
  lesson planning integration 167–168
  mini-lessons 168–171
  parking assistance/sensors/cameras 170–171
  reinforcing safe habits 168
AEB. *See* Automatic Emergency Braking (AEB)
alcohol 28, 67, 88, 182
all-round observations 133, 137, 139, 146, 150, 151, 155
ancillaries 126, 131
'apparent listening' 76

Approved Driving Instructors National Joint Council. *See* ADI NJC
Approved Driving Instructors. *See* ADIs
autism 29, 30–31, 33
Automatic Emergency Braking (AEB) 170
automatic gears 127
awareness 1, 38, 62, 72, 84, 162, 168, 172, 197, 209
  anticipation and 164, 248
  disability 244–245
  distractions 166
  driving situation 233
  effective questions 75–76
  mirror usage 134–135
  Pass Plus scheme 239
  perception and 11–13, *12*
  personal characteristics 233
  responsibility and 69–70
  risk 192
  risk-increasing factors 88
  see also coaching; self-awareness

barriers 24–33, 47, 69, 96
  ADHD 31
  autism 30–31
  colour blindness 25
  Dyslexia 31–32
  Dyspraxia 32
  hearing difficulties 26–27
  labels and individual differences 33
  lack of motivation 25
  language difficulties 25–26
  methodical approach 32–33
  neurodivergence and client-centred coaching 33
  neurodivergent pupils 29–30
  physical disabilities 28–29
  Standards Check 30
Bedfordshire 239
bends 38, 105, 112, 145
blind areas 132, 133, 136, 147
Blind Spot Monitoring (BSM) 169–170
blind spots 54, 222
body language 29, 45, 51–52, 68, 70–71, 156, 179, 188, 196, 206–207
  checking 114
  facial expressions 53
  gaze 53
  gestures 54–55
  personal appearance 57
  personal space 55
  posture 54
  rapport 89
  rules 57–59, *57*, *58*, *59*
  touches 55–56, *56*
boredom 16
brake lights 21, 137, 138
brakes 21, 139
  dual brake 73, 119–120, 198, 218
  emergency stop 149–151
  footbrake 127, 129, 133, 146
  handbrake 91, 121, 128, 129, 131, 139, 146, 202
braking distances 150–151
BSM. *See* Blind Spot Monitoring (BSM)
built-in sat nav 165
business costs 186
business records 235
business skills 229, 230, 231, 234
  customer care and 234–236

C licence (rigid goods vehicle) 249, 250
C+E licence (articulated large goods vehicle or large goods vehicle with trailer) 249, 250
C1 licence (medium goods vehicle) 249, 250
C1+E licence (medium-sized goods vehicle with trailer) 249, 250
cameras 170–171
car parks 148, 149, 170, 244
caravans 244, 248
Cardington 239, 251
Cardington test 229, 239–240
Carshalton 244
cash flow 229, 235
category B licence 248
category B+E licence 248
Certificate of Competence 231, 249
clarity 27, 32, 65, 83, 117
client-centred learning 2, 46, 62–63, 199, 205
  active listening 77
  agreed programme 123
  basic coaching-type questions 75–76
  coaching and 62–92
  communication skills 69–70
  effective questioning 70–77
  examples of 101
  feedback 78–82, 90
  Goals for Driver Education 86–88, *86–87*
  GROW model 63, 82–86
  identifying and agreeing goals 83–84
  instructing and 63–64
  key benefits 65–66
  main principles of 65
  options: alternative strategies 85
  prior knowledge and experience 84–85
  questioning technique 75
  rapport 66–69
  skills 66–70
  Standard Check 175

client-centred learning (*Continued*)
  summary 88–92
  way forward: plan summarizing 85–86
Client-centred questions 74, 89
client-centred relationship 47, 66, 68–69, 70–71, 89
client-centred skills 3, 122, 164
closed questions 19, 72, 75, 200
clutch 32, 128
  dual clutch 119–121
  emergency stop 150–151
coaching
  active listening 77
  basic coaching-type questions 75–76
  communication skills 69–70
  effective questioning 70–77
  feedback 78–82
  goal setting 83–84
  Goals for Driver Education 86–88, *86–87*
  GROW model 63, 82–86
  identifying and agreeing goals 83–84
  instructing and 63–64
  key benefits 65–66
  main principles of 65
  options: alternative strategies 85
  prior knowledge and experience 84–85
  questioning technique 75
  rapport 66–69
  skills 66–70
  summary 88–92
  way forward: plan summarizing 85–86
  see also instructors
communication skills
  body language 51–59
  briefings and explanations 49–51
  coaching 36–37
  coaching and instruction 38–39
  content of speech 41–42
  CPD and 250
  facial expressions 53
  feedback 59–61
  gaze 53
  gestures 54–55
  instruction 36
  listening skills 45–49
  neutral and non-judgemental 37–38
  personal appearance 57
  personal space 55
  pitch of your voice 44
  posture 54
  speed of speaking 43
  tone of voice 40
  touches 55–56, *56*
  use of emphasis 40–41
  use of figurative language 42
  use of humour 42–43
  use of implied speech 44–45
  use of pronunciation 43
  variety of methods 35
  see also active listening
community groups 247
complex junctions 106, 141, 183
conceptualization 10
Continuing Professional Development (CPD) 3
  ADI national organizations 237–238
  benefits of 230–232
  business opportunities 243–250
  business skills 235–236
  business skills and customer care 234–236
  City and Guilds 243
  customer care 236
  dealing with complaints 237
  definition and introduction 229–230
  driver trainer competence framework 232–234
  driving instructor training 241–242
  driving standards 239–241
  intensive courses 245
  LGV training 249–250
  Pass Plus 239, 246–247
  pre-driver training 244
  qualifications: driving instructors 242–243
  training for disability persons 244–245
  Tri-Coaching Partnership 242–243
  vocational driver training 247–249
coping strategies 91
CPD. *See* Continuing Professional Development (CPD)
criticism 31, 34, 37–38, 41, 81
customer care skills 229, 234, 235
cyclists 112, 135, 141, 144, 164, 169

'D' plates 174
defensive driving 22–24, 95
deliberateness 43
demonstrations 25, 27, 64, 113, 146–147, 160, 176, 184, 185, 204
disability 243, 244–245
  hearing difficulties 26–27
  physical disability 28–29
Driver and Vehicle Standards Agency (DVSA) 3, 174, 229, 230, 234, 237, 251
  Cardington test 239–240
  hazard-perception testing 22
  National Register of LGV Instructors 249–250
  Pass Plus 246–247

see also ADI Standard Check
Driver Certificate of Competence 231, 249
driver errors 108–109, 118
driver training
ADAS features 166–171, *167*, 173
ADAS mini-lessons: step-by-step teaching 168–171
advanced driving tests 239–241
anticipation 163–164
Cardington test 239–240
crossroads 140–141
driving standards 239–241
eco-driving and EVs 171–173
emergency stop 149–151
foot controls 127–128
GDE matrix 86–88, *86–87*
hand controls 128–130
handling of, traffic issues 142–145
independent driving and use of sat nav 165–172
indicators, horn and ancillary controls 130–131
Institute of Advanced Motorists 240
junctions 138–140
lesson structure 123–124
main car controls 124–131
manoeuvres 18, 133, 145–149
mirror usage 134–136
moving off and stopping 132–134, 165
pedestrian crossings 151–153
road positioning 161–163
RoSPA Advanced Driving Test 240–241
roundabouts and dual carriageways 154–161
types of main controls 126–131
using of signals 136–138
vehicle familiarization 125–126, 130
see also instructors; road users; traffic conditions
driveways 148
Driving Instructor 238
Driving Instructor's Handbook, The 1, 21, 29, 63, 93, 166, 245, 247
Driving Instructors Association (DIA) 237–238, 252
Driving Instructors' Group 237
Driving magazine 238
driving simulators 115
drugs 67, 88, 182, 193
dual brake 73, 119–120, 198, 218
dual carriageways 106, 141, 144, 171, 227–228
feedback 161
mini roundabouts 154–155
Model for Goal-Setting and Risk Management 227–228
Paas Plus scheme 246–247
roundabouts and 154–161
dual clutch 119–121
dual controls 54, 64, 102, 118, 119, 121, 194
dual mirrors 54, 119
'dual-fuel' vehicles 241
DVLA 252
DVSA Training and Development Centre 239, 251
DVSA. *See* Driver and Vehicle Standards Agency (DVSA)
dyslexia 29, 31–32, 33
dyspraxia 29, 32, 33

EDP (Explain – Demonstrate – Practice) 167, 201
effective questions 69, 78, 89, 111, 152, 158, 162
roundabouts 155–156
use of 70–77, 136, 140, 148–149
electric vehicle (EVs) 1, 171–173
emergency stop 23, 149–151, 249
emotional responses 30, 31
emotional states 90
empathy 32
EV. *See* electric vehicle (EV)
eye contact 53, 58, 68, 77, 89, 115, 137, 138

Face-to-face conversation 27
facial expressions 45, 51, 52–53
fatigue 16, 67, 241
faults 38, 47, 59, 79, 144, 153, 182, 191–192, 206, 215, 240, 249
analysing 79, 110
assessment 107–111
correction 110–111
dual carriageways 160
grading of errors 108–109
identification 79
identification, analysis and rectification 133–134
mini roundabouts 155
recognition 109–110
remedy 79
FCW. *See* Forward Collision Warning (FCW)
Fleet Driver Training Register 248
fleet training 248
Follow-up procedures 235
Follow-up questions 60, 74
footbrake 127, 129, 133, 146
emergency stop 150–151
formal training courses 250
Forward Collision Warning (FCW) 170
forward-planning skills 186
Freight Transport Association 249

fuel economy 229, 241

gas pedal 42, 119–120, 150
gaze 51, 52, 53
GDE 5, 64, 86–88, *86*, *87*
gears 21, 129–130, 131, 133
  changes 32, 223–224
  selector 127
General Purposes Committee 238
gestures 45, 51, 52, 54–56, 77
goal questions 71–72
Goals for Driver Education. *See* GDE
goal-setting 60, 72, 189
  dual carriageways 227–228
  goals and 95–101
  input 211–212
  lesson planning 220–221, *220*
  moving off and stopping 223–227
  over-instruction and under-instruction 210–211
  risk management 210–228, *212*, *215*, *221*
  risk outside the goal 218–220
  risk within the goal 217–218
  teaching and learning strategies 222
grading system 240
GROW (goals, reality, options, way forward) 9, 10, 63, 82–86

handbrake 91, 121, 128, 129, 131, 139, 146, 202
hands-free systems 166
Hazard perception 22, 31, 111–114, 150, 241, 250
headlights 137, 164
hearing impairment 245
Hierarchy of Needs 97–98
Highway Code, The 2, 17, 132, 248, 254
horn 23, 131, 137, 138
horse-riders 112
hyperbole 42, 115

IAM. *See* Institute of Advanced Motorists (IAM)
ill-health 186
impatience 16, 23
impulsivity 31
in-car noise 166
in-car systems 166
indicators 126, 130–131, 136
individual learning 1, 25, 65, 70
informal training 250
infotainment screens 165
Institute of Advanced Motorists (IAM) 240
instructions 37, 84, 138, 160, 165, 182, 184–185, 225
  autism 31
  communication and 35, 50
  directional 35, 51
  directions and 194–195, 216
  Dyspraxia 32
  intuition 91–92
  levels of 101–104
  over-instruction 102–103
  talk-through 103
  under-instruction 103–104
  verbal 114, 119
instructors
  accuracy of technical information 203–205
  appropriate, non-discriminatory manners 207–208
  business opportunities 243–250
  City and Guilds 243
  'client-centred' approach 175
  development of active problem solving 201–202
  directions and instructions 194–195
  dual carriageways 227–228
  feedback for safety-critical incidents 198–199
  goal-setting 212–214, *212*
  importance of reflection 209
  input 211–212, *212*
  inputs and interventions 196–198
  instructional errors 101–104
  intensive courses 245
  interpretation: assessment criteria 187–209
  learning goals and needs identification 187–189
  lesson planning 220–221, *220*
  lesson structure 189–190
  LGV training 249–250
  moving off and stopping 223–227
  observation skills 196
  over-instruction and under-instruction 210–211
  Pass Plus 239, 246–247
  perception of hazards 111–114
  practice areas 190–191
  pre-driver training 244
  qualification criteria 242–243
  questioning techniques 117
  response to queries 206–207
  reversing exercises 145–146
  risk management 117–121, 192–194, 215–228, *215*, *221*

risk outside the goal 218–220
risk within the goal 217–218
RoSPA 243
significance of timely feedback 205–206
standard of ability 109
teaching and learning strategies 199–209, 222
teaching style vs preferred style 199–201
training for disability persons 244–245
Tri-Coaching Partnership 242–243
use of opportunities and practical examples 202–203
visual aids 115–117
vocational driver training 247–249
see also driver training
insurance 235, 238, 246, 247
costs 5, 186
responsibilities 229
Intelligent Speed Assistance (ISA) 169
intensive courses 15, 245
Intermediate routes 106
intuition 48–49, 90, 91–92
iPad 98
'irradiation' 14, *15*
ISA. *See* Intelligent Speed Assistance (ISA)

junctions 8, 51, 141, 153, 162, 171, 183, 194, 219
colour blindness 25
complex junctions 106, 141, 183
emergency stop 149
intermediate routes 106
intuition 91–92
left and right turns 223–227
M S M rules on 160
manoeuvres 18, 146
overtaking 145
T-junctions 98–99, 154, 158, 159
turning and emerging 138–140, 211

Know Your Traffic Signs 254
Kolb, David 9–10

L A D routine 108
'L' plates 174
Lane Departure Warning (LDW) 168–169
Lane Keeping Assist (LKA) 168–169
LDW. *See* Lane Departure Warning (LDW)
Learning aids 94, 115
learning difficulties 245
learning (structured)
Hazard perception 111–114
levels of instructions 101–104
physical intervention 119–121
risk management 117–121
route planning 104–107
verbal intervention 118–119
visual aids 115–117
see also barriers; faults; goal-setting; Model for Goal-Setting and Risk Management
learning
activity and involvement 16
attention 15–16
awareness 11–13, *12*
consistency and predictability 30
developing long-term memory 17
importance of sight 11, *11*
memorizing 16–17
perception 14, *15*
technique of problem solving 19–20
transferability of 13–14
understanding 17–19
level crossings 25, 106
LGV training 249–250
life-long learning 185, 186
light conditions 126, 131, 164
light vans 174–175
lip-reading 27
LKA. *See* Lane Keeping Assist (LKA)
local associations 238
log book 98
loudness 44

M S M routine 17, 49, 108, 125, 132, 134, 141
application of 137, 143, 151, 153, 155–156
application on junctions 163
two-way roads 160
understanding of 152
main roads 106, 141
MAM. *See* maximum authorised mass (MAM)
Maslow, Abraham 97–98
maximum authorised mass (MAM) 248
memory prompts 119
metaphors 42, 115
Metropolitan Police principles 240
mind map 25
mini roundabouts 154–155, 157
minibuses 247
minor faults 109–110, 249
minor roads 8, 140, 154
mirrors 78, 108, 126, 132, 157, 203, 222, 224–225
checking 145, 155, 169
using of 134–137, 159, 219
see also dual mirrors
mnemonics 17, 49

Model for Goal-Setting and Risk Management
dual carriageways 227–228
goal-setting 212–214, *212*
input 211–212, *212*
lesson planning 220–221, *220*
moving off and stopping 223–227
over-instruction and under-instruction 210–211
risk management 215–228, *215*
risk management 221–222, *221*
risk outside the goal 218–220
risk within the goal 217–218
teaching and learning strategies 222
mopeds 174–175
MoT certificate 174
Motor Schools Association 238, 252
motorcycles 174–175
motorcyclists 112, 141, 144, 164
motorways 38, 95, 171, 185, 240, 246
MSA 252
MSPSL 224, 225, 226
multi-lane roads 106, 161

narrow roads 142
national associations 238
National LGV Instructor Register 249–250
National Standard for Driver and Rider Training 174–175, 183, 184
National Standard for Driver Training 181–182, 187
neurodivergence 1–2, 29–30, 33
non-verbal clues 188
non-verbal communication techniques 68–69, 89
non-verbal messages 46
non-verbal signals 16, 77
non-verbal signs 191
Northern Ireland 234
Norway 55
Nursery routes 105–106

Official DVSA Guide to Driving: The essential skills, The 17, 254
Official DVSA Guide to Learning to Drive, The 254
Official DVSA Theory Test for Car Drivers, The 254
Official Guide to Learning to Drive, The 17
Official Register of Driving Instructor Training. *See* ORDIT
oncoming vehicles 144, 145
1 Metcalf Avenue 244
one-way systems 106
on-road training 192
sessions 175
open questions 71, 73, 74, 89, 200
open-ended questions 19, 46, 83
ORDIT 242
out-of-hours work 246
Over-correction 169
over-instruction 33, 51, 102–103, 153, 210–211
over-steering 120, 147
overtaking 144–145, 152, 159, 164

P S L routine 108
'palming' method 130
parked vehicles 105, 142–144, 149, 158–160, 164, 197–198
parrot-fashion learning. See rote learning
Pass Plus scheme 239, 243, 246–247
pedal extensions 28
pedestrian crossings 105, 106, 151–153, 197, 203, 219
pedestrians 84–85, 112, 129, 130, 141, 143–144, 147, 164, 208
pelican crossing 152–153, 197
personal appearance 52, 57, 206, 236
personal dynamism 54
personal space 55, 208
physical disabilities 28–29, 245
physical skills 32
pick-up point 124
Police Advanced Drivers certificate 240
post-test learning 63
posture 51, 52, 54, 57
practice areas 190–191, 213, 214
pre-driver training 243, 244
pre-printed diagram 25
professionalism 231, 234
prompting 103–104, 113–114, 135, 155, 160
public liability 229, 235
'pull–push' 128

QEF Mobility Services 244
questioning techniques 50, 64, 117
types of 71–74
quietness 44

real-world situations 202
Rear Cross-Traffic Alert 169–170
rear wheels 129, 147
receptiveness 52
reflective questions 79–80, 218
reflective thinking 31
Reuvid, Jonathan 236
reverse parking 145–146
Road Haulage Association 249
road junctions 110, 112
road layout 25, 105
road positioning 137, 155, 161–163
road signs 141, 183, 248

Road Transport Industry Training Board (RTITB) 249–250
road users 34, 103, 110, 139, 141, 143, 207–208
  anticipation 111, 144, 163–164
  Cardington test 239–240
  gestures 54–55
  management of risk 192
  use of signals 132, 136–138
Roadcraft 240
role-play skills 242
RoSPA. *See* Royal Society for the Prevention of Accidents (RoSPA)
rote learning 16–17, 18
roundabouts 91, 105–106, 141, 164, 171, 183, 189
  dual carriageways 154–161
  risk management 214–219
routes 15, 30, 31, 94, 101, 141, 143
  on-road training sessions 175
  planning 104–107, 121, 156, 171, 175
  risk management 117
  sat nav 166
  selection 106–107, 141, 162
  training 107
Royal Society for the Prevention of Accidents (RoSPA) 240–241, 243
RTITB. *See* Road Transport Industry Training Board (RTITB)

safety margins 112
safety routines 106
safety-critical questions 72–73
sat nav (satellite navigation) 165–166
scaling 79, 80–81
  questions 59–60
seatbelts 67, 126, 174
self-appraisal 209
self-assessment 97
self-assurance 54
self-awareness 38, 60, 70, 101, 122
  coaching 65–66
  goal-setting 96
  GROW model 82–86
self-confidence 6, 54, 55, 69
self-discipline 54
self-esteem 6, 49, 97
self-evaluation 68, 74, 78, 81, 220
  feedback 59–61, 90
  goal-setting and 97
  reflection 59–61, 79, 209
  scaling and 80
self-learning 122
self-reflection 65
self-responsibility 97
sensors 169, 170–171
sensory overload 31, 197
sequencing 31
short-term memory 31
side roads 106, 141, 159, 164
signalling 108, 157, 160, 229, 241
  clearance 143
  mini roundabouts 154–155
  roundabouts 156
signals 19, 57, 139, 141, 152
  non-verbal 16, 77
  passive 54
  silent 46, 52
  using of 132, 136–138, 219
similes 42, 115
slip roads 158
SMART 213–214, 226
solo driving 63
speed limits 106, 138
Start Up and Run Your Own Business (Reuvid) 236
steering 13, 19, 36, 73, 126, 128, 168–169
  accuracy 32
  assistance with 119–120
  body language 58, 59
  common faults 144
  emergency stop 149–151
  flexibility 229, 241
  left and right turns 223–227
  manoeuvres 145–149
  mini roundabouts 155
stress 28, 40, 114, 118
supplementary questions 19, 20, 76
Surrey SM5 4AW 244

'talk-through' mode 20, 148, 155, 160
  over-instruction 102–103
  under-instruction 103–104
task-specific questions 73–74
taxi driving 248–249
test routes 106
theory of learning 9–10, 9
thinking distance 150–151
T-junctions 98–99, 139, 154, 158, 159
traffic conditions 104–106, 114, 163, 183, 241
  Cardington test 239–240
  challenges 122–123
  driving assessment 248–249
  evaluation of 232
  nature of 107
  Pass Plus scheme 246–247
traffic lights 43, 104, 105, 106, 152, 171
  colour blindness 25
  controlled junctions 141
trailers 248
training routes 104, 105, 107

Tri-Coaching Partnership 242–243
two-way roads 154, 158
  M S M rules 160

UK 26, 186, 237, 240
UK licence 186, 246
under-instruction 102, 103–104, 210–211
  see also over-instruction

VAT 235, 244
vehicle sympathy 130, 134
verbal feedback 148–149, 180–181
verbal messages 45, 46, 54–55
visual aids 25, 27, 50, 110, 115–117
  as communication tool 35
  dual carriageways 159
  power to speed ratio 129
  reversing 146
visual checks 108, 170
visual keys 12, 17, 50

Wales 174
weather conditions 14, 67, 86–88, 126, 131, 164
  dress code 57
  road accidents 23
Welsh 174
word associations 17, 50

youth associations 239
youth groups 244, 247

Also from Kogan Page

ISBN: 9781398630741

www.koganpage.com

From 4 December 2025 the EU Responsible Person (GPSR) is:
eucomply oÜ, Pärnu mnt. 139b – 14, 11317 Tallinn, Estonia
www.eucompliancepartner.com

www.ingramcontent.com/pod-product-compliance
Lightning Source LLC
LaVergne TN
LVHW010618190926
848399LV00034B/332

* 9 7 8 1 3 9 8 6 3 0 9 0 1 *